A COMPLETE DESCRIPTIVE GUIDE TO BRITISH MONUMENTAL BRASSES

A COMPLETE
DESCRIPTIVE GUIDE TO

BRITISH MONUMENTAL BRASSES

RICHARD le STRANGE

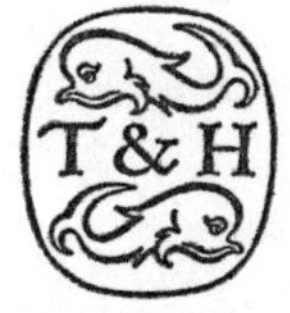

THAMES AND HUDSON
LONDON

To Liz, for all her help

PRINTED IN GREAT BRITAIN BY
BILLING AND SONS LIMITED, GUILDFORD AND LONDON

ISBN 0 500 01076 5 CLOTHBOUND
ISBN 0 500 27018 X PAPERBOUND

CONTENTS

INTRODUCTION

Monumental brasses first appear early in the thirteenth century. One of the first recorded in Britain, now lost, was to John de Beauchamp (*c.* 1210), mounted before the foot of the altar in St Paul's Church, Bedford. The earliest known surviving brass is in Germany in the church of St Andrew at Verden, a religious brass commemorating Bishop Ysowilpe and dated 1231.

In England we are fortunate indeed in having two remaining military brasses of the late thirteenth century, those of Sir John D'Aubernoun at Stoke D'Abernon, Surrey (1277), and Sir Roger de Trumpington (1289), at Trumpington, Cambs.

Stone memorials preceded the use of brass plate. At first the stone lid of the coffin was carved with an inscription or motif. This was replaced during the twelfth century by a figure in semi-relief, which evolved into the incised slab. The substitution of brass for stone seems to have taken place during the early thirteenth century, although the two methods existed together for some time after.

The material used for engraving effigies and inscriptions was called 'latten'. It consisted of approximately two-thirds copper and one-third zinc, with a little lead and tin added. This plate, sometimes called 'cullen plate', was in the main manufactured in Cologne and exported to the east coast ports, where it was distributed, engraved and laid down. The use of these latten plates as sepulchral monuments became very popular, perhaps owing to the fact that they were so durable, were easily moved from one place to another, and gave opportunity for more detailed engraving than stone.

In England the greatest number of brasses are found in the eastern counties, probably because of the density of the population at the time and the trade between the east coast ports and the Continent. In Scotland and Ireland they are rare indeed.

In eastern England there are to be found several brasses engraved by foreign workmen: the 'Flemish' brasses. These can be easily distinguished from the English brass, as the effigies are engraved in the centre of a large rectangular plate or plates joined together and the background completely filled with minute and delicate engraving. English brasses, however, have the figure cut out and inlaid in a setting of stone.

After the brass had been engraved, it was set in its indent, which had simply been filled with pitch. In later brasses, metal screws were used to secure the plates.

In some cases the brasses were coloured, but this was a very expensive form of decoration. Sometimes traces of colour can still be found in the grooves. The use of enamel was a more uncommon form of colouring, although this too can occasionally be found.

It was generally left to the engraver himself to draw up the design, and so, although the brass depicted the costume or military wear of the day, there were few attempts at portraiture. Certain engravers even developed a characteristic face which they used on brasses coming from their workshops. These schools of workmanship can be identified today in different parts of the country.

FOURTEENTH CENTURY

The earliest brasses depict only knights and their ladies and ecclesiastics. From about 1350 we find brasses to the middle classes, and, towards the end of the century, brasses to the richer tradesmen.

During this period the design and workmanship are very good, the engraving is on very thick plate, with simple lines deeply cut. Sometimes the effigies were life-size and placed under canopies, surrounded by a fillet or border from 1½″ to 2″ wide, on which was cut in Norman French the name, description and decease of the person memorialized.

Cross and bracket brasses appear, sometimes on a pedestal of steps, which in turn rests on the inscription plate.

FIFTEENTH CENTURY

The first half of the fifteenth century produced many examples of fine brasses, with the effigies well cut and beautifully drawn. At this time the art of engraving was at its peak, but as the use of brasses spread to people of no social significance the numbers laid down rapidly increased and so the standard began to deteriorate.

Military brasses in the first half of this period are generally exceptionally good. As time went on, however, the canopies and figures grew somewhat smaller, with the inscription fillet giving way to a foot inscription.

The bracket brasses of this time usually show the deceased standing on top of the bracket, or sometimes kneeling to the bracket on which would be a saint or saints.

From 1450 to the end of the century there is a marked decline. The recumbent figure concedes to poses and three-quarter views, as the ladies show off their butterfly head-dresses and the military man his ornate armour. Children are often shown in groups below their parents.

Above the effigies were often scrolls with texts, although these sometimes issued from hands or mouth.

During this century it became popular to commemorate the dead by showing them in their funeral shrouds; this developed into the gruesome, grinning skeletons with impossible bone structures. Between the two, the shroud and skeleton brasses, lay the cadavers, emaciated and shrunken corpses in shrouds.

Heart brasses were also introduced, either as a simple heart with scrolls, or held in the person's hands with an inscription.

During the latter part of this century the practice spread of engraving chalice brasses to priests, sometimes with the wafer, and an inscription below. This form of monument was most extensively used in Norfolk where the majority of such brasses is to be found.

At the end of this period more shading was attempted and the art of engraving began to decline.

SIXTEENTH CENTURY

In the early 1500s large quantities of brasses were engraved and laid down. They were more popular than ever before, but the workmanship was rapidly deteriorating. The figures lost their grace and, especially in the case of effigies in armour, were engraved out of proportion. Many brasses are spoilt by cross-hatch or line shading.

English now becomes the common language on inscriptions with the exception of those to ecclesiastics, which remain in Latin.

Infants who died before they were a month old are shown as chrysoms, looking like small Egyptian mummies.

Mural brasses come into fashion, most being rectangular in shape; husband and wife generally kneeling at desks with their children behind them, boys behind their father, girls behind their mother.

From 1550 not only the engravings but the plate itself deteriorates. Instead of the thick hard latten of previous times, imported from the Continent, we find a much softer and thinner metal, now being manufactured in England, a cheaper plate that could easily be bent, scratched and dented.

During the reign of Elizabeth I (1558–1603) brasses were still laid down in quantity, with the standing figures on pedestals or pavements.

There are many small mural brasses of this period, often spoilt by shallow engraving and an excess of shading, the brass itself looking overcrowded with its kneeling families in prayer.

SEVENTEENTH CENTURY

After the death of James I in 1625, the engraving of brasses seems to have become a lost art. Those that were laid down, with few exceptions, seem to be more poorly engraved than in the previous era.

In the eighteenth century the brass had all but disappeared, with only about four examples. The latest commemorates Benjamin Greenwood (1773), at Cray, St Mary, Kent. This rectangular plate, and another to his wife Philadelphia, appears merely to have been scratched on the metal.

DEMOLITION OF BRASSES

Up to the year 1536 most of the brasses in churches had been treated with respect and only rarely were they taken up and engraved on the reverse. In 1536, however, King Henry VIII sent a commission to inquire into the state of the monasteries. The larger ones were generally found to be in good order, but the smaller were sometimes full of abuses. Sufficient evidence was obtained for what Henry wanted, and in 1536 the smaller monasteries were dissolved by an Act of Parliament, all the property going to the Crown. In 1539 another Act was passed, authorizing the surrender to the king of all the remaining monasteries. This in turn made thousands of priests, monks and nuns homeless throughout the land.

Thus priory chapels and conventual churches were sacked, everything 'popish' being destroyed. This meant, of course, that brasses came in for special treatment. Great numbers were torn up, sold or melted down, or sometimes reversed, engraved on and laid down again. These are the palimpsest brasses, and this is why so many date between 1540 to 1600. Another type of palimpsest is the appropriated and converted brass, which has not been reversed but altered and re-used with the addition of a new inscription for a second occasion. There are not many of these in existence.

The destruction did not stop at the death of Henry VIII. In Edward VI's short reign (1547–53) commissioners were sent round to the churches with orders to destroy everything that was popish.

Queen Elizabeth in the second year of her reign issued 'a Proclamation against breaking or defacing of Monuments of Antiquitie' but this evidently did not stop their destruction, for twelve years later another proclamation was issued for the same purpose.

Oliver Cromwell, when he came to power, lost no time in despoiling the churches. He took the lead for bullets and the brasses were made into cannon. Anything in the churches was regarded as his troops' lawful plunder. Once again commissioners were appointed to examine the churches. Anything brazen, superstitious or popish was again ripped out. After Cromwell's day the demolition of brasses abated somewhat.

The religious troubles were not confined only to Britain. Many palimpsests consist of fragments of both foreign and English brasses, which could have come from the sacking of the Netherlands churches in 1566. Those brasses which escaped the melting pot were probably exported to Britain.

If a brass dating from about 1540 is engraved on thick, heavy plate instead of thin, it is almost certain to be a palimpsest.

The following list does not include the many brasses which have been destroyed or lost, but only those remaining in the churches. If, for example, a knight and his lady were originally engraved side by side and the knight is now lost, no mention of him is made, only of his lady. Similarly, if any children are missing from a group, only the remaining number are listed.

Foot inscriptions are omitted. Marginal and chamfer inscriptions are included, but most are to be found in a mutilated state. If such inscriptions are lost or badly mutilated, they are not listed. These inscriptions are not necessarily found near the effigies, but sometimes even at the opposite end of the church.

Remaining achievements are noted if with an effigy. These usually consist of a coat of arms, with sometimes a shield, helmet and crest.

The brasses have been listed in strict chronological order. In many cases where brasses have been taken up, they have been relaid incorrectly. The date given is the year or approximate year of engraving, not necessarily the date of the person's death. In some cases there was a lapse of up to 100 years between the deceased's commemorated death and the engraving of the plate.

No attempt has been made to locate the position of the brasses in the church, as these tend constantly to be moved. They are not only to be found on the floor of the church, i.e. the chancel or nave, but in the most unlikely places. Some of the more unusual locations found in the course of research for this book have included the foot of the pulpit, the screen, on pillars, on the vestry door, in a cupboard in the vestry, the church doorsteps, the roof of the crypt, on the rood loft door, on a swing door, several under organs, pews, pulpits, wooden floors, and even one in the churchyard on a tomb. Each reference is to a parish church, unless otherwise indicated.

Please remember when entering a church, and especially when looking for an elusive brass, that the church itself should be held in respect; it is in some people's estimation a holy place and should be treated as such, with due reverence.

If rubbings are required, permission should always be obtained first from the priest in charge or from one of his churchwardens, who will inform you of any fee. And remember to clear up any mess when finished. Do not leave it for someone else to do.

I would like to thank the local secretaries of the Monumental Brass Society who have helped with their lists of lost effigies, especially Mr D. G. Meara, BA, of Oriel College, Oxford, and Mr C. M. Byrom, of Gough Way, Cambridge. Also Miss R. M. R. Young, MA, Assistant Director of the City of Norwich Museums; The Keeper of Western MSS, Bodleian Library, Oxford; Mr A. R. E. North, of the Department of Metalwork, Victoria and Albert Museum; Mr John Cherry, Assistant Keeper of the Mediaeval Department, The British Museum; Mrs S. Harper of the Department of the Environment; Miss M. D. Cra'ster, MA, Assistant Curator, Cambridge University Museum of Archaeology and Ethnology; Miss P. M. Butler, MA, FMA, of Ipswich Museum; Mr D. T. D. Clarke, MA, FMA, FSA, of the Colchester and Essex Museums; and the Norfolk and Norwich Archaeological Society for the use of their library. I also owe a debt of gratitude to the many vicars and rectors throughout Great Britain who have willingly answered letters and checked brasses within their churches, and the Archaeological Societies that have kept me informed of any changes.

GLOSSARY

ACADEMICAL DRESS

The distinguishing costume of the University.

In the Middle Ages nearly all the Colleges of Cambridge and Oxford were under ecclesiastic or monastic rule, with the result that most academics were also priests. Their basic dress was the cassock, over which was a gown, which varied in shape somewhat according to the degree of the wearer. Over the shoulders could be a tippet (a cape of fur and cloth) and on the head a skull cap or doctor's cap. It is sometimes difficult to ascertain the exact degree of the person depicted (unless stated on the inscription), as in real life this would be shown by the colour and material used in his dress.

ACHIEVEMENT

A hatchment, consisting of the helm, crest, wreath and mantling, with a shield of arms. These are usually placed a little above the effigies.

ALMUCE

The almuce was worn in conjunction with the cope, being a large cape and hood of black cloth, lined with fur. At the shoulders it was turned back to show the fur lining, with the two ends hanging down in front to the knees. Many priests are depicted without the cope, but when it is worn, the almuce underneath gives the appearance of being a fur collar.

ANELACE

A short sword worn by civilians. Usually suspended from the belt or girdle around the waist.

CANOPIES

Many brasses are surrounded by a frame, the canopy, rising over and around the figures and reflecting the architectural style of the time. From the foot of the brass tall shafts rise to support an arch or arches, the side shafts continuing upwards in the form of pinnacles. These canopies are generally very graceful and take on many forms and patterns, with figures of saints, shields of arms and many other devices. Often the canopy arches are double or triple, with clustered pinnacles above.

CHAMFER INSCRIPTION

The sloped or slanted fillet or border, surrounding a brass, usually from 1½″ to 2″ wide. On this would be cut the name, description and date of death of the person portrayed. Mainly found on tomb brasses.

CHASUBLE

The chasuble was worn by priests over their other vestments. It was a large circular or oval garment with an opening for the head in the centre. When worn it hung down on all sides and covered the upper parts of the arms. It was made of the richest and most expensive material available, this depending on the status of the wearer; some were plain and without ornament, others made of velvet and gold cloth, the borders (or orphreys) richly decorated.

CHRYSOMS

These are small mummy-like figures of infants who died before they were a month old. They are depicted wrapped in their chrysoms, a white square of linen, bound by a cere-cloth, but still showing their faces.

COIF

The coif was a tight-fitting cap, tied under the chin, worn by members of the legal profession, the judges. Sometimes over the coif would be a skull cap of black velvet.

COLLAR OF SUNS AND ROSES

A metal collar or heavy necklace of alternating suns and roses, worn loosely around the shoulders. Favoured by the Yorkist knights and their ladies. Worn by followers of Edward IV.

COPE

The cope was a large cloak falling nearly to the ground, fastened at the throat by a morse (a clasp or large jewelled brooch). The garment itself was often decorated with two wide orphreys running down the straight edges in front, frequently richly embroidered, with texts in Latin, figures of saints and sometimes set with jewels. Occasionally the whole of the cope was richly diapered.

COTE-HARDIE

Sometimes another dress was worn over the kirtle, the cote-hardie. The sleeves were short, and long lappets were often attached, almost reaching the floor. Occasionally there were two pockets in front. This style developed into the sideless cote-hardie, where the sides of the dress were cut away as far as the hips, leaving a narrow piece forming the front, and a fur trimming around the shoulders. To this would be attached a skirt slit up the sides.

CROSIER

The crosier is usually depicted as a long staff with the end curved into a scroll, decorated with foliage. The pastoral staff finished in a crook, often ornamented with jewels.

EMBATTLED CANOPIES OR ENTABLATURES

Sometimes super-canopies were added to those described above, where the side shafts were continued upwards, beyond the pinnacles, to support a heavy embattled entablature at the top.

EPISCOPAL VESTMENTS

The higher religious orders wore certain distinctive vestments peculiar to their rank, although they were still entitled to wear the dress of their subordinates.

Bishops and mitred abbots were allowed to wear the tunicle, a plain garment slit up each side with fringed ends, reaching to about the knees. Over the tunicle was worn the dalmatic, slightly shorter, but almost identical in cut. The dalmatic was generally made of the same material and pattern as the chasuble, which was worn above.

Other episcopal insignia consisted of the mitre, the ring, white silk gloves, sandals and crosier.

FLOWING HAIR

Unmarried girls were frequently depicted with long flowing hair. There are also a few examples of married women shown this way.

HERALDIC DRESS AND HERALDIC MANTLE

Ladies sometimes bore their husband's arms, richly embroidered on their mantles, and that of their own family on their kirtles or, as more often found, both on the mantle, their own on the sinister, their husband's on the dexter.

JUDICIAL ROBES

Judicial dress varies little. Most judges are depicted wearing a long cassock-like robe with a fur-lined, hooded mantle, buttoned on the right shoulder. On the head would be a coif.

JUPON

A sleeveless tight-fitting outer garment worn over the hauberk (a long coat of mail). It was generally made of leather, lacing up at the sides, with an outside layer of silk or velvet, often charged with the wearer's arms. The lower edge reached half-way down the thighs; in most cases it was scalloped or fringed.

KIRTLE

A close-fitting dress, low-cut at the neck, with long tight fitting sleeves, these occasionally reaching halfway over the hands, bordered and trimmed with fur. The hem of the skirt always reached the floor. The hips were often girdled. Over the kirtle would be worn a cote-hardie or a mantle, later replaced by a long full robe.

K.G.

Knight of the Order of the Garter. Full insignia consisted of collar, hood, mantle, badge and garter buckled below the left knee.

MANTLE

The mantle was a long cloak worn over the shoulders, falling down each side. In the brasses of ladies it is generally secured by a cord in front, on the men by a button or buttons fastened on the right shoulder.

MARGINAL INSCRIPTION

The inscription placed around the slab, thus surrounding the effigies and usually engraved on a fillet, or narrow border of brass. On altar tombs marginal inscriptions were often inlaid in a chamfer or sloping edge, the words facing away from the brass, instead of towards it.

MASS VESTMENTS

These are the usual Eucharistic vestments as worn by the parish priest at the celebration of the Mass, consisting of the alb, amice, stole, maniple and chasuble. Brasses were often engraved without either the stole or maniple.

MITRE

On brasses the mitre appears as a peaked cap, richly embroidered and studded with jewels. Its height gradually increased until the Reformation, when it looked a tall and imposing headpiece.

MONASTIC HABIT

Usually showing simple Benedictine

dress, consisting of a cassock, a loose gown with wide, loose sleeves, and a cowl or hood.

ROCHET

The rochet was a type of alb made of white linen, over which was worn the chimere (a sleeveless gown), open in front, made of black or scarlet silk.

SALADE

A helmet with a movable visor in front. At the back it reached down low over the neck to guard and protect it.

SHROUDS

Sometimes shroud brasses were laid down while the person depicted was still alive.

This type of memorial showed the dead in their funeral shrouds, usually knotted above the head and below or between the feet, but left sufficiently open to reveal the breast, face and knees. Occasionally the sheets were left apart to show the naked body beneath. At first the deceased was portrayed as an emaciated but living person, which gradually evolved into the gruesome grinning skeleton.

SS COLLAR

The SS collar was worn around the shoulders by distinguished people of both sexes. Its origin and significance is obscure. It was a badge of the House of Lancaster.

STOLE

The stole was worn by those entitled to preach. It consisted of a long embroidered strip, passed around the neck so that the fringed ends came to within a foot of the floor. Only the two ends could be seen as it was worn beneath the chasuble.

SURPLICE

The surplice was worn over the alb. It was a long loose garment passed over the head, and had very deep sleeves. On brasses it appears as a pleated vestment.

TABARD

The tabard was a short coat of silk, reaching to the thighs, worn over the body armour. The wearer's arms were displayed on the front and back, and on each sleeve.

TONSURE

The round bare place on the heads of priests and monks, made by shaving the head.

TRINITY

The union of three in one, God the Father, God the Son and God the Holy Ghost. Often featured above the effigies.

WIMPLE

Worn by nuns, widows and vowesses. Consisting of a veil headdress, with a barbe or wimple hiding the neck and throat.

LIST OF ABBREVIATIONS

acad. dr. *academical dress*
ach. *achievement*
Annun. *Annunciation*
arm. *in armour*
b. *brother*
bad. mut. *badly mutiliated*
bp. *bishop*
br. *bracket*
B.V. *Blessed Virgin*
c. circa, *approximately*
can. *canopy*
c.d. *civil dress*
cent. *century*
ch. *chalice*
child. *children*
coll. *collar*
cond. *condition*
coron. *coronation*
dau. *daughter*
eff. *effigy*
emac. *emaciated*
entab. *entablature*
Ev. syms. *evangelistic symbols*
f. *father*
fam. *family*
fig. *figure*
Flem. *Flemish*
frag. *fragment*
ft *foot, feet*
her. dr. *heraldic dress*
her. mant. *heraldic mantle*
hf *half*
hf-eff. *half-effigy*
hus. *husband*
inscr. *inscription*
kng. *kneeling*
(L) *brass loose*
l. *left*
lge. *large*
liv. coll. *livery collar*
m. *mother*
mant. *mantle*
marg. *marginal*
mass vests. *mass vestments*
mcht. *merchant*
miss. *missing*
mut. *mutilated*
orig. *original*
pal. *palimpsest*
poss. *possibly*
quad. can. *quadruple canopy*
rect. pl. *rectangular plate*
rest. *restored*
s. *sister*
sin. can. *single canopy*
sm. *small*
SS coll. *collar with design of letter 'S'*
St J.B. *St John the Baptist*
stg. *standing*
tab. *tabard*
Trin. *Trinity*
trip. can. *triple canopy*
v. *very*
vests. *vestments*
w. *wife*
wf. *wafer*
wid. *widow*
wid. dr. *widow's dress*
wn. *worn*

A LIST OF DEGREES TO BE FOUND IN THE TEXT

B.A.	Bachelor of Arts
B.C.L.	Bachelor of Civil or Canon Law
B.D.	Bachelor of Divinity
D.C.L.	Doctor of Civil Law
D.D.	Doctor of Divinity
LL.B.	Bachelor of Laws
LL.D.	Doctor of Laws
M.A.	Master of Arts
M.B.	Bachelor of Medicine
M.D.	Doctor of Medicine
S.T.B.	Bachelor of (Sacred) Theology
S.T.D.	Doctor of (Sacred) Theology
S.T.P.	Professor of (Sacred) Theology

Entries in the text refer to parish churches unless otherwise indicated. No attempt has been made to locate the position of the brasses in a church, since this tends constantly to be changed.

BEDFORDSHIRE

AMPTHILL
1450 Wm. Hicchecok, mcht., c.d., mut.
w. Agnes, wid. dr.
1485 Margt. Lodyngton, c.d., sm., wn.
1506 John Barnard, c.d., sm.
w. Ellen, c.d., both wn.
1532 Sir Nich. Harve, arm.

ASPLEY GUISE
*c.*1410 Priest, acad. dr., kng. with St J.B. stg.
*c.*1501 Sir John Guise, arm., SS coll.

BARFORD, GREAT
*c.*1525 Man, arm.
w., c.d.

BARFORD, LITTLE
1535 Thos. Perys, c.d.
w. Agnes, c.d.

BARTON-IN-THE-CLAY
*c.*1396 Rich. Brey, rector, mass vests., hf-eff.
*c.*1490 Man, c.d., sm., wn.

BEDFORD, ST MARY
1627 Robt. Hawse, mayor, c.d. (covered).
1663 Mary Thorne, c.d., with 3 daus., rect. pl.

BEDFORD, ST PAUL
1573 Sir Wm. Harper, arm., mant.
2nd w. Margt., c.d., partly rest.

BIDDENHAM
*c.*1490 Wm. Faldo, c.d.
w. Agnes, c.d.
*c.*1490 John Faldo, c.d.
*c.*1520 Man, in shroud.
w., in shroud.
1639 Helen Boteler,c.d., hf-eff., rect. pl.

BIGGLESWADE
1449 Wm. Halsted, c.d. (head miss.).
w. Alice, c.d., both wn.

BLUNHAM
1506 Rich. Maulaye, mercer, c.d.
w. Alice, c.d.

BROMHAM
1535 Sir John Dyve, arm., SS coll.
m. Eliz., c.d.
w. Isobel, c.d., trip. can., marg. inscr., both mut; lge. (Orig. commem. Thos. Widville, 1435, and 2 ws., Eliz. and Alice.) [Pal.]

CADDINGTON
1505 John Hawtt, alias Cryscyan, c.d.
w. Eliz., c.d., with 4 sons, 4 daus.
1518 Edw. Dormer, yeoman, c.d.
1st w. Joan, c.d., with 7 sons, 7 daus.
2nd w. Eliz., c.d.

CAMPTON
c. 1489 Rich. Carlyll, c.d.
w. Joan, c.d., sm.

CARDINGTON
c. 1540 Sir Wm. Gasgoine, arm., tab.
1st w. Eliz., her. dr.
2nd w. ?, her. dr.
1638 Sir Jarrate Harvye, arm.
w. Dorothy, c.d., with 6 sons, 5 daus.

CLIFTON
1528 John Fysher, arm.
w., c.d.

COPLE
c. 1410 Nichol Roland, sergeant-at-law, in robes.
w. Pernel, c.d.
1415 Walter Roland, arm.
1435 John Launcelyn, arm.
w. Margt., c.d.
c. 1507 Thos. Grey, arm.
w. Benet, c.d., with 4 sons, 7 daus.
1544 Sir Walter Luke, justice of the common pleas, in robes.

w. Anne, nurse to Hen. VIII, her. mant., kng.
1556 Robt. Bulkeley, arm., with 4 sons, rect. pl., ach.
w. Joan, c.d., with 4 daus., all kng.
1563 Nich. Luke, baron of the exchequer, in judicial robes, kng.
w. Cecyle, c.d., with 5 sons, 4 daus., kng.

DEAN
1501 Thos. Parker, rector, in almuce.

DUNSTABLE
1450 Laur. Pygot, woolman, c.d. (ft miss.).
w. Alice, c.d.
1463 W. of John Pedder, c.d.
1502 John Blunte, c.d.
w. Eliz., c.d.
1516 Rich. Pynfold, c.d.
w. Margt., c.d., with 4 sons.
1518 4 daus. of Robt. Alee, sm.
1640 Rich. Fynche, tailor, c.d.
f. Thos. Fynche, c.d.
m. Eliz., c.d.

EATON BRAY
1558 Lady Jane Bray, with 1 son, 10 daus.

EATON SOCON
c.1450 Woman, c.d., sm., wn.
c.1570 2 sons, 1 shield, mut.

ELSTOW
1427 Margery Argentine, wid. dr., marg. inscr., mut.
c.1520 Dame Eliz. Herwy, abbess of Elstow, with crosier, marg. inscr., mut.

EYWORTH
1624 Rich. Gadburye, c.d.
2nd w. Margt., c.d., with 1 dau., Magdalenna, aged 5.

FELMERSHAM
c.1610 Man, c.d.
w., c.d., both sm., wn.

FLITTON
1434 Dame Eleanor Conquest, wid. (head miss.).
1544 Eliz. Waren, c.d., sm.
1545 Harry Grey, arm. [Pal.]
1628 Thos. Hill, aged 101, c.d.

GODLINGTON
1507 Rich. Fyssher, c.d.
1585 Robt. Hatley, arm., kng.

GRAVENHURST, LOWER
1606 Benj. Piggott, J.P., c.d.
1st w. Mary, c.d., with 1 son.
2nd w. Anne, c.d., with 2 sons, 2 daus.
3rd w. Bridget, c.d., with 2 sons, 7 daus.

HATLEY COCKAYNE
c.1430 Man, arm. (Poss. John Cockayne.)
c.1430 5 sons and 5 daus. (Poss. of above.)
c.1480 Woman, c.d. (Poss. w. of above.)
c.1480 3 sons, 1 dau. (Poss. of above.)
1515 Edm. Cockayne, arm.
w. Eliz., c.d., with 12 sons, 4 daus.
c.1525 2 sons, c.d.
1527 Wm. Cockyn, arm.
1st w. Dorothy, c.d.
2nd w. Kath., c.d., wn.

HAWNES (HAYNES)
1568 Anth. Newdigate, c.d., kng., ach.

HIGHAM GOBIAN
1602 Kath. Browne, c.d., with 9 sons, 6 daus.
1603 Jane Cason, c.d., with 1 son, 1 dau.

HOUGHTON CONQUEST
1493 John Conquest, arm., with 1 son,

Richard, arm., and his w. Isabel, c.d., with 9 sons, 5 daus.
1500 Rich. Conquest, arm.
w. Eliz., c.d., sm.

HOUGHTON REGIS
1410 John Waleys, vicar, mass vests., hf-eff.
1506 Wm. Walley, vicar, mass vests.

HUSBORNE CRAWLEY
1600 John Carter, c.d.
w. Agnes, c.d., with 2 sons, 6 daus., sm., wn.

KEMPSTON
1605 7 sons of Wm. Carter, c.d.

LANGFORD
1520 Thos. Hundon, vicar, mass vests., wn.

LEIGHTON BUZZARD
1597 Wm. Jackmann, c.d., with 2 sons, kng., rect. pl.
1636 Francis Welles, c.d.
w. Margt., c.d., rect. pl.

LIDLINGTON, NEW CHURCH
c. 1490 Wm. Goldyngton, c.d.
w. Margt., c.d., with 2 sons, 4 daus., Trin., marg. inscr., mut.

LUTON, ST MARY
c. 1415 Hugh atte Spetyll, c.d., with 1 son, John, priest, mass vests. (head rest.).
1455 Isabel Hay, c.d. [Pal.]
c. 1490 Woman, wid. dr., trip. can., mut. (Poss. of the Rotherham fam.)
1500 Man, c.d.
1512 4 daus. of John Lamar, c.d.
1513 John Sylam, arm.
1st w. Eliz., c.d.
2nd w. Joan, c.d.
1513 John Acworth, arm., with 8 sons, 9 daus.
1st w. Alys, c.d.
2nd w. Amy, c.d. (All repaired, relaid, 1911.)
1515 Agnes Barbar, c.d. (Inscr. reads 1415, engraver's error.)
c. 1515 Edw. Sheffeld, LL.D., in almuce, cap.
c. 1520 Robt. Su—?, c.d. (head miss.).
1st w., c.d.
2nd w., Annys, c.d., broken and mut.
1593 Woman, c.d.
Part eff. of another, ws. of Geo. Rotherham, with 3 sons, 1 dau., also 2 sons, 1 dau., his child.

MARSTON MORTAINE
1420 Walter Papley, rector, mass vests., hf-eff.
1451 Thos. Reynes, arm.
w. Alice, wid. dr., with 9 sons (2 heads miss.).

MAULDEN
1576 Rich. Faldo, arm.
w. Amphelice, c.d., with 4 sons, marg. inscr., mut., ach.
1594 Anne, dau. of above, c.d., kng., sm.

MEPSHALL (MEPPERSHALL)
1440 John Mepertyshale, arm., wn.
1441 John Boteler, arm.
w. Eliz., c.d., mut., wn.

PODDINGTON
1518 John Howard, c.d.

POTTESGROVE
1535 Rich. Sawnders, c.d.
w. Joan, c.d.
1563 Wm. Saunders, c.d. (lower hf miss.).
w. Issabel, c.d. (centre part only), mut. [Pal.]

PULLOXHILL
1608 Geo. Fittz, arm.
w. Anne, c.d., kng., rect. pl.

RENHOLD
1518 Edw. Wayte, c.d., dog at ft.
w. Agnes, c.d., sm.

SALFORD
1505 John Peddar, c.d.
w. Alice, c.d., with 6 sons, 5 daus.

SHARNBROOK
1522 Wm. Cobbe, smith, c.d.
w. Alice, c.d., with 1 son, Thos.

SHILLINGTON
1400 Matthew de Asscheton, rector, in cope, marg. inscr., mut., lge.
1485 Thos. Portyngton, rector, in cope, hood, sm., wn.

SOULDROP
1608 John Hangar, c.d., kng., rect. pl.

STAGSDEN
1617 John Cocke, arm., with 1 dau., Eliz., aged 11, rect. pl.

STEVINGTON
1422 Thos. Salle, arm.

THURLEIGH
c. 1420 John Harvey ?, arm., wn.

TILBROOK
c. 1400 Man, c.d., anelace.
w., c.d.

TINGRITH
1611 Robt. Hogeson, c.d., with 2 chrysoms, rect. pl., ach.

TODDINGTON
c. 1480 Two pieces of a shrouded fig., with 3 daus. and 1 chrysom.

TOTTERNHOE
1524 John Warwekhyll, vicar, mass vests., ch., wf.
1621 Wm. Michell, c.d., sm.

TURVEY
c. 1480 Man, c.d., sm.
c. 1500 John Crosse?, priest, acad. dr.
1606 Alice Bernard, c.d.

WILLSHAMPSTEAD
c. 1450 Wm. Carbrok, chaplain, mass vests., hf-eff.

WYMINGTON
1391 John Curteys, c.d., anelace.
w. Aubrey, wid. dr., mant., dble. can., marg. inscr.
1407 Margt. Brounflet, c.d., mant.
1430 Sir Thos. Brounflet, cup bearer to Rich. II., arm.
c. 1510 John Stokys, rector, mass vests., ch., wf.

YELDEN
1433 John Heyne, rector, mass vests.
1617 Thos. Barker, M.A., rector, kng., rect. pl.
1628 Christ. Strickland, c.d., rect. pl.

In the Victoria and Albert Museum are brasses from Dunstable Priory Church to
1521 Alys, w. of Nich. Purvey, c.d.
c. 1516 Hen. Fayrey, in shroud.
w. Agnes, in shroud, with 5 sons.

BERKSHIRE

ABINGDON, ST HELEN
1417 Geoff. Barbur, mcht., c.d., hf-eff.
1501 Wm. Herward, S.T.D., vicar, acad. dr., wn.

APPLETON
1518 John Goodryngton, emac. eff. in shroud.

ASHBURY
c. 1360 John de Walden, in cape and hood (head mut.), hf-eff., sm.
1409 Thos. de Busshbury, rector, in cope (head miss.).
1448 Wm. Skelton, LL.B., rector, in cope.

Basildon
1497 John Clerk, c.d., sm.
w. Lucy, c.d.

Binfield
c. 1361 Walter de Annefordhe, rector, mass vests., hf-eff.

Bisham
1517 Thos. Crekett, fishmonger, c.d.
1581 John Brinckhurst, mcht., c.d.
1st w. Eliz., c.d.
2nd w. Jane, c.d.

Blewbury
1496 John Balam, vicar, mass vests.
c. 1515 Man, arm. (Poss. of the Latton fam.)
2 ws., c.d., with 3 daus.
1523 Sir John Daunce, arm., tab.
w. Alice, her. mant., with 5 sons, 2 daus.
1548 John Latton, arm., tab.
w. Anne, c.d., with 9 daus.

Bray
1378 Sir John de Foxle, arm.
1st w. Maud, her. dr.
2nd w. Joan, her. dr. on br., dble. can., bad. mut.
1475 Sir Wm. Laken, justice of the king's bench, in robes, anelace, rosary.
c. 1490 Wm. Smyth, c.d.
1st w. Agnes, c.d.
2nd w. Maud, c.d., with 7 sons, 5 daus.
c. 1610 Arthur Page, c.d.
w. Sessely, c.d., kng., with 1 son, Edw., chrysom, rect. pl.
1621 John Rixman, M.A., c.d.
w. Mary, c.d., rect. pl., ach.

Brightwalton
1517 John Newman, c.d., sm.

Brightwell
1507 John Scoffyld, priest, mass vests. ch., wf.
1509 Robt. Court, c.d.
w. Jane, c.d.
1512 Rich. Hampden, c.d.
w. Jane, c.d., sm.

Buckland
1578 John Yate, c.d.
w. Mary, c.d., with 5 sons, 7 daus., ach.

Burghfield
1568 Nich. Williams, arm.
2nd w. Mabel, c.d.

Buscot
c. 1500 Man, c.d. (head miss.).
w., c.d.

Childrey
1444 Wm. Fynderne, arm., tab.
w. Dame Eliz., her. dr., dble. can., mut., ft inscr., marg. inscr., lge.
c. 1480 Priest, mass vests.
c. 1480 Wm. Walrond, c.d.
w. Eliz., c.d.
c. 1490 Priest, mass vests. (head miss.), ch., sm.
1477 Joan Strangbon, on tomb in shroud, Trin., lge.
1514 John Kyngeston, arm.
w. Susan, c.d., Trin.
1516 Wm. Feteplace, in shroud.
w. Eliz., in shroud, both rising from tombs.
c. 1520 Thos. Walrond, c.d.
w. Alice, c.d., Trin.
1529 Bryan Roos, LL.D., parson, acad. dr.

Cholsey
1471 John Mere, vicar, mass vests., ch., sm., wn.

Compton Parva
c. 1520 Rich. Pygott, c.d.
w. Alice, c.d.

Cookham
1458 John Babham, c.d., sm.

1503 Margt. Andrew, c.d.
1st hus. John Monkeden, c.d.
2nd hus. Wm. Andrew, c.d., all sm.
1510 Robt. Pecke, arm.
w. Annes, c.d., Trin., sm.
1527 Rich. Babham, arm.
w., c.d., both kng.
1577 Raffe More, c.d.
w. Mary, c.d., bad. mut. [Part pal.]
1615 Dau. of Edw. Woodyore, c.d., sm.

COXWELL, GREAT

c. 1509 Wm. Morys, c.d., with 2 sons, 1 dau.
c. 1510 Joan, w. of Wm. Morys, c.d.

CUMNOR

c. 1572 Anth. Forster, arm., ach.
w. Anne, with 3 sons, all kng.
1577 Kath. Staverton, c.d., with 1 son, bad. mut. [Pal.]
1599 ? Staverton, c.d.
w. Yedythe, c.d.

DENCHWORTH

1516 Olyver Hyde, arm.
w. Agnes, c.d.
1562 Wm. Hyde, arm.
w. Margery, c.d., with 12 sons, 8 daus.
1567 Wm. Hyde, arm.
w. Alice, c.d.

EASTHAMSTEAD

1443 Thos. Berwyk, c.d., hf-eff.

FARINGDON

1443 Thos. Faryndon, arm., liv. coll. (head miss.).
w. Margt., c.d., with 1 dau., Kath. Pynchepole.
1485 John Parker, c.d.
w. Margt., c.d., wn.
1505 John Sadler, vicar, mass vests., sm.
1547 Sir Alex. Unton, arm., tab., with 7 sons.
1st w. Mary, her dr.
2nd w. Lady Cecyll, her. dr., with 3 daus. (heads of both ws. mut.), all kng.

FAWLEY

1621 Mary Gunter, c.d., with 1 son, kng, rect. pl.

FINCHAMPSTEAD

1635 Eliz. Blighe, c.d., with 1 dau., Jane, aged 5, rect. pl.

HAGBOURNE, EAST

1627 Hugh Keate, arm.
w. Christian, c.d., with 4 sons, 4 daus., all kng., rect. pl.

HANNEY, WEST

c. 1370 John Seys, rector, mass vests., lge. (lower hf and br. miss.), marg. inscr., mut.
1557 Humf. Cheynie, arm., marg. inscr.
1592 John Ayshcombe, c.d.
1st w., c.d.
2nd w. Margery, c.d.
1599 Sir Christ. Lytcot, arm.
1602 Francis Wellesborne, arm.
1st w. Alice, c.d.
2nd w. Eleanor, c.d., with 3 daus., ach.
1611 Oliver Ayshcombe, c.d.
w. Martha, c.d., with 4 sons, 2 daus.

HARWELL

1599 John Jennens, c.d.
w. Margt., c.d., with 6 sons, 5 daus.

HENDRED, EAST

1439 Roger Eldysley, mcht., c.d.
1589 John Eyston, arm.
w. Jane, c.d., with 4 sons, 1 dau.

HURST

1574 Rich. Warde, c.d., with 8 sons.

w. Colibury, c.d. (head miss.), with 9 daus., all kng., ach.
c. 1600 Alice Harison, in bed, rect. pl. (Died in childbirth).

KINTBURY
1626 John Gunter, c.d.
w. Alice, c.d.

LAMBOURNE
c. 1406 John de Estbury, c.d., hf-eff.
w. Agnes, c.d., hf-eff.
c. 1410 John Estbury, c.d., hf-eff., with 1 son, Thos., c.d., hf-eff.
c. 1485 John Estbury, arm., tab., mut., chamfer inscr.
1619 Thos. Garrard, c.d.
w. Anne, c.d., ach.

LANGFORD
1609 Walter Prunes, c.d.
w. Mary, c.d., marg. inscr., ach.

LETCOMBE REGIS
c. 1440 Alice Estbury, c.d. (head miss.), v.sm.

LOCKINGE, EAST
1624 Edw. Keat, c.d.
w. Joan, c.d.
1628 Mary Nedham, aged 16, c.d., sm.

LONGWORTH
1422 John Henele, rector, mass vests., hf-eff.
1500 Rich. Yate, in shroud.
w. Joan, in shroud, with 3 sons, in shrouds, 2 c.d.
1509 8 daus. of John Yate, 4 in shrouds.
1566 Elynor Goodolphyn, c.d.

MARCHAM
1540 Edm. Fetyplace, arm., with 5 sons.
w. Margt., c.d., with 6 daus., all kng.

MORETON, NORTH
c. 1500 4 sons, 1 a priest, in almuce, were (L).

MORTIMER STRATFIELD
1441 Rich. Trevet, alias Hasylwode, arm.
w. Joan, c.d. (head miss.).

NEWBURY
1519 John Smalwode, alias Wynchcom, c.d.
w. Alice, c.d., with 2 sons, 1 dau.

READING, ST GILES
1521 John Bowyer, tanner, c.d.
w. Jone, c.d., both wn.

READING, ST LAURENCE
c. 1415 John Kent, burgess, c.d., hf-eff.
w. Joan, c.d., hf-eff.
1538 Walter Barton, c.d. [Pal.]
1584 Edw. Butler, c.d.

REMENHAM
1591 Thos. Maryet, arm. (head miss.), sm., ach.
1622 John Newman, pastor, in gown.

SANDHURST
1608 Rich Geale, c.d.
w. Eliz., c.d., with 4 sons, 5 daus., both sm.

SHEFFORD, LITTLE, OLD CHURCH
1524 John Fetyplace, arm.
w. Dorothy, c.d., kng., with 4 daus.

SHOTTESBROOKE
c. 1370 Priest, mass vests.
Man, c.d., anelace, dble. can., mut., lge.
1401 Margt. Pennebrygg, c.d.
1511 Rich. Gyll, arm.
1567 Thos. Noke, c.d., badge on shoulder.
1st w., c.d.
2nd w., c.d., with 3 sons, 3 daus.
3rd w. Julian, c.d.

SONNING

1434 Laur. Fyton, bailiff, arm.

1546 Anth. Barker, c.d., sm.

1549 Wm. Barker, c.d.
w. Anne, c.d., with 1 dau., Anne.

1575 Anne Barker, c.d., with 6 sons, 5 daus.

1585 Anne Staverton, c.d., with 4 sons.

1627 Eliz. Chute, c.d., aged 3½, sm.

SPARSHOLT

1353 Wm. de Herleston, rector, mass vests., in head of cross (nearly all miss.).

*c.*1495 Thos. Bothe?, c.d. (lower hf miss.), with 2 sons.

*c.*1510 Woman, c.d., sm.

1602 John Fettiplace, c.d.

STANFORD-DINGLEY

1444 Margt. Dyneley, c.d.

1610 John Lyford, tailor, c.d.

*c.*1620 Man, c.d., kng., sm.

STANFORD-IN-THE-VALE

1398 Roger Campedene, rector, mass vests., hf-eff., lge.

STEVENTON

1476 Rich. Do, c.d.
w. either Agnes or Joan, c.d., sm.

1584 Edm. Wiseman, arm.
w. Anne, with 4 sons, 4 daus., 2 ach.

STREATLEY

1570 Margt. Byryngton, c.d.

1583 Griffen Clarke, c.d., sm. [Pal.]

1600 Thos. Clarke, c.d.
w. Eliz., c.d., with 1 son, 3 daus. (Brasses buried under chancel floor.)

1603 Thos. Buriton, c.d.
w. Joan, c.d.

SWALLOWFIELD

1466 Margery Letterford, c.d., sm.

1544 Christ. Lytkott, arm.
w. Kath., c.d., with 3 sons, 1 dau.

TIDMARSH

1499 Margt. Wode, c.d.

1517 Hen. Leynham, arm., tab. (head mut.).

TILEHURST

1469 Gauwyn More, marshall of the king's hall, c.d., sm.
w. Isabel, c.d., with 3 sons, 2 daus.

UFTON NERVET

1627 Wm. Smith, c.d., sm.
w. Constance, c.d., ach.

WALTHAM, WHITE

1445 Margt. Hille, c.d. (head miss.), (L).

1506 Joan Decons, c.d., sm.

WANTAGE

*c.*1370 Priest, mass vests., hf-eff.

1414 Sir Ivo Fitzwaryn, arm., lge.

1512 Wm. Geddyng, vicar, acad. dr., marg. inscr., mut.

1522 Walter Tawbott, c.d.
1st w. Agnes, c.d.
2nd w. Alice, c.d., with 5 sons.

1619 Cecily Willmott, c.d., marg. inscr., mut.

WARFIELD

1592 Humf. Staverton, c.d.

WELFORD

*c.*1490 John Westlake, priest, acad. dr., sm.

*c.*1530 John Younge, c.d., sm.

WINDSOR, OLD

1621 Humf. Michell, c.d.
2nd w. Frances, c.d., with 1 son, Samuel, c.d., servant to Jas. I.

WINDSOR, ST GEORGE'S CHAPEL

1475 Sir Thos. Sellynger, arm., tab.
w. Anne, s. to Edw. IV, mant., both kng., rect. pl., Trin., repaired.

1522 Robt. Honywode, canon of Windsor, in almuce, kng., rect. pl., can. with St Kath. and B.V. with Child.

1630 Dorothy King, aged 8 months, in cradle.

1633 Wm. 2nd son of John and Mary King, aged 10 weeks.

WINKFIELD

1630 Thos. Mountagu, yeoman of the guard, in habit of the guard, distributing bread to poor, hf-eff., rect. pl.

WITTENHAM, LITTLE

1433 John Churmound, rector, mass vests.

1454 David Kidwelly, porter of the palace to Hen. VI, c.d., sm.

1472 Cecily Kydwelly, c.d.

1483 Geoff. Kidwelly, c.d.

c. 1585 Wm. Dunche, auditor of the mints to Hen. VIII, Edw. VI, c.d., kng.
w. Marie, c.d., kng. rect. pl.

1588 John Barnes, arm., kng., rect. pl., ach.

1683 Anne Dunch, aged 9 months, rect. pl., sm.

WOKINGHAM

c. 1520 Man, c.d. (ft miss.).
w., c.d.

c. 1610 Clement? Dawbnie, c.d.
w., c.d., kng., rect. pl.

WYTHAM

c. 1455 Man, arm.
w., c.d. (lower hf of both effs. miss.). (Poss. Wm. Browning and w. Agnes.)

BUCKINGHAMSHIRE

AMERSHAM

1430 Hen. Brudenell, c.d., anelace.
w. Eleanor, c.d.

1439 Thos. Carbonell, c.d.
w. Eliz., c.d.

1450 Man, c.d. (head miss.), wn.

1521 John de la Penne, c.d.
w. Eliz., c.d.

1623 John Drake, aged 4, kng., sm.

ASTWOOD

1534 Thos. Chibnale, c.d.
1st w. Emme, c.d.
2nd w. Alice, c.d.

BEACHAMPTON

1600 Wm. Bawdyn, blacksmith, c.d.

1611 Alice Baldwyn, c.d., with 2 sons, 2 daus., sm.

BEACONSFIELD

1609 John Warren, c.d.
w. Eliz., c.d., with 4 sons, 2 daus.

BLEDLOW

1525 Wm. Herun, B.A., vicar, mass vests., sm.

BLETCHLEY

1616 Thos. Sparke, rector, bust in oval, with 3 sons, 2 daus.

BRADENHAM

1521 Rich. Redberd, rector, mass vests.

BURNHAM

c. 1500 Gyles Eyre, c.d.
w. Eliz., c.d., sm.

c. 1520 15 daus. of Wm. and Agnes Aldriche.

1563 Edm. Eyre, c.d.
w., c.d., with 3 sons, 2 daus., ach. [Pal.]

1581 Thos. Eyer, c.d.
1st w., c.d.
2nd w., c.d., with 4 sons, 3 daus.
3rd w., c.d. [All pal.]

Calverton

1519 John Rokys, c.d.
w. Joan, c.d.

Chalfont St Giles

c. 1470 Priest, mass vests., sm.

c. 1500 3 sons.

c. 1510 Woman, c.d.

c. 1540 Man, c.d. (Poss. of Gardyner fam.)
2 ws., c.d.

c. 1558 Wm. Gardyner, arm.
w. Anne, c.d., with 5 sons, 4 daus.

1570 Thos. Fletewood, arm.
1st w. Barbara, c.d., with 2 sons, 2 daus.
2nd w. Brigett, c.d., with 8 sons, 6 daus., all kng., ach.

Chalfont St Peter

c. 1446 Wm. Whappelode sen., arm.
w. Eliz., c.d.

1446 Wm. Whappelode jun., arm.
w. Margery, c.d.

c. 1440 Priest, mass vests., sm. [Pal.]
Fig. slightly altered, inscr. added, appropriated to

1545 Robert Hanson, vicar.

Chearsley

1462 John Frankeleyn, c.d.
w. Margt., c.d., with 3 sons, 4 daus., sm.

Chenies

1469 John Waliston, c.d.
1st w. Isabel, c.d.
2nd w. Joan, c.d., all wn.

1484 Edm. Molyneux, arm., salade.
w. Agnes, mant., dble. can., wn.

1494 Rich. Newland?, rector, mass vests., sm., wn.

1510 Dame Anne Philip, wid. dr., holding heart, sin. can., wn.

1511 Agnes Johnson, wid. dr.

1524 Eliz. Broughton, c.d., flowing hair, marg. inscr.

Chesham Bois

1516 Eliz. Cheyne, c.d.

1552 Robt. Cheyne, arm.

Chicheley

1558 Anth. Cave, arm. (head mut.).
w. Eliz., c.d.

c. 1560 Anth. Cave, skeleton in shroud, rect. pl., sm.

Claydon, Middle

1523 Isabel Gifford, c.d.

1526 Alex. Anne, priest, $\frac{3}{4}$-eff., mass vests., ch., wf.

1542 Roger Gyfford, arm.
w. Mary, c.d., with 13 sons, 7 days., lge.

Clifton Reynes

1428 Sir John Reynes, arm., legs mut.

c. 1500 John Reynes, in shroud.
2nd w. Agnes, in shroud.

Crawley, North

1589 John Garbrand, parson, in gown and hood, kng., rect. pl.

Crendon, Long

1468 John Canon, c.d.
w. Agnes, c.d., with 3 sons, 8 daus.

Datchet

1593 Rich. Hanbery, goldsmith, c.d.
w. Alice, c.d., with 2 daus., rect. pl.

Denham

1494 Walter Duredent, arm.
1st w. Agnes, c.d., with 9 sons, 10 daus.
2nd w. Margt.. c.d., with 3 sons, 4 daus., ach., wn.

c. 1540 Dame Agnes Jordan, abbess of Syon, monastic dr.

1528 3 sons, 1 dau., of Thos. Bedyll.
1545 Amphillis Pekham, c.d., flowing hair. [Pal. on reverse, eff. of friar, in gown and hood, with hands folded in sleeves, *c.* 1440.]
1560 Leonard Hurst, parson, in surplice.

DINTON

1424 John Compton, arm.
w. Margery, c.d., with 4 sons, 7 daus., child. kng., sm.
1486 Wm. Lee, c.d.
w. Alice, c.d. (head miss.).
1551 Thos. Greneway, arm.
w. Eliz., c.d.
1551 Rich. Greneway, arm., son of above.
w. Joan, c.d., both mut.
1558 Francis Lee, c.d. [Pal.[
w. Eliz., c.d., sm.
1628 Simon Mayne, arm.
w. Colubery, c.d., with 2 child., Simon and Colubery, ach.

DRAYTON BEAUCHAMP

1368 Thos. Cheyne, arm., shield-bearer to Edw. III, lge.
1375 Wm. Cheyne, arm., marg. inscr., mut., lge.
1531 Hen. Fazakyrley, priest, mass vests. (head miss.), ch., wf., sm.

DRAYTON PARSLOW

1535 3 sons, 11 daus. of Agnes and Benet Blacknolle.

DUNTON

c. 1420 Man, c.d.
w., c.d., sm.
c. 1510 ? Collys, c.d., with 1 son stg. behind, sm.

EDLESBOROUGH

1395 John de Swynstede, rector, mass vests., lge.
1540 John Rufford, arm.
3 ws. Brygett, Anne, Elynore, c.d., all on 1 pl.
1592 John Pigott, c.d.
w. Wenefrid, c.d.

ELLESBOROUGH

1544 Thos. Hawtrey, arm.
w. Sybell, c.d., with 11 sons, 7 daus.

EMBERTON

c. 1410 John Mordon, alias Andrew, rector, mass vests.

ETON COLLEGE CHAPEL

1489 Thos. Barker, S.T.D., fellow, in cap and almuce, sm.
1503 Hen. Bost, provost, in almuce, trip. can., partly rest., lge.
1509 Rich. Ardern, fellow, mass vests., ch., wf., sm., wn.
1521 Rich. Grey, arm., sm.
1522 Wm. Boutrod, pety-canon of Windsor, in cope.
1525 Walter Smith, M.A., fellow, acad. dr.
1525 ? Horman, mass vests., ch., wf.
1528 W. of Hen. Smyth, c.d. (Poss. Agnes.)
c. 1540 Roger Lupton, provost of Eton, canon of Windsor, mant., with garter badge.
1545 Thos. Edgcomb, fellow, vice-provost, in hood, ¾-eff. [Pal.]
c. 1560 Eliz. Stokys, c.d.
1636 Thos. Allen, fellow of Eton, in gown, kng.

HADDENHAM

c. 1420 Priest, in choir cope, wn.
1428 Thos. Nassh, vicar, mass vests., hf-eff.

HALTON

1553 Hen. Bradschawe, baron of the exchequer, in robes.
w. Joan, with 4 sons, 4 daus., all kng.

HAMBLEDEN
1457 John Shipwash, c.d. (lower hf miss.), with 4 sons.
1497 John White, c.d.
w. Alice, c.d.
1500 Kath. Scrop, wid., mant.
c. 1600 Man, c.d.
w., c.d. (upper hf miss.).
1634 John Saunders, c.d., rect. pl.
2 ws., c.d.

HAMPDEN, GREAT
c. 1525 John Hampden, arm.
w. Eliz., c.d., with 4 sons, 6 daus.
1553 Sir John Hampden, arm.
1st w. Eliz., c.d., with 3 daus.
2nd w. Philippa, c.d.
1626 5 sons, 3 daus. of Sir Jerome Horsey.

HANSLOPE
1602 Mary Birchmore, aged 6, sm.

HARDMEAD
1556 Francis Catesby, c.d. (ft miss.).

HAVERSHAM
1427 Alice Payn, c.d.
1605 John Maunsell, skeleton, rect. pl.

HEDGERLEY
1498 Robt. Fulmer, c.d.
w. Joan, c.d., with 2 sons, 2 daus., sm.
1540 Margt. Bulstrode, c.d., with 10 sons, 3 daus. [All pal.]

HITCHAM
1510 Thos. Ramsey, arm.
w. Margt., c.d., with 4 sons, 3 daus.
1551 Nich. Clarke, arm., with 2 sons, Wm. and John.

HORWOOD, GREAT
1487 Hen. Upnore, rector, acad. dr., sm., wn.

HUGHENDEN
1493 Robt. Thursbe, chaplain, in mass vests., sm.

IVER
1508 Rich. Blount, arm.
w. Eliz., c.d., with 3 sons, 3 daus., marg. inscr.

IVINGHOE
1517 Rich. Blackhed, c.d.
w. Maud, c.d., sm.
1531 Thos. Duncombe, c.d. (head rest.), with 4 daus.
1576 Wm. Duncombe, c.d., with 3 sons, 2 daus. by 1st w. Mary, and 6 sons by 2nd w. Alice.
1594 John Douncombe, c.d.
w. Alice, c.d., with 4 sons, 3 daus.

LANGLEY MARSH
1608 John Bowser, c.d.

LECKHAMSTEAD
c. 1500 Woman, c.d.
1506 Regenolde Tylney, c.d., with 3 daus., Eliz., Joan and Joan, separate.

LILLINGSTONE DAYRELL
1491 Paul Dayrell, arm.
w. Margt., c.d.
1493 Rich. Blakysley, rector, mass vests., sm. (head miss.).

LILLINGSTONE LOVELL
c. 1460 Thos. Clarell, c.d., suns and roses on coll.
w. Agnes, c.d., with 1 son, 2 daus.
1513 Wm. Rysley, c.d.
w. Agnes, c.d.

LINFORD, GREAT
1473 Roger Hunt, c.d.
w. Joan, c.d., marg. inscr.
1536 Thos. Malyn, c.d.
w. Eliz., c.d., with 1 dau.

1611 John Uvedall, c.d., sm.
w. Anne, c.d., with 5 sons, 3 daus.

LINSLADE, OLD CHURCH
c.1500 Man, c.d.
3 ws., c.d., with 5 sons, 7 daus.

LOUGHTON
1514 Hugh Parke, rector, mass vests., hf-eff.

LUDGERSHALL
c.1600 Ann, w. of Mihil Englishe, c.d. Anne Englishe, w. of John Gyfford, with 1 dau., Anne Neele, aged 4, ach.

MARLOW, LITTLE
1430 Alice Ledewich, c.d.

MARSTON, NORTH
1602 Rich. Sanders, c.d., rect. pl.

MARSWORTH
1586 Nich. West, arm. (legs only). [Pal.]
4 sons (legs only), 2 daus., ach.
1606 Mary West, c.d., with chrysom.
1618 Edm. West, arm., reclining on tomb, fig. of Death behind.
w. Theodosia, kng., with 1 son, 6 daus, 2 infants in cradle, rect. pl.

MILTON KEYNES
1427 Adam Babington, rector, mass vests.

MISSENDEN, GREAT
c.1510 Woman, c.d., sm.

MISSENDEN, LITTLE
1613 John Style, c.d.
1646 Portion of 2 daus. of Francis Style.

MOULSOE
1528 Rich. Rowthall, arm.
w., c.d.

MURSLEY
1570 Cecily Fortescue, c.d., marg. inscr., mut.

NETTLEDEN
1545 Sir George Cotten, arm. [All pal. by alteration.]

NEWPORT PAGNELL
c.1440 Man, c.d., v. wn., lge.

PENN
1540 Eliz. Rok, in shroud.
1597 John Pen, arm.
w. Ursula, c.d., with 6 sons (lower hf of both effs. miss.).
1638 Wm. Pen, arm.
w. Martha, c.d., with 1 son, 2 daus.
1640 Lady Susan Drury, c.d., ach.
1641 John Penn, arm.
w. Sarah, c.d., with 5 sons, 5 daus.

PITSTONE
c.1315 Woman, c.d., sm.

QUAINTON
c.1360 Joan Plessi, c.d., hf-eff., sm.
1422 John Lewys, rector, acad. dr., kng., sm.
1485 John Spence, rector, in cope, marg. inscr.
1509 Margery Verney, c.d., with 1 son, 3 daus.
1510 Rich. Iwarby, c.d.
1593 Eliz. Chester, c.d., sm.

RADNAGE
1534 Wm. Este, c.d., with 8 sons, 1 a priest, and 5 daus., mut.

RISBOROUGH, MONKS
1431 Robt. Blundell, rector, mass vests.
c.1460 Man, c.d., hf-eff.
w., c.d., hf-eff.
c.1520 2 sons, 5 daus.

SAUNDERTON

c. 1430 Isabel Saunterton, c.d., hf-eff., sm.

SHALSTON

1540 Dame Susan Kyngeston, vowess.

SLAPTON

1462 Reginald Mauser, rector, mass vests., hf-eff.

1519 Jas. Torney, c.d., badge on shoulder.
1st w. Amye, c.d., with 3 sons, 2 daus.
2nd w. Eliz., c.d., with 4 sons, 5 daus.

1529 Thos. Knyghton, parson, mass vests., ch., wf., sm.

SOULBURY

1502 John Turnay, c.d.
w. Agnes, c.d.

1516 Agnes Mallet, c.d., with 8 daus., wn.

STOKENCHURCH

1410 Robt. Morle, arm.

1415 Robt. Morle, arm.

1632 Barth Typping, c.d., rect. pl.
w. Martha, c.d., rect. pl.

STOKE POGES

1425 Sir Wm. Molyns, arm.
w. Dame Margery, wid. dr.

c. 1577 Edm. Hampdyn, c.d.
w. Isabel, c.d., marg. inscr., mut.

STONE

1472 Wm. Gurney, in shroud (head miss.).
w. Agnes, c.d.

1520 Thos. Gorney, c.d. [Pal.]
w. Agnes, c.d., with 6 sons, 3 daus.

STOWE

c. 1479? Alice Saunders, c.d., sm.

1592 John Temple, aged 2 months, sm.

SWANBOURN

1626 Thos. Adams, c.d.
w. Eliz., c.d., with 2 sons, 2 daus.

TAPLOW

c. 1350 Nichole de Aumberdene, sm. eff. in head of fine floriated cross, stem resting on dolphin. (Eff. and cross slightly mut.)

1455 Rich. Manfeld, aged 19, c.d., liv. coll., with maiden s. Isabel, in mant., flowing hair, young b. John, in shroud.

1540 Thos. Manfeld, arm. (r. ft miss.).
1st w. Agnes, c.d.
2nd w. Kath., wid., c.d. [All pal.]

THORNBOROUGH

c. 1420 Wm. Barton, c.d.
w., c.d.

THORNTON

1472 Robt. Ingylton, arm.
1st w. Margt., c.d., with 3 sons, 5 daus.
2nd w. Clemens, c.d., with 2 sons, 3 daus.
3rd w. Isabel, c.d., with 1 son, 2 daus., quad. can.

1557 Jane Seynct Johns, c.d., marg. inscr.

TINGEWICK

1608 Erasmus Williams, rector, in ruff and gown, kng., rect. pl.

TURWESTON

c. 1450 Priest, mass vests.

c. 1490 Thos. Grene, c.d.
1st w. Joan, c.d.
2nd w. Agnes, c.d., v. sm.

TWYFORD

1413 John Everdon, rector, mass vests., hf-eff.

1550 Thos. Giffard, arm. [Pal.]

Tyringham

c. 1484 John Teringham, arm., tab., salade.

1508 Mary Catesby, c.d.

Upton

1472 Agnes Bulstrode, in shroud, kng.

1517 Edw. Bulstrode, arm., with 2 ws., c.d., either Mary, Ellen or Margt., with 2 groups of child., 4 sons, 6 sons, 2 daus.

1599 Edw. Bulstrod, arm.
w. Cecil, c.d., with 4 sons, 6 daus.

Waddesdon

1490 Roger Dynham, arm., tab., trip. can., marg. inscr., bad. mut.

1543 Rich. Huntyngdon, rector, mass vests., ch., wf., sm.

1548 Hugh Brystowe, parson, in shroud.

1561 Robt. Pygott, arm.
w. Mary, c.d., with 6 sons, effs. mut.

Wendover

1537 Wm. Bradschawe, c.d., kng.
w. Alice, c.d., with 2 sons, 7 daus., 1 unmarried, 3 of child. in shrouds.

Weston Turville

c. 1580 Man, c.d.

Weston Underwood

1571 Eliz. Throkmarton, c.d. (head miss.), with 5 daus.

Whaddon

1519 Thos. Pygott, serjeant-at-law, in robes.
1st w. Agnes, c.d., with 2 sons, 3 daus.
2nd w. Eliz., c.d., with 3 sons, 2 daus.

1612 Margt. Myssenden, c.d., kng., with 1 son, a skeleton.

Winchendon, Nether

c. 1420 John Hampden?, arm.

c. 1420 Woman, c.d.

1487 John Barton, c.d. (head miss.).
w. Margt., c.d., sm.

Winchendon, Over

1502 John Stodeley, in habit of Austin canon.

Wing

1489 Harry Blaknall, c.d.
w. Agnes, c.d., both wn.

c. 1490 Man, c.d.
w., c.d., wn.

1648 Thos. Cotes, c.d., kng., rect. pl.

Winslow

1578 Thos. Fige, c.d.
w. Jane, c.d., with 2 sons, 5 daus., sm.

1634 Dorothy Barnard, c.d., wn.

Wooburn

1488 John Godwyn, c.d.

c. 1500 Christ. Askowe, c.d.
w. Margery, c.d., wn.

1519 Thos. Swayn, S.T.B., in cope.

c. 1520 Christ. Grantham, in shroud, Trin.

1642 Arthur Wharton, aged 9 months, reclining on altar tomb, rect. pl.

Worminghall

1592 Philip Kinge, c.d.
w. Eliz., c.d., with 5 sons, 6 daus., kng., and dead infant, rect. pl.

Wotton Underwood

1587 Edw. Greneville, c.d.
w. Alice, c.d., with chrysom.

Wyrardisbury (Wraysbury)

1488 John Brecknock, arm., dble. can.

1512 John Stonor, scholar, c.d., sm.

CAMBRIDGESHIRE

ABINGTON-PIGOTTS

c. 1460 Man, c.d., with 8 sons, 8 daus. (Poss. of the Pigott fam.)

BALSHAM

1401 John Sleford, rector, in cope with SS, B.V. Mary and Child, arms of England, etc., marg. inscr., trip. can., lge., fine.

1462 Dr John Blodwell, canon, in gown, cap, with saints, marg. inscr., sin. can., entab., lge., wn.

c. 1480 Man, arm., wn.

BARTON

c. 1600 John Martin, c.d., sm.
w. Margt., c.d.

BASSINGBOURN

1683 Edw. Turpin, c.d.
w. Eliz., c.d.

BRINCKLEY

1521 Son and dau. of Wm. Stutfield.

BURWELL

c. 1520 John Laurence, Benedictine abbot of Ramsey, in surplice, almuce, trip. can., lge. [Part pal.] (Altered from mass vests. to almuce after the Dissolution.)

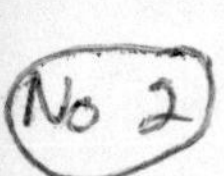

CAMBRIDGE, CHRIST'S COLLEGE

c. 1520 Thos. Fowler, arm.
w. Edith, c.d., marg. inscr.

c. 1509 John Sycling, priest, acad. dr.

CAMBRIDGE, GONVILLE AND CAIUS COLLEGE

c. 1500 Man, arm., wn.

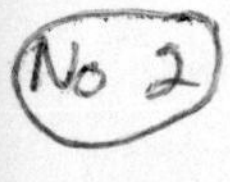

CAMBRIDGE, KING'S COLLEGE

1496 Wm. Town, D.D., fellow, acad. dr., cap, scroll from hands.

1507 John Argentein, D.D., M.D., rector, provost, acad. dr., cap, mouth scroll, marg. inscr.

1528 Robt. Hacombleyn, provost, in almuce, marg. inscr., scroll from hands.

1558 Robt. Brassie, S.T.P., provost, in almuce, cap.

CAMBRIDGE, QUEEN'S COLLEGE

c. 1480 Priest in cope (head miss.).

c. 1535 Priest, acad. dr.

1591 Robt. Whalley, fellow, c.d., marg. inscr., ach.

CAMBRIDGE, ST JOHN'S COLLEGE

1414 Eudo de la Zouche, acad. dr., (head miss.), trip. can., lge., wn.

c. 1430 Priest, mass vests., mut., v. wn.

CAMBRIDGE, TRINITY HALL

c. 1510 Walter Hewke, D.C.L., master, in cope (head rest. 1895).

c. 1530 Priest, acad. dr.

1598 Thos. Prestone, LL.D., master, acad. dr.

CAMBRIDGE, ST BENEDICT

1442 Rich. Billingford, D.D., master, kng., acad. dr.

CAMBRIDGE, ST MARY-THE-LESS

1436 John Holbrook, acad. dr. (bottom hf only.)

c. 1500 Doctor of divinity or law, acad. dr., cap, ¾-eff.

CROXTON

1589 Edw. Leeds, LL.D., c.d., text from Job.

DRAYTON, DRY

c. 1540 Man, arm. (Poss. of the Hutton fam.)
w., c.d.

ELY CATHEDRAL

1554 Thos. Goodryke, bp. of Ely, in episcopal vests., holding Bible and great seal, lge.

1614 Umphrey Tyndall, D.D., in gown, cap, ach., marg. inscr., mut., v. lge.

FORDHAM

1521 Wm. Cheswryght, c.d., wn.
w. Maud, c.d.

FULBOURNE

c. 1390 Priest, mass vests., scroll from hands. (Poss. Roger Grymm.)

1391 Wm. de Fulburne, canon, in cope, sin. can., mut., marg. inscr., mut., lge.

c. 1470 Woman, c.d.

c. 1477 Geoff. Bysschop, vicar, mass vests., hands crossed.

c. 1480 Woman, c.d., with 2 sons, kng., 1 a priest, acad. dr.

GIRTON

1492 Wm. Malster, prebendary of Fenton, in cope.

1497 Wm. Stevyn, canon of Lincoln, in cope.

HADDENHAM

1454 John Godfrey, c.d.
w. Margt., c.d. (head miss.).

HATLEY, EAST, NEW CHURCH

1520 Kath. Dockra, c.d.

HATLEY ST GEORGE

1425 Sir Baldwin Seyntgeorge, arm.

HILDERSHAM

1408 Robt. Parys, c.d.
w. Eleanor, c.d., kng. to floriated cross with Trin. in head.

1427 Hen. Paris, arm.
w. Margt., c.d.

1466 Hen. Parice, arm., sin. can., mut., with Trin.

c. 1530 Skeleton, in shroud.

HINXTON

1416 Sir Thos. de Skelton, arm.
1st w. Margt., c.d.
2nd w. Kath., c.d., marg. inscr., mut.

HORSEHEATH

1365 Wm. de Audeley, arm., frag. of can., lge.

1552 Robt. Alington, c.d. (head miss.).

IMPINGTON

1505 John Burgoyn, arm., tab.
w. Margt., her. dr., with 7 sons, 2 daus., marg. inscr.

ISLEHAM

1451 Sir John Bernard, arm., SS coll.
w. Ellen, c.d., dble. can., mut.

1484 Thos. Peyton, arm.
1st w. Margt., c.d.
2nd w. Margt., c.d., trip. can., mut.

1574 Rich. Payton, student, c.d., holding book.
w. Mary, c.d.

KIRTLING

1553 Edw. Myrfin, c.d., kng., sm.

LINTON

1424 Nich. Paris, arm.

MARCH

1501 Wm. Andrew, yeoman, c.d.
w. Joan, c.d., both v. wn., sm.

1517 Anth. Hansart, arm., tab. (legs mut.).
w. Kath., her. dr., with 1 son (head miss.), kng., Annun., sm.

MILTON

1553 Wm. Coke, justice of the common pleas, in robes.
w. Alice, c.d., with 2 sons, 3 daus., marg. inscr., ach.

1660 John Harris, c.d., with 4 sons, 3 daus., rect. pl.

OVER

c. 1530 7 daus., wn., sm.

SAWSTON

c. 1420 Man, c.d. (ft miss.).

c. 1480 Man, arm. (head miss.).

c. 1500 Robt. Lockton, in shroud.
w. Joan, in shroud, with 5 daus.

1527 Wm. Richardson, rector, mass vests., holding ch., sm.

Shelford, Great
1418 Thos. Patteslie, rector, in cope, name on orphreys (lower hf miss.), sin. can., mut.

Shelford, Little
c. 1410 Robt. de Frevile, arm.
w. Clarice, c.d., holding hands.
1410 Thos. Frevile, arm.
w. Margt., wid. dr., holding hands.
c. 1480 Priest, acad. dr.

Stapleford
1617 Wm. Lee, vicar, in gown, rect. pl., sm.

Stow-cum-Quy
1460 John Ansty, arm., with 12 sons, in tabs., and 4 daus., kng., marg. inscr., mut.

Stretham
1497 Dame Joan, wid. of John Swan, wid. dr.

Swaffham Prior
1462 John Tothyll, arm.
w., c.d., sm.
1515 Rich. Water, c.d.
w. Alice, c.d., with 4 sons.
1521 Wm. Water, c.d.
w. Alice, c.d., with 6 sons.
c. 1530 Man, c.d.
w., c.d.
1638 Robt. Chambers, c.d., v. sm.

Trumpington
1289 Sir Roger de Trumpington, arm., shield, lge.

Westley Waterless
c. 1325 Sir John de Creke, arm., shield.
w. Alyne, c.d., dble. can., lge.

Weston Colville
1427 Rich. Leverer, arm.
w. Isabel, c.d., with son, John, c.d. (lower hf miss.).
1636 Abraham Gates, S.T.B., rector, in gown.
w. Mary, c.d., kng., rect. pl.

Wicken
1414 Margt. Peyton, c.d., sm.
c. 1520 John Peyton, c.d., sm. (new head).

Wilbraham, Little
1521 Wm. Blakwey, M.A., rector, acad. dr., kng., sm.

Wilburton
1477 Rich. Bole, archdeacon of Ely, in cope, sin. can., marg. inscr., lge., rest.
1506 John Hyll, c.d.
w. Margt., with 5 sons, 2 daus., 4 Ev. syms.
1516 Wm. Byrd, c.d.
w. Margt. with 3 sons, 5 daus.

Wimpole
c. 1500 Man, c.d.
1501 Thos. Worsley, LL.B., in cope, with B.V. Mary and Child, lge.
c. 1535 Woman, c.d., with 6 daus.

Wisbech
1401 Thos. de Braunstone, constable of Wisbech Castle, arm., marg. inscr., mut., lge., wn.

Wood Ditton
1393 Hen. Englisshe, arm.
w. Margt., c.d. (head miss.), lge.

CHESHIRE

Chester, St Peter
c. 1460 Lawyer, c.d., cap, wn.

Macclesfield
1506 Roger Legh, c.d., kng., with 6 sons, representation of the mass of St Gregory, pardon inscr. below.

MIDDLEWICH

1591 Eliz. Venables, c.d., with 1 son, Thos., aged 11, and 2 daus., Eliz. and Mary, rect. pl.

OVER

c.1510 Hugh Starky, usher to Hen. VIII, arm.

WILMSLOW

1460 Sir Robt. del Bothe, arm.
w. Douce, c.d., flowing hair, hands clasped, sin. can., mut., marg. inscr., wn.

WYBUNBURY

1513 Rafe Dellvys, arm.
w. Kath., c.d.

CORNWALL

ANTHONY, EAST

1420 Margery Arundell, c.d., sin. can.

BLISLAND

1410 John Balsam, rector, mass vests.

BUDOCK

1567 John Killigrew, captain of Pendennis castle, arm.
w. Eliz., c.d., ach.

CALLINGTON

1465 Nich. Assheton, justice of the common pleas, in robes.
w. Margt., c.d., marg. inscr., mut.

CARDYNHAM

c.1400 Thos. Awmarle, rector, buttoned cassock, tonsure, sm.

COLAN

1572 Francis Bluet, c.d.
w. Eliz., c.d., with 13 sons, 9 daus., rect. pl.

1575 John Cosoworth, mercer, arm.
w. Dorothy, c.d., with 7 sons, 1 dau., marg. inscr., ach.

CONSTANTINE

1574 Rich. Gerveys, c.d., rect. pl. [Pal.]
w. Jane, c.d., with 8 sons, 8 daus., marg. inscr., detached.

1616 John Pendarves, c.d., with 1 son, Samuel.
w. Melior, c.d., with 1 dau., Mary, all kng., rect. pl., sm.

CROWAN

c.1420 Geoff. Seyntaubyn, sheriff of Cornwall, arm. (ft miss.).

c.1490 Man, of the Seyntaubyn fam., arm.
w., c.d., with 4 sons.

c.1550 Legs and feet of man, arm.
w. (lower hf only), c.d., marg. inscr., mut.

c.1599 John St Aubyn(?), arm. (head miss.), with 4 sons, portion of marg. inscr.

1626 4 daus. of Thos. St Aubyn (all relaid incorrectly).

FOWEY

c.1450 Man, c.d., head rest.
w., c.d.

c.1450 Man, c.d. (Poss. of Treffrey fam.)

1582 John Rashleigh, c.d., with 6 daus.

1602 Alice Lanyon, c.d., w. of above.

GORAN

c.1510 Woman, c.d., kng.

GRADE

1522 Jas. Eryssy, arm.
w. Margt., c.d., with 5 sons, 5 daus.

HELSTON

1606 John Bougins, mcht., c.d.
w. Alice, c.d., with 2 sons, 1 dau.

ILLOGAN

1603 Jas. Bassett, arm.
w. Jane, c.d., with 5 sons, 5 daus.

LANDRAKE

1509 Edw. Cowrtney, arm., sm.

LANTEGLOS-NEAR-FOWEY

*c.*1440 Thos. de Mohun, arm., marg. inscr.

*c.*1525 John Mohun, arm.
w. Anne, c.d., with 5 sons, 4 daus. (the latter rest.).

LAUNCESTON

*c.*1620 Woman, c.d.

LOSTWITHIEL

1423 Tristram Curteys, arm., wn.

MADRON

1623 John Clies, mcht., c.d.
w. Blanche, c.d., with 1 son, 5 daus., marg. inscr.

MAWGAN-IN-PYDER

*c.*1420 Priest, in cope, sm.

1573 Geo. Arundell, arm.
w. Isabel, wid., c.d.

1578 Cysselle Arundell, c.d.

*c.*1580 Man, c.d.

MINSTER

1602 Hender, son of Rich. Robarts, aged 1.

PROBUS

1514 John Wulvedon, c.d.
w. Cecily, c.d.

QUETHIOC

1471 Roger Kyngdon, c.d.
w. Joan, c.d., with 11 sons, the eldest a priest, in almuce, 2nd a yeoman, 5 daus.

1631 Rich. Chiverton, c.d.
w. Isabel, c.d., with 11 child.

ST BREOCK

*c.*1510 Man, c.d. (Poss. of the Tredenick fam.)
w., c.d., with 7 daus.

ST COLUMB MAJOR

1545 Sir John Arundell, K.B., arm.
1st w. Eliz., c.d.
2nd w. Kath., with 1 son, arm. (head miss.), 2 daus., marg. inscr., mut.

1633 Sir John Arundell, arm.
w. Anne, c.d., with 2 sons, 5 daus., ach.

1633 John Arundell, son of above, arm., ach.
w. Anne, c.d., with 4 sons, 7 daus.

ST ERME

1596 Robt. Trencreeke, J.P., c.d.
w. Anis, c.d., with 4 daus., all kng., ach.

ST GLUVIAS

*c.*1485 Thos. Kyllegrew, c.d.
w. either Joan of Eliz., c.d.

ST IVES

1462 Agnes Trevnwyth, c.d., kng., wn., with fig. of St Michael.

ST JUST IN ROSELAND

*c.*1520 Priest, in choir cope.

ST MELLION

1551 Peter Coryton, arm.
w. Jane, c.d., with 17 sons, 7 daus., marg. inscr.

ST MICHAEL PENKIVEL

1497 John Trenowyth, arm.

1515 John Trembras, M.A., parson, acad. dr.

1619 Edw. Boscawen, c.d., mouth scroll.
w. Jane, c.d.

1622 Marie Coffin, c.d.

1634 John Boscawen, arm., kng., rect. pl., ach.

ST MINVER

1517 Roger Opy, c.d., mouth scroll, marg. inscr.

STRATTON

1561 Sir John Arundell, arm.

1st w. Mary, c.d.
2nd w. Julian, with 4 sons, 7 daus., marg. inscr.

TINTAGEL

c. 1430 Joan Kelly, c.d., hf-eff.

TRURO, CATHEDRAL

1585 Rich. Singleton, c.d., 2 sons, 4 daus., ach.

1630 Cuthbert Sydnam, wool draper, c.d.

WENDRON

1535 Warin Penhalluryk, vicar, in cope (head miss.), marg. inscr.

c. 1580 Man, c.d.
w., c.d., with 7 sons, 8 daus. (lower parts of effs. miss.). [Pal.]

CUMBERLAND

BOOTLE

1562 Sir Hugh Askew, arm.

CARLISLE, CATHEDRAL

1496 Rich. Bell, bp., full vests., with crosier, mitre, holding book, trip. can., mut., marg. inscr., mut., lge.

1616 Hen. Robinson, bp., provost of Queen's College, Oxford, in robes, kng., rect. pl.

CROSTHWAITE

1527 Sir John Ratclif, arm. (head rest.).
w. Alice, c.d.

EDENHALL

1458 Wm. Stapilton, arm., tab.
w. Margt., c.d.

GREYSTOKE

1526 John Whelpdall, LL.D., rector, in almuce, hf-eff., v. sm.

c. 1540 Margt. Morisby, c.d., sm.

1547 Wenefride Newport, c.d., flowing hair, v. sm.

1551 Rich. Newport, c.d., sm.

DERBYSHIRE

ASHBOURNE

1538 Francis Cokayne, arm., tab.
w. Dorothy, c.d., with 3 sons, 3 daus., trip. can., rest., marg. inscr.

ASHOVER

1504 Philip Eyre, rector, mass vests., ch. above head.

1507 Jas. Rolleston, arm.
w. Anne, c.d., with 4 sons, 9 daus., marg. inscr.

BAKEWELL

1648 Latham Woodroofe, servant to the Earl of Rutland, c.d., rect. pl., v. sm., ach.

BEELEY

1710 John Calvert, rect. pl. with recumbent fig. in shroud.

CHESTERFIELD

1451 Anne Foljambe, c.d., effaced.

1529 Sir Godfrey Foljambe, king's councillor, arm., tab.
w. Kath., her dr., with child., marg. inscr. (rest. 1879).

DRONFIELD

1399 Thos. Gomfrey, rector, mass vests.
b. Rich. Gomfrey, rector, mass vests.

1580 John Fanshawe, c.d.
w. Margt., c.d., with 6 child.

EDENSOR

1570 John Beton, rect. pl., with recumbent eff. arm., ach.

ETWALL

1512 Eliz. Porte, with 9 sons, 8 daus., shields with figs. of Our Lord, B.V. Mary and Child.

1557 Sir John Porte, arm., tab.

1st w. Eliz., her. mant., with 2 sons, 3 daus.
2nd w. Dorothy, her. mant., all kng.

HATHERSAGE

1463 Robt. Eyr, arm.
w. Joan, c.d., with 10 sons, 4 daus. (rest. 1852).

1493 Ralph Eyr, arm.
w. Eliz., c.d.

c. 1500 Robt. Eyre, arm., tab.
w. Eliz., her. mant., with 4 sons, 2 daus., all kng.

c. 1560 Sir Arthur Eyre, arm., tab.
1st w. Margt., her. mant., kng.

HOPE

1685 Hen. Balgay, c.d., holding pen and book, rect. pl., sm.

KEDLESTON

1496 Rich. Curzon, arm.
w. Alice, c.d., with 8 daus., marg. inscr., mut.

LONGSTONE, GREAT

1624 Rowland Eyre, c.d.
w. Gertrude, c.d., rect. pl., both kng., defaced crucifix between effs.

MORLEY

1454 John Stathum, arm.
w. Cecily, c.d., kng., with fig. of St Christopher.

1470 Sir Thos. Stathum, arm.
1st w. Eliz., c.d.
2nd w. Thomasine, c.d., with St Anne, B.V. Mary and Child and St Christopher.

1481 Henry Stathum, arm.
1st w. Anne, c.d.
2nd w. Eliz., c.d.
3rd w. Margt., wid. dr., with 1 son, 4 daus.

c. 1525 John Sacheverell, killed at Bosworth field, arm., with 3 sons.
w. Joan, c.d., with 5 daus., all kng., fig. of St Christopher above.

1558 Sir Hen. Sacheverell, arm.
w. Isabel, c.d.

MUGGINTON

c. 1475 Nich. Kniveton, arm., SS coll.
w. Joan, c.d., flowing hair, detached effs. of 4 sons, 1 dau., marg. inscr., mut.

NORBURY

1538 Sir Anth. Fitzherbert, justice of the common pleas, in robes (head miss.).
2nd w. Maud, her. mant., with 5 daus. [All pal.]

SAWLEY

1467 Roger Bothe, arm.
w. Kath., c.d., with 7 sons, 10 daus., marg. inscr., mut.

1478 Roger Bothe, arm., suns and roses on coll.
w. Margt., wid. dr., with 6 daus., marg. inscr., mut.

1510 Rich. Shylton, mcht., c.d., mut.
w. Alys, c.d.

STAVELEY

c. 1480 Peter Frechwell, arm., tab. (head and shoulders miss.), Trin., marg. inscr.

1503 Peyrs Freychwell, esq. to Hen. VI, arm., with 8 sons.
w. Mawde, c.d., with 7 daus., all kng., with B.V.Mary and Child above.

TADDINGTON

1505 Rich. Blakwall, c.d.
w. Dame Agnes, wid., c.d., with 6 sons, 5 daus.

TIDESWELL

c. 1500 Robt. Lytton, c.d.
w. Isabel, c.d., marg. inscr.

1579 Robt. Pursglove, prior of Gisburn,

Yorks., bp. of Hull, in episcopal vests., with crosier, ft inscr., marg. inscr.

WALTON-ON-TRENT

1492 Robt. Morley, rector, mass vests., blessing ch. and wf.

WILNE

1513 Hugh Wylloughbye, arm., tab., with 1 son, Thos., arm., tab.
w. Anne, c.d., with 4 daus., all kng., Trin., ach. (Damaged by fire 1917, relaid in orig. slab 1925).

WIRKSWORTH

c.1510 Man, c.d.
w. c.d., with 8 sons, 10 daus.

1525 Thos. Blakewall, c.d.
w. Maude, with 6 sons, 1 dau.

YOULGRAVE

1604 Fridswide Gilbert, c.d.

At Tideswell the brass to
1385 John Foljambe, arm.
was completely renewed in 1875.

DEVONSHIRE

ALLINGTON, EAST

c.1540 Woman, c.d., kng. (head. mut.).

1595 John Fortescue, c.d.
w. Owner, c.d.

ATHERINGTON

1539 Sir John Basset, arm.
1st w. Honor, c.d., with 1 son, 4 daus.
2nd w. Anne, c.d., with 3 sons, 4 daus.

BIGBURY

c.1440 Woman, c.d.

c.1460 Dame Eliz., wid. of Wm. Bigbury.

BLACKAWTON

1582 Nich. Forde, c.d.
w. Margt., c.d.

BRAUNTON

1548 Lady Eliz. Bowcer, c.d., kng. [Pal., c.1370.]

CHITTLEHAMPTON

1480 John Cobleigh, c.d.
1st w. Isabel, c.d.
2nd w. Joan, c.d., with 1 dau.

CLOVELLY

1540 Robt. Cary, arm.

c.1540 Sir Wm. Cary?, arm.

CLYST ST GEORGE

1614 Julian Osborne, aged nearly 100, c.d., kng.

DARTMOUTH, ST PETROCK

1609 John Roope, mcht., c.d., marg. inscr., mut., lge.

1610 Barbara Plumleighe, c.d., with 2 sons, 4 daus., marg. inscr., mut.

1617 Dorothy Rous, c.d., sm., rect. pl.

DARTMOUTH, ST SAVIOUR

1408 John Hauley, arm., holding hand of 1st w. Joan, c.d.
2nd w. Alice, c.d., mut., trip. can., mut., lge.

1470 Lady, c.d., sm.

1637 Gilbert Staplehill, mayor, c.d., marg. inscr., rest.

ERMINGTON

1583 Wm. Strachleigh, c.d.
w. Anne, c.d., with 1 dau., Christian, kng.

EXETER, CATHEDRAL

1409 Sir Peter Courtenay, K.G., arm., effaced, sin. can., marg. inscr., mut., wn.

1413 Wm. Langeton, canon, in cope, kng.

FILLEIGH

1570 Rich. Fortescue, arm., kng., sm.,

rect. pl., ach. (There is a similar but coarser brass to the same person also in the church.)

HACCOMBE

1469 Nich. Carew, arm.

1586 Thos. Carewe, arm.

1589 Mary Carewe, c.d.

1611 Eliz. Carewe, c.d.

1656 Thos. Carewe, arm.
w. Anne, c.d., with 5 sons, 1 in arm., 1 dau., deceased, all kng., lge., rect. pl., ach.

HARFORD

1566 Thos. Williams, speaker in Parliament, arm.

1639 John Prideaux, c.d.
w. Agnes, c.d., with 7 sons, 4th in doctor's gown, 3 daus., rect. pl., all kng.

HARTLAND

1611 Anne Abbott, c.d., kng., painted and gilded.

LUPPITT

c. 1440 Fragment of woman, wid. dr. [Pal., c. 1400.]

MONKLEIGH

1566 Jas. Coffyn, arm., kng.

OTTERTON

1641 3 sons, 5 daus. of Robt. and Sarah Duke, sm. effs., kng.

OTTERY ST MARY

c. 1620 John Sherman, c.d., with 1 son, William, c.d., and 1 grandson, Rich., c.d.

PETROCKSTOW

1591 Hen. Rolle, arm., with 10 sons.
w. Margt., c.d., with 8 daus., all kng., 2 rect. pls. (poss. engraved at different dates), ach.

ST GILES-IN-THE-WOOD, NR TORRINGTON

1430 Eleanor Pollard (upper hf miss.).

1592 Margt. Rolle, c.d., with 8 sons, 2 daus., marg. inscr., mut.

1610 Joan Risdon, c.d., kng., inscr., rect. pl.

SAMPFORD PEVERELL

1602 Margt. Poulett, c.d., with 4 sons, 3 daus., rect. pl.

SANDFORD, NR CREDITON

1604 Mary Dowrich, with 1 son, Thos., and 3 daus., rect. pl. with recumbent eff. on tomb.

SHILLINGFORD

1499 Sir Wm. Huddesfeld, arm., tab.
w. Kath., her. mant., with 1 son, 2 daus., kng., rect. pl., sm.

STAVERTON

1592 John Rowe, c.d., hf-eff., rect. pl.

STOKE-FLEMING

1391 John Corp, c.d., anelace, with 1 grand-dau., Eleanor, c.d., on pedestal, dble. can., lge.

STOKE-IN-TEIGNHEAD

c. 1370 Priest, mass vests. (Poss. John Symon.) (Once in cross.)

TEDBURN ST MARY

1580 Wm. Smith, M.A., in gown and hood, kng.

1613 Edw. Gee, rector, in gown.
w. Jane, c.d., with 1 son, 3 daus., rect. pl.

TIVERTON

1529 John Greenway, mcht., c.d.
w. Joan, c.d., lge.

TOR MOHUN

1581 Wilmot Cary, c.d., with 3 daus.

UGBOROUGH

c. 1500 Woman, c.d.

WASHFIELD

1606 Hen. Worth, c.d.
w., c.d., with 1 dau., ach.

Yealmpton

1508 Sir John Crokker, standard-bearer to Edw. IV, arm.

1580 Inscr. to Isabel Copleston. (On reverse, portion of Flem. brass, 15th cent., with heads of St James, the B.V. Mary, scroll, seated fig. of God the Father holding soul in sheet.)

DORSETSHIRE

Bere Regis

1596 John Skerne, c.d.
w. Margt., c.d., kng., ach.

Church Knowle

1572 John Clavell, arm.
1st w. Millicent, c.d., with 3 sons, 1 dau.
2nd w. Susan, c.d., all kng., ach.

Compton Valence

*c.*1440 Thos. Maldon, rector, mass vests., hf-eff., wn.

Corfe Mullen

1437 Rich. Hert, c.d., v. wn.

Crichel More

1572 Isabel Uvedale, c.d.

Evershot

1524 Wm. Grey, rector, mass vests., ch., wf.

Fleet, old church

1603 Robt. Mohun, arm., with 9 sons.
w. Margt., c.d., with 8 daus., all kng., rect. pl.

1612 Maximilian Mohun, arm., son of above, with 5 sons.
w. Anne, c.d., with 8 daus., all kng., rect. pl.

Langton

1467 John Whitewod, c.d.
1st w. Joan, c.d.
2nd w. Alice, c.d.

Lytchett Matravers

*c.*1470 Thos. Pethyn, rector, in shroud, sm.

Melbury Sampford

1562 Sir Gyles Strangwayes, arm., tab.

Milton Abbey

1565 Sir John Tregonwell, D.C.L., arm., tab., kng., ach.

Moreton

1523 Jas. Frampton, arm., kng.

Piddlehinton

1617 Thos. Browne, parson and clerk, in gown and hat, holding book and staff, rect. pl., sm.

Piddletown

1517 Roger Cheverell, c.d. (lower hf miss.).

1524 Christ. Martyn, arm., tab., kng., Trin., rect. pl.

1595 Nich. Martyn, arm.
w. Margt., c.d., with 3 sons, 7 daus., all kng., ach.

Pimperne

1694 Dorothy Williams, rect. pl. with fig. of recumbent skeleton.

Puncknowle

*c.*1600 Wm. Napper, arm., kng., ach.

Purse, Caundle

*c.*1500 Man, arm. (Poss. Wm. Long.)

1527 Eliz. Longe, c.d., flowing hair, sm.

1536 Rich. Brodeway, rector, mass vests., looped maniple, sm. (head miss.).

Rampisham

1523 Thos. Dygenys, c.d.
w. Isabel, c.d.

Shapwick

*c.*1440 Mary Oke, c.d.

*c.*1520 Rich. Chernok, alias Hogeson, vicar, in cassock and scarf over c.d.

STURMINSTER-MARSHALL

1581 Hen. Helme, vicar, c.d., sm

SWANAGE

c. 1490 Margt., c.d.
Anne, c.d., ws. of Wm. Clavell, sm.

THORNCOMBE, NEW CHURCH

1437 Sir Thos. Brook, c.d., with SS coll.
w. Joan, c.d., with SS coll., marg. inscr., rest., lge.

WIMBORNE MINSTER

c. 1440 St Ethelred, King of the West Saxons, martyr, in regal robes with sceptre and crown, hf-eff.

WOOLLAND

1616 Mary Argenton, c.d., kng.

YETMINSTER

1531 John Horsey, esq. to Hen. VIII, arm.
w. Eliz., c.d.

DURHAM

AUCKLAND ST ANDREW

c. 1380 Priest, in cope (head mut.).

AUCKLAND ST HELEN

c. 1470 Man, c.d.
w., c.d., with 6 sons, 3 daus., sm. (upper hf of w. miss.).

BILLINGHAM

c. 1485 Robt. Brerley, vicar, in almuce (head miss.), wn.

BRANCEPETH

c. 1400 Man, arm., wn.
1456 Rich. Drax, rector, acad. dr., hf-eff., wn.

CHESTER-LE-STREET

1430 Alice Lambton, wid. dr.

HARTLEPOOL

1593 Jane Bell, c.d., rect. pl.

HAUGHTON-LE-SKERNE

1592 Dorothy Parkinson, c.d., holding twin chrysoms, Rich. and Marmaduke.

HOUGHTON-LE-SPRING

1587 Margery Belassis, c.d., kng., with 8 sons, 4 daus., rect. pl.

SEDGEFIELD

c. 1315 Lady, c.d., kng., sm.
c. 1500 Man, skeleton in shroud.
w., skeleton in shroud.

ESSEX

ALTHORNE

1502 2 daus., 1 a nun, of Margt. Hyklott, kng., B.V. Mary and Child above, sm.
1508 Wm. Hyklott, c.d., Trin. above.

ARKESDEN

1439 Rich. Fox, arm.

ASHEN

c. 1440 Man, arm.
w., c.d., sm.

AVELEY

1370 Ralph de Knevynton, arm., under can., sm. rect. pl., Flem.
c. 1520 6 sons, 2 daus. (Poss. of the Belhouse fam.)
1588 Nathaniell, aged 3.
Eliz., aged 2, child. of Edw. Bacon. (Both died 1588.)

BADDOW, GREAT

1614 Jane Paschall, c.d.

BARDFIELD, GREAT

1584 Eleanor Bendlowes, c.d.

BARKING

c. 1480 Priest, acad. dr., ch., wn.
1485 Rich. Malet, chaplain, mass vests., surname engraved on eff.

1493 Thos. Broke, c.d.
w. Alice, c.d., with 1 son, 1 dau.
1596 John Tedcastell, c.d.
w. Eliz., c.d., with 9 sons (5 chrysoms), ach.

BELCHAMP ST PAUL
1587 Wm. Golding, arm., with 1 son, 3 daus., ach.
1591 1 son, 1 dau., and 1 son, 3 daus. of Eliz. Golding, sm.

BENTLEY, LITTLE
1490 Sir Wm. Pyrton, arm., SS coll. (lower hf miss.).
wid. Kath., with 5 sons, 5 daus.

BERDEN
1473 Wm. Turnor, c.d.
1st w. Margt., c.d.
2nd w. Margery, c.d.
1607 Thos. Thompson, c.d.
w. Anne, c.d., with 9 sons, 4 daus.

BLACKMORE
*c.*1420 Man, c.d. (lower hf miss.).

BOCKING
1430 John Doreward, arm.
w. Isabel, c.d.
1613 Oswald Fitch, c.d.

BOREHAM
1573 Alse Canceller, c.d., with 1 son, 5 daus.

BOWERS GIFFORD
1348? Sir John Gifford, arm., lge. (head miss.).

BRADFIELD
1598 Joan Rysbye, c.d.

BRADWELL-ON-THE-SEA
1526 Margt. Wyott, c.d.

BRAXTED, LITTLE
1508 Wm. Roberts, auditor to Hen. VII, arm.
1st w. Joyce, c.d., with 1 son, 2 daus.
2nd w. Margt., c.d., with 1 son, 1 dau.

BRIGHTLINGSEA
1496 John Beryf, c.d.
2nd w. Amy, c.d., with 5 sons, 5 daus. of 1st w. Margt.
1505 Mary Beryf. c.d., with 4 sons, 1 dau.
1514 Margt. Beryf, c.d.
1521 John Beriff, c.d.
1st w. Mary, c.d., with 4 sons, 1 dau.
2nd w. Alice, c.d., with 2 sons, 3 daus.
1525 Wm. Beryff, mariner, c.d.
w. Joan, c.d., lge.
1536 Dame Alice Beriffe, wid. dr., with 1 dau., Margt., flowing hair, on br. *c.*1420. [Pal.]
1578 Wm. Beriffe, c.d.

BROMLEY, GREAT
1432 Wm. Byshopton, rector, mass vests., sin. can., mut.

CANFIELD, GREAT
*c.*1530 Woman, c.d.
1558 John Wyseman, auditor to Hen. VIII, arm.
w. Agnes, c.d., with 4 sons, 6 daus., all kng.
1588 Thos. Fytche, arm.
w. Agnes, c.d., with 3 sons, 3 daus. (Heads of these effs. rest.)

CANFIELD, LITTLE
1578 Eliz., c.d., with 2 sons, 3 daus.
Anne, c.d., with 4 sons, ws. of Wm. Fytch.
1593 Ann Fyttche, c.d., with 1 son, in cloak, below.

CHESTERFORD, GREAT
*c.*1530 Agnes Holden?, c.d.

CHESTERFORD, LITTLE

1462 Isabel, wid. of Geo. Langham, wid. dr.

CHIGWELL

1631 Sam. Harsnett, archbp., in cope, with mitre and crosier, marg. inscr., lge.

CHRISHALL

c. 1380 Sir John de la Pole, arm.
w. Joan, c.d., holding hands, trip. can., marg. inscr.

c. 1450 Woman, c.d., sm.

c. 1480 Man, c.d.
w., c.d., kng., wn.

CLAVERING

c. 1480 ? Songar, c.d. (upper hf miss.).
w., c.d., with 4 sons, 1 a priest, acad. dr., 9 daus.

c. 1520 3 daus. of Joan Smith.

1591 Thos. Welbore, c.d.
w. Ursula, c.d., with 1 son, 5 daus.

1593 ? Day, c.d.
w. Joan, c.d.

COGGESHALL

c. 1490 2 women, c.d.

c. 1520 Man, c.d.
w., c.d. (Poss. of the Peacock fam.)

1533 John Paycock, c.d.
w. Joan, c.d.

1580 Thos. Paycocke, c.d., marg. inscr., mut.

COLCHESTER, ST JAMES

1569 John Maynarde, clothier, c.d.

1584 Ales Maynarde, c.d. (upper hf miss.). [Pal.]

COLCHESTER, ST PETER

1530 John Sayre, civic mant.
w. Eliz., c.d., with 4 sons, 1 dau., all kng., rect. pl.

1553 Agnes Leache, c.d., with 4 sons, 5 daus.
1st hus. Aleyn Dister, c.d.
2nd hus. Robt. Leache, civic mant., all kng., rect. pl.

1563 John Sayer, c.d., kng., rect. pl.

1572 Wm. Brown, c.d., with 6 sons.
w. Margt., c.d., with 2 daus., all kng.

1610 Rich. Sayer, c.d.
1st w. Ailse, c.d., with 1 son.
2nd w. Ellen, wid. dr., with 1 dau., Jane, all kng., rect. pl., ach.

COLD NORTON

c. 1520 Woman, c.d.

CORRINGHAM

c. 1340 Rich. de Beltoun, rector, mass vests., hf-eff.

c. 1460 Man, c.d., mut., wn.

CRESSING

1610 Dorcas Musgrave, c.d., seated fig. with chrysom at ft. (Died in childbirth.)

DAGENHAM

1479 Sir Thos. Urswyck, recorder of London, mant.
w., mant., with 9 daus., the eldest a nun.

DENGIE

c. 1520 Woman, c.d., mut., with 5 sons, 3 daus.

DONYLAND, EAST

1621 Nich. Marshall, c.d.

1627 Mary Marshall, c.d.

DOVERCOURT

c. 1430 Man, c.d., with scroll.

DUNMOW, GREAT

1579 Philipe Glassock, c.d.

EASTER, GOOD

1610 Margt. Norrington, c.d., with 1 dau., mut.

EASTON, LITTLE

c. 1420 Robt. Fyn, rector, mass vests.

1483 Hen. Bourchier, K.G., 1st Earl of Essex, arm.
w. Isabel, c.d., both with suns and roses on coll., coloured.

EASTWOOD

1600 Thos. Burrough, yeoman, c.d.

ELMDON

*c.*1460 Wm. Lucas, c.d.
w. Kath, c.d., with 4 sons, eldest an abbot of Waltham, 4 daus. (These brasses came from Wendon Lofts church.)

*c.*1530 Man, c.d.
1st w., c.d., with 5 sons, 4 daus.
2nd w., c.d., with 4 sons, 6 daus., marg. inscr. (Poss. John Cooke and ws.)

1559 4 sons, 8 daus. of Thos. Crawley.

ELSENHAM

1615 Anne Fielde, c.d., kng., rect. pl.

1619 Alice Tuer, c.d., kng., rect. pl.

EPPING

1621 Thos. Palmer, in gown, ach.

FAMBRIDGE, NORTH

1590 Wm. Osborne, c.d.
w. Annes, c.d. (head miss.), with 8 sons, 8 daus.

FAULKBOURNE

1576 Hen. Fortescue, esq. to Eliz. I, arm., with 4 sons, 5 daus. by his 1st w., Eliz., and 1 son by his 2nd w., Dame Mary Darrel, marg. inscr.

1598 Dame Mary Darrel, wid. dr.

FELSTED

*c.*1415 Man, arm.

1420 Cristine Bray, c.d., hf-eff.

FINCHINGFIELD

1523 John Berners, arm., tab.
w. Eliz., her. mant.

FINGRINGHOE

*c.*1600 John Alleyn, c.d., with dau., Ailse.

FRYERNING

1563 Leonard Berners, arm. (l. ft only). [Pal., *c.*1500.]
w. Mary, c.d. [Pal., *c.*1460.]

GOLDHANGER

1531 Woman, c.d., one of the ws. of Thos. Heigham.

GOSFIELD

1440 Thos. Rolf, serjeant-at-law, in robes, coif.

HALSTEAD

*c.*1420 Barth., Lord Bourchier, arm.
1st w. Margt., c.d.
2nd w. Iden, wid. dr., lge.

1604 Eliz. Watson, c.d., with 2 sons, 3 daus. and chrysom, kng., rect. pl.

HANNINGFIELD, WEST

1361 Isabel Clonvill, c.d., hf-eff.

HARLOW

*c.*1430 Man, arm.
w., c.d., sm.

*c.*1490 Man, c.d.
w., c.d., with 4 sons, 5 daus.

1518 Thos. Aylmer, c.d.
w. Alys, c.d., with 7 sons, 4 daus.

1559 Wm. Sumner, c.d., sm., mut.

1582 Edw. Bugge, c.d.
w. Jane, c.d., with 3 sons, 2 daus.

*c.*1585 Man, c.d.
w., c.d., sm., mut.

1602 Wm. Newman, c.d., with fig. of Death, rect. pl., sm.

1615 John Gladwin, c.d., sm.

1636 Rich. Bugges, arm., holding staff.
1st w. Vahan, c.d.
2nd w. Eliz., c.d., ach.

1642 Francis Reve, c.d.
w. Joan, c.d., kng., sm., ach.

Hatfield Broadoak

c.1395 Head of woman (in church library).

Hatfield Peverell

1572 John Allen, c.d.
1st w., c.d., with 3 sons, 4 daus., all kng.

Hempstead

c.1475 Man, c.d.
w., c.d.
c.1480 Man, c.d., with 5 sons, 2 daus.
1498 Thos. Huntingdon, arm.
w. Margt., c.d.
1518 Wm. Mordaunt, c.d., with 10 sons.
1530 Man, c.d.
w., c.d., with 4 sons, 5 daus., sm., wn.

Henny, Great

c.1530 Wm. Fyscher, c.d.
w. Annes, c.d., with 6 sons, 9 daus.

Heybridge

1627 John Whitacres, c.d.

Horkesley, Little

1412 Sir Robt. Swynborne, arm., with 1 son, Sir Thos., capt. of Fronsac castle, arm., with SS coll., both under trip. can., marg. inscr.
1502 Kath. Leventhorpe, in shroud.
1549 Dame Brygete Marnay, her. mant.
1st hus. Thos. Fyndorne, arm., tab.
2nd hus. John, Lord Marnay, arm., tab.

Hornchurch

c.1500 5 sons.
1591 Thos. Drywood, c.d.
w. Anne, c.d., with 8 sons, 3 daus., sm., mut.
1602 Two women, c.d., either Eliz., Alice or Joan, ws. of Wm. Drywoode.
1604 Thos. Hone, c.d.
w., c.d., with 6 sons, 6 daus., sm. (Most brasses incorrectly relaid.)

Horndon, East

1476 Dame Anne Tyrell, wid. dr., marg. inscr., mut.
c.1520 Man, arm. (head miss.), with 8 sons, kng.

Hutton

c.1525 Man, arm.
w., c.d., with 8 sons, 8 daus.

Ilford, Little

1517 Thos. Heron, c.d., penner and inkhorn.
1630 Anne Hyde, c.d., sm.

Ingrave

1466 Margt. Wake, c.d., marg. inscr., mut.
1528 Sir Rich. Fitzlewes, arm., tab.
1st w. Alice, her. mant.
2nd w., c.d.
3rd w. Eliz., her. mant.
4th w. Joan, her. mant.

Laindon

c.1470 John Kekilpenny, rector, mass vests., ch., wf.
c.1510 Priest, mass vests., ch., wf., sm. (Poss. Rich. Bladwell, rector.)

Lambourne

1546 Robt. Barfott, c.d.
w. Kath., c.d., with 4 sons, 1 dau. and 4 sons, 10 daus.

Latton

1467 Sir Peter Arderne, chief baron of the exchequer, in robes, coif.
w. Kath., c.d.
c.1490 Wm. Harper, arm.
w. Anne?, c.d., with 3 sons.

*c.*1600 Emanuell Wollaye, c.d.
w. Margt., c.d., ach.
1604 Frances Franklin, c.d., with 1 son, 1 dau.

LAVER, HIGH

*c.*1495 Edw. Sulyard, arm.
w. Myrabell, c.d., with 4 sons, 1 dau.

LEIGH, NR ROCHFORD

1453 Rich. Haddok, c.d.
w. Cristine, c.d., with 7 sons, 3 daus., and 1 son, John, c.d.
w. Alice, c.d., with 8 sons, 3 daus.
1632 Rich. Chester, mariner, c.d.
w. Eliz., c.d., with 4 sons, 1 dau.
*c.*1640 Man, c.d.
w., c.d.

LEIGHS, GREAT

*c.*1370 Head of priest, *now fastened to fig. of*
1414 Ralph Strelley, rector, mass vests., hf-eff. (head previously miss.).

LEYTON, LOW

1493 Ursula, dau. of Luke Gasper, c.d., sm.
*c.*1620 Tobias Wood, c.d.
w. Eliz., c.d., with 7 sons, 5 daus.

LINDSELL

1514 Thos. Fytche, c.d.
w. Agnes, c.d., with 6 sons, 5 daus.

LITTLEBURY

*c.*1480 Man, c.d.
*c.*1510 Priest, mass vests., ch., wf.
*c.*1510 Man, c.d.
w., c.d.
*c.*1520 Man, c.d.
1578 Jane Bradbuirye, c.d.
1624 Anne Byrd, c.d.

LOUGHTON

1541 John Stonnard, c.d.
1st w. Joan, c.d.
2nd w. Kath., c.d.
1558 Geo. Stonnard, arm.
w. Mary, c.d., rect. pl., with arched can.
1594 Wm. Nodes, c.d., with 8 sons.
1637 Abel Guilliams, c.d.
w., c.d., with 6 sons, 4 daus., all kng., rect. pl.

MARGARETTING

*c.*1550 Man, arm. (head miss.).
w., c.d., with 3 sons, 4 daus.

MATCHING

1638 John Ballett, c.d.
w. Rose, c.d., with 2 sons, 6 daus.

MESSING

*c.*1540 Woman, c.d.

NETTESWELL

1522 Thos. Laurence, c.d.
w. Alice, c.d., with 2 sons, 5 daus.
1607 John Bannister, c.d.
w. Eliz., c.d., with 3 sons, 1 dau., a chrysom.

NEWPORT

1515 Thos. Brond, c.d.
w. Margery, c.d., with 2 sons, 2 daus., marg. inscr.
1608 Geoff. Nightingale, c.d.
w. Kath., c.d., ach.

OCKENDON, NORTH

1502 Wm. Poynz, arm.
w. Eliz., c.d., with 6 sons, 6 daus.
1532 Thomasyn Badby, c.d.

OCKENDON, SOUTH

1400 Sir Ingam Bruyn, arm., scroll on chest (head miss.), bad. mut., sin. can.

1602 Margt. Barker, c.d.

ONGAR, HIGH

c. 1510 Man, c.d.

ORSETT

1485 1 son, 2 daus. of Thos. Latham.
c. 1520 6 daus.
c. 1535 Man, c.d., kng., sm.

PARNDON, GREAT

1598 Rowland Rampston, c.d.

PEBMARSH

c. 1323 Sir Wm. Fitzralph, arm., shield, cross-legged, lge.

RAINHAM

c. 1480 Woman, c.d.
c. 1500 Man, c.d.
w., c.d.

RAWRETH

1576 Edm. Tyrell, arm.
w. Susan, c.d., kng. (upper hf rest. 1882).

RAYLEIGH

c. 1450 Man, c.d. (head miss.).
w., c.d., wn. (Poss. of the Barrington fam.)

RETTENDON

c. 1535 Man, c.d.
1st w., c.d.
2nd w., c.d., also group of 3 sons, 4 daus.
1605 Rich. Cannon, c.d.
1607 Rich. Humfrie, c.d., with 3 sons.

ROCHFORD

1514 Mary Dilcok, c.d., sm.

ROYDON

1471 Thos. Colte, arm., with coll.
w. Joan, mant., suns and roses on coll.
1521 John Colte, arm., tab.
1st w. Eliz., her. mant., with 4 sons, 8 daus.
2nd w. Mary, her. mant., with 3 sons, 3 daus., marg. inscr., mut.
1570 John Swifte, c.d., ach.
1589 Eliz. Stanley, c.d., with 5 child., rect. pl.

RUNWELL

1587 Eustace Sulyard, arm.
w. Margt., c.d., kng.

SAFFRON WALDEN

c. 1430 Priest, mass vests.
c. 1480 Two women, c.d.
c. 1490 Woman, c.d.
c. 1500 Woman, c.d.
c. 1510 Man, c.d.
c. 1530 Man, c.d. (ft miss.).
c. 1530 Woman, c.d.
c. 1530 Man, in gown, holding book.

SAFFRON WALDEN, ALMSHOUSES

c. 1475 Master Thos. Byrd, rector, with parents, Agnes and Thos., also b. John, with w. Joan (above fireplace in hall).

SANDON

1588 Patrick Fearne, rector, clerk, in gown, kng.
w., c.d., kng.

SOUTHMINSTER

c. 1560 Man, c.d.
w., c.d., with arms of City of London.
1634 John King, c.d.

SPRINGFIELD

1421 Thos. Coggeshall, arm.

STANFORD RIVERS

1503 Robt. Borrow, arm.
w. Alys, c.d.
c. 1540 Man, arm.
w., c.d. (Under floor.)
1584 Anne Napper, c.d., kng., with 6 sons.

STEBBING

c. 1390 Woman, wid. dr., lge.

STIFFORD

1378 Ralph Perchehay, rector, mass vests., hf-eff.

c. 1480 Priest, in shroud, holding inscribed heart. (Poss. Robt. Oldfield.)

1504 John Ardalle, c.d.
w. Anne, c.d.

1622 Wm. Lathum, c.d.
w. Susan, c.d.

1627 Anne, dau. of Thos. Lathum, aged 17, sm.

1630 Eliz., w. of Thos. Lathum, c.d., sm.

STISTED

1584 Eliz. Wyseman, c.d., kng., with 1 dau.

STOCK

1574 Rich. Twedye, arm., ach.

STONDON MASSEY

1570 John Carre, ironmonger, c.d.
1st w., c.d.
2nd w., c.d.

1573 Rainold Holingworth, arm.
w., c.d., ach. [Effs. pal.]

STOW MARIES

1602 Mary Browne, c.d., with 3 sons, 4 daus.

STRETHALL

c. 1480 Priest, acad. dr.

SUTTON

1371 Thos. Stapel, arm. (miss. from knees down). (From Shopland church.)

TERLING

c. 1500 Robt. Rochester?, arm.
w. Eliz?, c.d., with 9 sons, 9 daus.

1584 Wm. Rochester, c.d., with 6 sons.
w. Eliz?, c.d., with 4 daus., all kng.

1584 John Rochester, c.d.
1st w. Philippe, c.d., with 3 sons, 7 daus.
2nd w. Joan, c.d., with 1 son, 1 dau., all kng.

THAXTED

c. 1450 Priest, M.A., acad. dr.

THEYDON GERNON

1458 Wm. Kirkeby, rector, in cope.

c. 1520 Man, arm., with 2 sons.
w., c.d., with 3 daus., kng.

1567 Ellen Braunche, c.d., kng.

THORRINGTON

1564 Kath. Clare, c.d., with 2 sons, 3 daus.

THURROCK, GRAYS

c. 1510 1st w., c.d.,
2nd w., c.d., with 6 daus.

THURROCK, WEST

1585 Humph. Heis, c.d., with 1 son, Humph., c.d.

TILLINGHAM

1584 Edw. Wiott, c.d., kng.

TILTY

1520 Gerard Danet, councillor to Hen. VIII, arm.
w. Mary, c.d., with 5 sons, 6 daus., marg. inscr., lge.

1562 Geo. Medeley, arm.
w. Mary, c.d., with 3 sons, 2 daus., marg. inscr.

1590 Margt. Tuke, c.d., with 3 sons, 3 daus., all kng., also 3 chrysoms, sm.

TOLLESBURY

1517 Thos. Freshwater, c.d.
w. Margt., c.d., with 9 daus.

TOLLESHUNT DARCY

c. 1420 Man, arm. (head mut.).
w., c.d. (Poss. John de Boys and w.)

c.1535 Kath. Darcy?, c.d. [Pal., c.1400.]
1540 Anth. Darcy, J.P., arm. (rest. 17th cent.).
1559 Philipe Darcy, c.d.

TOPPESFIELD
1534 John Cracherood, c.d.
w. Agnes, c.d., with 4 sons.

TOTHAM, GREAT
1606 Eliz. Coke, c.d., and only child, Eliz., c.d., w. of Thos. Wilde.

TWINSTEAD
1610 Isake Wyncoll, c.d.
w. Mary, c.d., with 5 daus.

UPMINSTER
1455 Eliz. Dencourt, mant.
c.1530 Man, c.d. [Pal., 15th cent.]
1545 Nich. Wayte, c.d.
w. Ellyn, c.d. [Both pal. Flem., late 15th cent.]
c.1560 Eliz. Latham?, c.d., holding book.
1591 Geerardt D'Ewes, arm.
1626 Grace Latham, unmarried dau. of Wm. Latham, c.d.

WALTHAM ABBEY
1565 Edw. Stacy, c.d., with 1 son, Francis.
w. Kath., c.d., all kng., rect. pl.
1576 Thos. Colte, c.d.
w. Magdalen, c.d., with 6 sons, 4 daus., all kng.

WALTHAM, GREAT
1580 Thos. Wyseman, c.d.
w., c.d., with 1 son, 2 daus., mut., ach.
c.1580 Man, c.d. (Poss. of the Wyseman fam.)
1617 Rich. Everard, c.d.
w. Clemence, c.d., ach.

WALTHAM, LITTLE
1447 John Maltoun, arm.

WARLEY, LITTLE
1592 Anne Hanmer, c.d., hf-eff.

WEALD, NORTH
1606 Walter Larder, c.d.
w. Marie, c.d., with 3 sons, 2 daus.

WEALD, SOUTH
c.1460 Woman, c.d., with 6 sons, 6 daus.
c.1500 7 sons, 7 daus.
1567 Sir Anth. Browne, justice of the common pleas, in robes (upper hf miss.), ach.
1634 Robt. Picakis, aged 7, kng.
Allen Talbot, aged 2¾, kng.
c.1450 Man, c.d.
c.1480 Man, c.d.
c.1600 Arthur Crafford, c.d. (These 3 brasses lost in 1868, but found in Noak Hill church and returned.)

WENDENS AMBO
c.1410 Wm. Loveney, arm.

WIDDINGTON
c.1450 Man, c.d. (ft miss.).

WILLINGALE-DOE
1442 Thos. Torrell, arm.
1582 Anne, wid. of John Sackville, wid. dr.
1613 Dorothy Brewster, c.d.

WIMBISH
1347 Sir John de Wautone, arm. (ft miss.).
w. Ellen, c.d., sm., in head of cross (nearly all miss.).

WIVENHOE
1507 Wm., Viscount Beaumont, Lord Bardolph, arm., trip. can., marg. inscr., mut., lge.
1535 Thos. Westeley, priest, chaplain, mass vests., ch., wf., sm.
1537 Lady Eliz., 2nd w. of John de Vere, her. mant., with coronet, trip. can., mut., marg. inscr., lge.

Woodham Mortimer

1584 Dorothy Alleine, aged 3, sm. (head miss.).

Wormingford

c. 1460 Man, c.d., liv. coll. (Poss. Thos. Bowden.)

c. 1590 Man, c.d.
1st w., c.d.
2nd w., c.d.

Writtle

c. 1500 Man, arm., of the Bedell fam.
w., c.d., with 6 sons, 2 daus.

c. 1510 Man, c.d.
Four ws., all c.d., with 3 groups of child.:
2 sons, 4 daus.; 1 son, 5 daus.; 7 sons, 2 daus.

1513 Thomasine, c.d., with f., Thomas Heveningham, arm., and grandf., Thomas Heveningham, arm., with w. Thomasine, c.d.

1524 Constans Berners, c.d., flowing hair, sm.

1576 Edw. Bell, c.d.
w. Margt., c.d., with 3 sons.

1592 Rose Pinchon, c.d., with 6 sons, ach.

1606 Edw. Hunt, c.d.
w., c.d., kng., rect. pl.

1609 Edw. Bowland, c.d.

1616 w. Joan, c.d.

Yeldham, Great

1612 Rich. Symonds, c.d.
w. Eliz., c.d., with 5 sons, 1 dau., all kng., rect. pl., lge.

In Cambridge University Museum of Archaeology and Ethnology is a fragment of a brass from Little Chesterford, Essex.

In the Castle of Colchester and Essex Museum are a few fragments from Essex churches and one piece from St Martins, Colchester.

In Essex Records Office is

c. 1530 4 sons, 1 dau., sm. (From Clavering, Essex.)

GLOUCESTERSHIRE

Abbenhall

1609 Rich. Pyrke, c.d.
w. Joan, c.d., with 2 sons, Thos., Robt.

Berkeley

1526 Wm. Freme, c.d., holding heart (ft miss.), marg. inscr., mut.

Bibury

1707 John Mathews, recumbent skeleton, rect. pl.

1717 Mary Benning, skeleton on mattress, aged 13 weeks, rect. pl.

Bisley

1515 Kath. Sewell, c.d., with 5 sons, 7 daus.

Blockley

1488 Philip Warthym, M.A., vicar, acad. dr., kng.

1510 Wm. Neele, rector, mass vests., kng.

Bristol, Grammar School

c. 1570 Nich. Thorne, mcht., founder of the school, c.d.
1st w. Mary, c.d., with 5 sons, 3 daus.
2nd w. Bridget, c.d., with 1 son, 1 dau., all kng.

Bristol, St James

1636 Hen. Gibbes, mayor, c.d., with 4 sons.
w. Anne, c.d., with 4 daus., all kng., rect. pl.

Bristol, St John

1478 Thos. Rowley, mcht., sheriff, c.d.
w. Margt., c.d.

Bristol, St Mary Redcliff

c. 1400 Man, c.d., hf-eff.

c. 1460 Priest, in cope. [Pal. on reverse, lady, mant., c. same date.]
1439 Sir John Juyn, recorder of Bristol, in robes, coif, marg. inscr.
1475 Philip Mede, arm., tab.
1st w., c.d.
2nd w., her. mant., all kng., with hf fig. of Our Lord issuing from clouds above, rect. pl.
c. 1480 John Jay, sheriff, c.d.
w. Joan, c.d., with 6 sons, 8 daus.
1522 John Brook, serjeant-at-law, in robes, coif.
w. Joan, c.d.

BRISTOL, ST STEPHEN

1594 Robt. Kitchin, alderman, c.d., with 3 sons.
w., c.d., with 3 daus., all kng., rect. pl.

BRISTOL ST WERBURGH

1586 Wm. Gyttyns, mcht., c.d., with 6 sons.
w. Mary, c.d., with 4 daus., all kng., rect. pl.

BRISTOL, TRINITY OR BARSTAPLE ALMSHOUSE CHAPEL

1411 John Barstaple, burgess, founder of the almshouse, c.d., anelace, sin. can., sm.
1411 Isabel, w. of above, c.d., sm. eff., sin. can., rest.

CHELTENHAM, ST MARY

1513 Wm. Greville, justice of the common pleas, in robes, coif.
w., c.d., with 3 sons, 8 daus. marg. inscr., mut., v. wn.

CHIPPING CAMDEN

1401 Wm. Grevel, c.d., anelace.
w. Marion, c.d., dble. can., marg. inscr., v. lge.
1450 Wm. Welley, mcht., c.d.
w. Alice, c.d.
1467 John Lethenard, mcht., c.d.
w. Joan, c.d.
1484 Wm. Gybbys, c.d.
1st w. Alice, c.d.
2nd w. Margt., c.d.
3rd w. Marion, c.d., with 7 sons, 6 daus.

CIRENCESTER

c. 1400 Vinter, c.d., with letter T on end of girdle.
w. Margery, c.d., both stg. on wine casks (head of man and upper hf of w. miss.), dble. can., lge., wn.
1438 Rich. Dixton, arm., sin. can., marg. inscr., mut., lge.
1440 Robt. Pagge, wool-mcht., c.d., stg. on woolpack.
w. Margt., c.d., with 6 sons, 8 daus., mut., dble. can.
1442 Reginald Spycer, c.d.
1st w. Margt., c.d.
2nd w. Julian, c.d.
3rd w. Margt., c.d.
4th w. Joan, c.d.
1462 Wm. Prelatte, arm.
1st w. Agnes, c.d.
2nd w. Joan, c.d.
c. 1470 Wm. Notyngham, c.d. (head miss.).
w. Cristine, c.d.
1478 Ralph Parsons, mass vests., ch., wf., wn.
c. 1480 Priest, in cassock, sm.
1480 Man, c.d. (head mut.).
w., mant., wn.
c. 1480 Woman, c.d. (upper hf miss., new head set on waist).
1497 John Bennett, c.d. (head miss.).
w. Agnes, c.d.
c. 1500 Man, c.d., mut. (head rest.).
c. 1500 Man, c.d., kng., with 4 sons, 1 a priest, acad. dr.

w., c.d., kng., with 3 daus. (Poss. John and Alice Avenyng.)
c.1530 Two women, c.d.
1587 Phillip Marner, clothier, c.d., staff in hand, dog at ft, shears by head.
1626 John Gunter, c.d.
w. Alice, c.d.

CLIFFORD CHAMBERS
1583 Hercules Raynesford, arm.
w. Eliz., c.d., with 2 sons, 1 dau., ach.
1601 Eliz. Marrowe, dau. of above, holding chrysom.

COALEY
1630 Daniel Stayn, M.A., pastor, with 1 son.
w., c.d., with 2 daus., all kng., rect. pl.

DEERHURST
1400 Sir John Cassy, baron of the exchequer, in robes, coif, lion at ft.
w. Alice, dog, Terri, at ft, dble. can., marg. inscr., lge.
c.1520 Woman, c.d. (lower hf miss.).
1525 Eliz. Rowdon, c.d.

DOWDESWELL
c.1520 Priest, in cope.

DOYNTON
1529 Wm. att Wode, c.d.
w. Margt., c.d.

DYRHAM
1401 Sir Morys Russell, arm.
w. Isabel, c.d., lge.

EASTINGTON
1518 Eliz. Knevet, her. mant., marg. inscr., mut.

FAIRFORD
1500 John Tame, arm.
w. Alice, c.d., chamfer inscr.
1534 Sir Edm. Tame, arm., tab.
1st w. Agnes, her. mant., with 2 sons, 3 daus.
2nd w. Eliz., her. mant., marg. inscr.
(The above are also represented on another brass, but with only 1 son, all kng., Trin.)

GLOUCESTER, ST JOHN BAPTIST
c.1520 Man, c.d. (lower hf miss.).
w., c.d.

GLOUCESTER, ST MARY DE CRYPT
1529 John Cook, alderman, c.d., mant.
w. Dame Joan, wid. dr., trip. can., fig. of St J.B., mut.
1519 Alys, c.d.
Agnes, c.d., ws. of Wm. Henshawe, bell founder. (These effs. came orig. from St Michael, Gloucester.)

KEMPSFORD
1521 Walter Hichman, c.d.
w. Cristyan, c.d., with 2 sons, marg. inscr.

LECHLADE
c.1450 Wool mcht., c.d. (Poss. John Townsend.)
w., c.d.
c.1510 Man, c.d.

LECKHAMPTON
1598 Wm. Norwood, c.d., with 9 sons.
w. Eliz., c.d., with 2 daus., all kng., rect. pl.

MICHELDEAN
c.1500 Margery, c.d.
Alice, c.d., ws. of Thos. Baynham.

MINCHINHAMPTON
c.1500 Man, c.d.
w., c.d.
c.1510 John Hampton, in shroud.
w. Elyn, in shroud, with 6 sons, the eldest a monk, and 3 daus., the eldest, Dame Alice, a nun.

1519 Edw. Halyday, c.d.
w. Margery, c.d.

NEWENT

1523 Roger Porter, arm., sm.

NEWLAND

1443 Robt. Greyndour, arm. (legs miss.).
w. Joan, c.d., also crest, showing miner with candle in mouth, pick in hand and bag of ore on back.

NORTHLEACH

c. 1400 Wool mcht., c.d., anelace, letter T on girdle.
w., c.d.

1447 Agnes Fortey, c.d. (head miss.).
1st hus. Wm. Scors, tailor, c.d.
2nd hus. Thos. Fortey, woolman, c.d. (head miss.), with 2 daus. and 2 sons, 4 daus., sin. can., marg. inscr., v. wn., mut.

1458 John Fortey, woolman, c.d., sin. can., mut., marg. inscr., mut., lge.

c. 1485 Woolman, c.d.
w., c.d., mut., with 2 sons, 2 daus., marg. inscr.

c. 1490 John Taylour, woolman, c.d.
w. Joan, c.d., with 8 sons, 7 daus., marg. inscr., mut., design of sheep on woolpack.

1500 2 sons, 2 daus. of Wm. and Margt. Bicknell.

1501 Robt. Serche, c.d.
w. Anne, c.d., with 3 sons, 1 dau.

1526 Thos. Bushe, woolman, c.d.
w. Joan, c.d., dble. can., marg. inscr.

c. 1530 Wm. Lawnder, priest, surplice, kng., marg. inscr., mut.

OLVESTON

1505 Morys Denys, arm., tab., and 1 son, Sir Walter Denys, arm., tab., both kng., holding scrolls.

QUINTON

c. 1430 Dame Joan, w. of Sir Wm. Clopton, vowess, sin. can., marg. inscr.

RODMARTON

1461 John Edward, lawyer, c.d., with lge. round cap.

SEVENHAMPTON

1497 John Camber, c.d.

THORNBURY

1571 Avice Tyndall, c.d.

TODENHAM

1614 Wm. Molton, c.d.
w. Millicent, c.d., rect. pl., ach.

TORMARTON

1493 John Ceysyll, servant, c.d., marg. inscr.

WESTON-SUB-EDGE

1590 Wm. Hodges, c.d.

WESTON-ON-AVON

1546 Sir John Greville, arm., tab.

1559 Sir Edw. Greville, arm., tab.

WHITTINGTON

1560 Rich. Coton, c.d.
w. Margt., c.d.

WINTERBOURNE

c. 1370 Woman, c.d. (Poss. Agnes Bradeston.)

WORMINGTON

1605 Anne Savage, in bed with chrysom, marg. inscr., mut. (Died in childbirth.)

WOTTON-UNDER-EDGE

1392 Thos., Lord Berkeley, arm., with mermaids on coll.
w. Margt., c.d., lge.

YATE

1590 Alex Staples, c.d.
1st w. Anis, c.d., with 2 sons, 3 daus.
2nd w. Eliz., c.d., with 4 sons, 2 daus., rect. pl.

HAMPSHIRE

(for ISLE OF WIGHT, see p. 66)

ALTON

c. 1510 Woman, c.d.
c. 1510 3 daus.

BASINGSTOKE

1606 Robt. Stocker, yeoman, c.d.
w. Ursula, c.d., with 9 sons, 2 daus.
1621 John, a child, son of Thos. Hilliard, sm.

BRAMLEY

1452 Wm. Joye, yeoman, c.d., with 6 sons stg. by his side, v. wn.
1504 Gwen Shelford, c.d.
1529 Rich. Carter, c.d.
w. Alys, c.d.

BRAMSHOTT

c. 1430 John Weston, c.d.
w. Eliz., c.d.

CANDOVER, BROWN

c. 1490 Man, c.d.
w., c.d., arm in arm.

CANDOVER, PRESTON, OLD CHURCH

1607 Kath. Dabrigecourt, c.d.

CRONDALL

1381 Nich. Kaerwent, rector, mass vests., lge.
1563 John Gyfford, arm., kng., with 8 daus., ach.
1641 John Eager, skeleton, rect. pl.

DEAN, PRIOR'S

1605 John Compton, c.d.
w. Joan, c.d., ach.

DOGMERSFIELD

1590 Anne Sutton, c.d., kng., with 3 daus., kng., and chrysom, rect. pl.

DUMMER

c. 1580 Wm. at Moore, clerk, c.d., with 1 son (head miss.), both kng., ach.

FORDINGBRIDGE

1568 Wm. Bulkeley, arm., with 3 sons.
w. Jane, c.d., with 5 daus., all kng., rect. pl., ach.

FROYLE

1575 John Lighe, c.d., ach.

HAVANT

1413 Thos. Aileward, rector, in cope.

HEADBOURNE WORTHY

c. 1430 John Kent, scholar of Winchester, c.d., sm.

HEADLEY

c. 1510 Man, c.d.
w., c.d., sm.

HECKFIELD

1514 Eliz. Hall, c.d.

ITCHEN STOKE

c. 1500 Woman, c.d., kng., sm.
1518 Joan Batmanson, c.d.

KIMPTON

1522 Robt. Thornburgh, arm.
1st w. Alys, c.d., with 1 son, 1 dau.
2nd w. Anne, c.d., with 1 son, 6 daus., all kng., sm. cross.

KINGSCLERE

1503 Cesily Gubard, c.d., sm., v. wn.
1519 Wm. Estwood, vicar, mass vests., sm.

MAPLEDURWELL

c. 1520 John Canner, c.d.
w. Agnes, c.d., with 4 sons, 6 daus., sm., wn.

MONXTON

1599 Alice Swayn, c.d., with 1 son, Arthur, c.d., both kng.

OAKLEY, CHURCH

1487 Robt. Warham, c.d.
w. Eliz., c.d., with 4 sons, 1 a priest, acad. dr.

Odiham
c.1480 Man, c.d., anelace.
w., c.d.
1498 Wm. Goode, rector, mass vests.
c.1520 Woman, c.d., with 6 daus.
c.1520 Woman, c.d., with 9 daus.
c.1530 Man, c.d.
c.1540 Man, arm. (ft miss.). (Poss. Rich. Vass.) [Pal.]

Ringwood
1416 John Prophete, dean of Hereford and York, in cope, SS on orphreys., marg. inscr., sin. can., mut., lge.

Sherborne, St John
c.1360 Raulin Brocas, c.d.
s. Margt., c.d., hf-effs., sm.
1488 Bernard Brocas, arm., tab., kng. to cross (miss.), with skeleton in shroud below, marg. inscr., mut., ach.
1492 John Brocas, arm.
1st w. Anne, c.d., with 2 sons, 3 daus.
2nd w. Anne, c.d., with 5 sons, 1 dau.
1492 John Brocas, arm., kng., Trin.
1540 Wm. Brocas, arm., kng., sm.

Sherfield-on-Loddon
1595 Mary Palmes, c.d., with 11 child., all kng., rect. pl.
1600 Stephen Hadnall, one of the privy chamber to Q. Mary, c.d., kng., ach.

Sombourne, King's
c.1380 Man, c.d.
Man, c.d.

Southampton, God's House
c.1500 Priest, in cope (head miss.).

Southwick
1548 John White, arm.
w. Kath., c.d., with 5 sons, 4 daus., chamfer inscr. [Poss. pal. approp. effs., c.1520.]

Stoke Charity
1482 Thos. Wayte, arm., with fig. of Our Lord in Pity.
1483 Thos. Hampton, arm.
w. Isabel, c.d. (upper hf miss.), with 2 sons, 6 daus., Trin.

Sutton, Bishop's
c.1520 Man, arm., mut.
w., c.d.

Thruxton
c.1425 Sir John Lysle, arm., trip. can., marg. inscr., lge.

Tytherley, West
1480 Anne Whitehede, c.d.

Wallop, Nether
1436 Dame Mary Gore, prioress of Amesbury, veil, barbe, mant.

Warnborough, South
1512 Robt. Whyte, arm., kng., with lge. hand pointing to scroll.

Whitchurch
1603 Rich. Brooke, c.d.
w. Eliz., c.d., with 3 sons, 3 daus.

Winchester, College Chapel and Cloisters
1413 John Morys, 1st warden, in almuce, facsimile.
1432 John Wyllynghale, fellow, in cope, hf-eff., facsimile.
1445 Nich. North, fellow, in cope, facsimile.
1450 Robt. Thurberne, warden, in cope, facsimile, lge.
1473 Edw. Tacham, fellow, in cope, hf-eff.
1494 John Taknell, fellow, mass vests., $\frac{3}{4}$-eff.
1498 John Bedell, scholar, mayor, c.d., facsimile.

1509 Thos. Lyrypyn, fellow, priest, mass vests., ¾-eff., facsimile.
1514 John Gylbert, fellow, mass vests., ¾-eff.
1514 John Erewaker, fellow, mass vests., ¾-eff.
1524 John Barratte, B.A., fellow, acad. dr., kng., sm., facsimile.
c.1548 John White, warden, in cope, facsimile. (The orig. effs. disappeared during rest. of chapel in 1875. Facsimiles placed in position 1882.)

WINCHESTER, ST CROSS
1382 John de Campeden, warden of the hospital, in cope, marg. inscr., v. lge.
1493 Rich. Harward, warden, in almuce, cap.
1518 Thos. Lawne, rector, mass vests.

YATELEY
1517 Wm. Lawerd, c.d.
w. Agnes, c.d., with 9 sons, 1 dau.
1532 Wm. Rygg, c.d.
w. Tomysyn, c.d., with 4 sons, 7 daus.
1578 Eliz. Smith, c.d. (lower hf miss.).
c.1590 Man, c.d.

HEREFORDSHIRE

BRAMPTON ABBOTS
1506 Joan Rudhale, c.d., sm.

BURGHILL
1616 John Awbrey, c.d., with 1 son.
w. Rachell, c.d., with 1 dau., all kng., rect. pl.

CLEHONGER
c.1470 Man, arm.
w., c.d. (Poss. Sir John Barre and w. Eden.)

COLWALL
1590 Anth. Harford, arm., with 6 sons.
w. Eliz., c.d., with 4 daus., rect. pl., ach.

HEREFORD, CATHEDRAL
c.1290 St Ethelbert, king and martyr, seated fig. holding crown, sm. (From brass to Bp. Thos. de Cantilupe, died 1282.)
1360 John Trilleck, bp., episcopal vests., with mitre and crosier, super can., sin. can., marg. inscr., lge.
1386 Rich. de la Barre, canon, in cope, in head of cross (stems and finials mut.).
1394 Man, c.d., once in head of cross (cross miss., ft of eff. mut.).
1428 Edm. Ryall, canon, in cope (head miss.).
1434 Priest, in cope, v. wn.
1435 Rich. Delamare, arm.
w. Isabel, c.d., dble. can., entab., lge.
1476 Rich. Rudhale, archdeacon, in cope, with SS.
1480 John Stockton, mayor, c.d., cask beneath ft, v. wn.
c.1480 Man, arm. (ft mut.).
1490 Thos. Chawndiler, dean of Hereford, in cope (head, ft miss.).
1514 Sir Richard Delabere, arm.
1st w. Anne, c.d., with 1 son, 4 daus.
2nd w. Eliz., c.d., with 10 sons, 6 daus., marg. inscr.
c.1520 Priest, mass vests., ch., wf., sm.
1529 Edm. Frowsetoure, prebendary, in cope, cap, trip. can., with SS, marg. inscr., lge., wn.
c.1600 ? Wilson, c.d.
w., c.d. (From St George's Chapel, Windsor.)

The following fragments remain from the brass to Wm. Porter, S.T.B., Warden of New College, Oxford:
Annun., several SS and 2 angels, part of can.

KINNERSLEY

1421 Wm. Dermot, rector, mass vests., hf-eff., v. wn.

LEDBURY

*c.*1410 Wm. Calwe, priest, acad. dr., kng., sm.
1490 Thos. Caple, arm., liv. coll.
1614 John Hayward, arm., rect. pl.

LUDFORD

1554 Wm. Fox, arm.
w. Jane, c.d., with 9 sons, 5 daus.

LUGWARDINE

1622 Jane Best, c.d., kng., rect. pl.

MARDEN

1614 Dame Margt. Chute, with 2 daus., Anne, Frances, 1 a chrysom.

WESTON-UNDER-PENYARD

1609 Walter Nurse, c.d., rect. pl.

HERTFORDSHIRE

ALBURY

*c.*1475 Hen. Barley, arm., salade,
w. Kath., c.d., with 4 daus., ach.
1588 Thos. Leventhorpe, high sheriff, c.d.
w. Dorothy, c.d., with 1 son, 5 daus.
1592 John Scrogs, arm.
w., c.d., with 1 son, Edw., rect. pl.

ALDBURY

1478 John Davers, c.d., sm.
1547 Sir Ralph Verney, arm., tab.
w. Eliz., her. mant., with 9 sons, 3 daus.

ALDENHAM

*c.*1520 Man, c.d.
w., c.d.
*c.*1520 Man, c.d. (head miss.).
*c.*1520 Man, c.d.
w., c.d., with 2 sons, 6 daus.
*c.*1520 Man, c.d., with 6 sons, 5 daus.
*c.*1525 Man, c.d.
2 ws., c.d., 1 mut., with 1 son, 2 daus.
*c.*1525 Parts of 2 women, with 4 sons, 1 dau.; 4 sons, 8 daus.; and 1 son, sm.
*c.*1535 Woman, c.d., sm.
1538? Joan Warner, c.d., with 1 dau., sm.
1547 Lucas Goodyere, in shroud, with 1 son, Edm., sm.
1608 Edw. Brisko, c.d.
1st w. Helen, c.d.

AMWELL, GREAT

*c.*1490 Man, c.d. (head miss.).
1st w., c.d., with 4 sons, 3 daus.
2nd w., c.d.

ARDELEY

*c.*1420 Eliz. Clerk, c.d. (upper hf miss.).
1515 Philip Metcalff, vicar, mass vests.
1599 Thos. Shotbolt, c.d.
w. Mary, c.d., with 4 sons, 2 daus.

ASPENDEN

1500 Thos. Goodriche, c.d.
w. Alice, c.d.
1508 Sir Robt. Clyfford, knight for the body to Hen. VII, arm., tab.
w. Eliz., her. mant., with 2 daus., all kng., marg. inscr.

ASTON

1592 John Kent, royal servant, in habit of yeoman of the guard.
w. Mary, c.d.

BALDOCK

*c.*1410 Woman, c.d. (lower hf miss.).

*c.*1420 Man, in dress of huntsman, with horn, knife, rope (legs, ft miss.). w., mant.

*c.*1480 Man, in shroud. w., in shroud.

*c.*1480 Man, c.d. w., c.d. (Poss. Wm. Crane, with w. Margt. or Joan.)

*c.*1500 Ft of man.

BARKWAY

1561 Robt. Poynard, c.d. 1st w. Joan, c.d. 2nd w. Bridget, c.d., with 4 daus.

BARLEY

1621 Andrew Willet, rector, in gown, cap.

BAYFORD

*c.*1545 John Knighton?, arm. w., c.d., middle portion only. [All pal.]

*c.*1630? Man, arm. (Poss. John Knighton.)

BENNINGTON

*c.*1420 Priest, in cope, with badge (lower hf miss.).

BERKHAMSTEAD, GREAT

1356 Rich. Torryngton, c.d. w. Margt., c.d., holding hands.

*c.*1365 Man, arm.

*c.*1370 Margt. Briggs?, c.d.

*c.*1400 Thos. Brydde?, priest, mass vests., hf-eff.

1485 Rich. Westbroke, c.d.

1520 Kath. Incent, in shroud.

BRAUGHING

*c.*1480 Man, c.d., v.wn. w., c.d. [Pal., *c.*1440.]

*c.*1490 Woman, c.d. (upper hf. miss.).

1561 Barbara Hanchett, c.d.

BROXBOURNE

*c.*1470 Robt. Ecton?, priest, mass vests., ch.

1473 Sir John Say, arm., tab., with suns and roses on coll. (head miss.). w. Eliz., her. mant., marg. inscr., mut., ach.

*c.*1510 Priest, acad. dr., with scroll.

1531 John Borrell, serjeant-at-arms to Hen. VIII, arm., holding mace (legs miss.), with 3 daus.

BUCKLAND

1451 Alice Boteler, c.d.

1478 Wm. Langley, rector, in cope, ch., wf.

1499 John Gyll, c.d., with 6 sons.

BUNTINGFORD

1620 Alex. Strange, vicar, sm. rect. pl.

CHESHUNT

1449 Wm. Prike, c.d. (head miss.). w. Elen, c.d., wn.

1453 Joan Clay, c.d., v. wn.

1502 Constance Parre, c.d.

1609 Eliz. Collen, c.d., kng., sm.

CLOTHALL

1404 John Vynter, rector, mass vests.

1519 John Wryght, rector, mass vests., ch., wf., Trin.

*c.*1535 Thos. Dalyson, rector, in cope.

1578 Anne Bramfeld, c.d. (covered).

1602 Wm. Lucas, rector, in gown.

DIGSWELL

1415 John Peryent, pennon-bearer to Rich. II, arm., leopard at ft. w. Joan, lady-in-waiting to Queen Joan, hedgehog at ft, swan on coll. of dress, both with SS coll., marg. inscr., mut., lge.

1442 John Peryent, son of above, arm.

1484 Wm. Roberts, auditor, in shroud. w. Joyes, in shroud, with 2 sons.

1495 Thos. Hoore, mercer, c.d. w. Alice, c.d., with 4 sons, 8 daus.

*c.*1530 Man, c.d.

w., c.d., *re-used by addition of inscr. to*
1557 Robt. Batyll and w. Margt., with 1 son, Wm., his w. Joan with 4 sons, 6 daus. (effs. added).

EASTWICK
1564 Joan Lee, c.d.

ESSENDON
1588 Wm. Tooke, c.d.
w. Alice, c.d., with 9 sons, 3 daus., all kng., ach.

FLAMSTEAD
1414 John Oudeby, canon, in cope.
c. 1470 Man, c.d.
w., c.d., with 2 sons, 2 daus., v.wn.

GADDESDEN, GREAT
1506 Wm. Croke, c.d.
w. Alice, c.d.
c. 1525 Man, c.d.
w., c.d., sm.

HADHAM, GREAT
c. 1420 Priest, acad. dr., cap, hf-eff.
c. 1520 Man, c.d.
w., c.d.
1582 Clement Newce, c.d.
w. Mary, c.d., with 8 sons, 9 daus.
1610 Wm. Newce, c.d.
1st w., c.d., with 6 sons, 7 daus.
2nd w., c.d.

HADHAM, LITTLE
c. 1470 Rich. Warriner, parson, in cope, sm., v. wn.
c. 1485 Ralph Bawde?, arm.
w. Margt.?, c.d., with 4 daus.

HARPENDEN
1456 Wm. Anabull, c.d.
w. Isabel, c.d., v. wn.
1571 Wm. Cressye, c.d.
w. Grace, c.d., kng., ach.

HEMEL HEMPSTEAD
1390 Robert Albyn, arm.
w. Margt., c.d.

HERTFORD, ALL SAINTS
1435 John Hunger (all miss., except ft).

HINXWORTH
c. 1450 Man, c.d.
w., c.d.
1487 John Lambard, mercer, alderman, c.d.
w. Amy, c.d., with 4 sons, eldest, Wm., in almuce, and 2 daus.

HITCHIN
c. 1420 Man, c.d.
1421 John Pulter, draper, (ft only).
w. Alice, c.d., v. wn.
1452 Mcht. of the staple of Calais.
w. Alice, c.d., with 4 sons, 6 daus.
c. 1470 Woman, c.d., wn.
1477 Margery Beel, in shroud, with 4 sons, 4 daus.
c. 1480 Man, c.d.
w., c.d., wn.
c. 1480 6 sons, kng.
1481 Thos. Abbot, mercer, c.d.
w. Joan, c.d.
1485 Eliz. Mattock, in shroud, mut., with 2 sons, 1 dau.
c. 1490 Man, in shroud.
w., in shroud, with 3 sons, 5 daus. (Poss. John Wisbeard and w. Ellen.)
c. 1490 Thos. Abbot?, in shroud.
w., in shroud, with 3 sons, 2 daus.
c. 1490 4 sons, 4 daus.
1498 Jas. Hert, vicar, in cope, bleeding heart above.
c. 1530 Man, c.d.
3 ws., c.d.
c. 1535 Man, c.d.
w., c.d.

HUNSDON
1495 Margt. Shelley, in shroud. Trin.
1591 Jas. Grey, hunting dress, shooting a stag while Death strikes him with a dart, rect. pl.

ICKLEFORD

c. 1400 Thos. Somer, c.d., hf-eff.
w. Marion, c.d., hf-eff., wn.

IPPOLYTS

1594 Ryce Hughes, haberdasher, c.d.
w. Alice, c.d., with 1 son, 2 daus.

KELSHALL

1435 Rich. Adane, c.d.
w. Marion, c.d., wn.

KIMPTON

c. 1450 Woman, c.d., flowing hair.

KNEBWORTH

1414 Simon Bache, canon of St Paul's, in cope, with SS, B.V. Mary on orphreys.

1582 Roland Lytton, arm.
1st w. Margt., c.d.
2nd w. Anne, c.d., ach.

LANGLEY, ABBOTS

1498 Eliz., c.d.
Joan, c.d., ws. of Rauffe Horwode, with 3 sons, 3 daus., sm.

1607 Thos. Cogdell, yeoman, c.d.
1st w. Jane, c.d.
2nd w. Alice, c.d.

LANGLEY, KING'S

1528 Alice Carter, c.d., sm.

1578 Margt. Cheyne, c.d. [Pal. 2 portions Flem. brasses, 14th, 15th cents.]

1588 John Carter, c.d.
2 ws., c.d.

LETCHWORTH

c. 1400 Wm. Overbury, c.d., hf-eff.
w. Isabel, c.d., hf-eff., wn.

1475 Thos. Wyrley, rector, mass vests., holding heart.

MIMMS, NORTH

c. 1370 Priest, mass vests., ch. and paten on chest, stg. on stag under can., with God the Father, SS, angels, etc., resting on br. Flem.

1458 Eliz. Knolles, c.d. (head miss.), with 2 daus.

1488 Hen. Covert, arm.

c. 1490 Man, c.d.
w., c.d., with 4 sons, 6 daus.

c. 1560 Rich. Butler, arm.
w. Martha, c.d., ach.

NEWNHAM

c. 1490 Man, c.d.
1st w., c.d.
2nd w., c.d., with 1 son, 3 daus.

1607 Joan Dowman, c.d., with 8 child.

OFFLEY

1529 John Samwell, c.d.
1st w. Eliz., c.d., with 1 son.
2nd w. Joan, c.d.

c. 1530 Man, c.d.
3 ws., c.d., with 9 sons.

PELHAM, BRENT

1627 Mary, c.d.
Anne, c.d., ws. of Francis Rowley, sm.

PELHAM, FURNEUX

c. 1420 Robt. Newport?, c.d., anelace.
w. Margery?, wid. dr., child beside mother, dble. can., mut.

1518 Robt. Newport, arm.
w. Mary, c.d., with 2 sons, 3 daus., all kng.

RADWELL

1487 Wm. Wheteaker, c.d.
w. Joan, c.d., with 1 son, Thos., mass vests., ch., between parents, sm.

1516 John Bele, c.d.
1st w. Anne, c.d., with 2 sons.
2nd w. Agnes, c.d.

1602 Eliz. Parker, c.d.

REDBOURN

c. 1490 8 daus., kng. (Poss. of the Pecok fam.)

1512 Rich. Pecok, c.d. (ft miss.), with 4 sons, mut., peacock below, mut.
1560 Sir Rich. Rede, arm.
w. Anne, c.d., with 3 sons, 3 daus. all kng., ach.

RICKMANSWORTH
1613 Thos. Day, c.d., with staff, book.
1st w. Alice, c.d.
2nd w. Joan, c.d.

ROYSTON
1421 Wm. Taveram, rector, acad. dr. (lower hf miss.), sin. can., mut.
c.1500 Man, c.d.
w., c.d.

ST ALBANS, ABBEY
c.1375 Thos. de la Mare, abbot, rich vests., fine can., with God the Father, angels, SS etc., marg. inscr., lge. rect. pl. Flem.
c.1400 Abbot (upper hf miss.). (Poss. John de la Moote.) [Pal., same date.]
1411 Thos. Fayreman, mcht., c.d.
w. Alice, c.d., v. wn.
c.1450 Reginald Bernewelt?, monk.
c.1460 Robt. Beauner, monk, holding bleeding heart.
c.1465 Man, c.d.
1468 Barth. Halley or Halsey, arm. (upper hf miss.).
w. Florens, c.d.
c.1470 Man, c.d. (head miss.).
c.1470 Monk hf-eff.
1480 Sir Anth. Grey, arm., suns and roses on coll.
1519 Rauff Rowlatt, mcht, c.d., with 6 daus., marg. inscr., mut.
1521 Thos. Rutlond, sub-prior, monastic dr.
1521 Robt. Fairfax, c.d.
w. Agnes, c.d. (renewed 1921).

ST ALBANS, ST MICHAEL
c.1380 John Pecok, c.d.
w. Maud, c.d.
c.1380 Man, arm. (Of the Pecok fam.)
c.1400 Man, c.d., in head of cross, mut.

ST ALBANS, ST PETER
1627 Roger Pemberton, c.d., high sheriff.
w. Eliz., c.d., with 3 sons, 3 daus.

ST ALBANS, ST STEPHEN
1482 Wm. Robins, clerk to the signet of Edw. IV, arm.
w. Kath, c.d., with 4 sons, 5 daus.

SANDON
1480 John Fitzgeffrey, arm., liv. coll.
w. Eliz., c.d., with 6 daus.

SARRATT
c.1500 Jas. Hedon?, c.d.
w. Joan?, c.d. (lower hf of both miss.), v. sm.

SAWBRIDGEWORTH
1437 John Leventhorpe, arm., liv. coll.
w. Kath., wid. dr., lge.
1470 Geoff. Joslyne, c.d.
1st w. Kath., c.d.
2nd w. Joan, c.d.
c.1480 12 sons, 6 daus. of John Chauncy.
1484 John Leventhorpe, in shroud.
w. Joan, in shroud, both holding engraved hearts.
1527 Joan Leventhorpe, her. mant.
c.1600 Edw. Leventhorpe, arm., son of above.
w. Eliz., c.d.
c.1600 Mary Leventhorpe, c.d.

SHENLEY
1621 Ralph Allway, c.d.
w. Dorothy, c.d.

STANDON
1412 John Ruggewyn, arm., kng. on helmet (upper hf miss.).
c.1465 Man, c.d.
1477 John Feld, mcht., alderman, c.d., mant., with 2 sons, 1 dau.

John Feld, son of above, arm., tab., with 2 sons, 2 daus., marg. inscr., mut.
1557 Guy Wade, arm., helmet.

STANSTEAD ABBOTS
c. 1490 Man, arm.
c. 1540 Man, c.d.
w., c.d. (head miss.), hand in hand, 1 pl. [Pal.]
1581 Wm. Saxaye, c.d., ach.

STEVENAGE
c. 1500 Stephen Hellard, canon, in cope.

TEWIN
1610 Thos. Pygott, c.d.

WALKERN
c. 1480 Man, c.d.
w., c.d.
1583 Edw. Humbarstone, c.d.
w. Annas, c.d., with 5 sons, 3 daus., ach. [All pal. various Flem., c. 1474, 1400, 1500.]
1636 Wm. Chapman, haberdasher, c.d.
w. Anne, c.d., with 6 sons, 6 daus., wn.

WARE
c. 1400 Jean Lucas?, c.d.
1454 Ellen Warbulton, c.d.
c. 1470 Wm. Pyrry, c.d.
1st w. Agnes, c.d., with 5 sons, 5 daus.
2nd w. Alice, c.d., with 5 sons, 5 daus.

WATFORD
1415 Sir Hugh de Holes, justice of the king's bench, in robes, coif, lge., mut.
1416 Margt., wid. of above, c.d., lge., mut.
1613 Hen. Dickson, c.d.
Geo. Miller, c.d.
Anth. Cooper, c.d., all servants to Sir Chas. Morrison, rect. pl.

WATTON-AT-STONE
1361 Sir Philip Peletoot, arm., lge. (Legs, can., inscr., rest. 1851.)
c. 1370 Priest, in cope, lion at ft, lge. (Poss. John Brigenhall.)
c. 1450 Man, c.d.
1455 Joan Bardolf, c.d.
c. 1470 Man, c.d. (head miss.).
1514 John Butler, arm., ach.
1545 Eliz. Butler, c.d. (lower hf miss.).

WHEATHAMPSTEAD
c. 1450 Hugh Bostok, c.d.
w. Margt., c.d.
c. 1480 Man, arm. (ft and 1 leg only).
w., c.d. (head mut.), with 4 daus.
1520 John Heyworth, c.d.
w. Eliz., c.d., with 4 sons, 5 daus.
c. 1510 Man, c.d.
c. 1510 Woman, c.d., profile, with 2 sons, 6 daus.

WILLIAN
1446 Rich. Goldon, rector, mass vests., holding heart.

WORMLEY
1479 Edm. Howton, c.d.
w. Annes, c.d.
c. 1490 John Cok, yeoman, c.d. (lower hf miss.).
w. A—?, c.d., with 10 sons, Trin., sm. pl. of dog hunting hare, etc., marg. inscr., mut.
1598 Walter Tooke, c.d.
w. Angelett, c.d., with 8 sons, 4 daus.

WYDDIALL
1532 Geo. Canon, c.d. (upper hf miss.).
1546 John Gille, c.d.
w. Margt., c.d., with 8 daus. (eff. engraved 1520).?
1575 Dame Margt. Plumbe, c.d., with open book, hf-eff., lge.

HUNTINGDONSHIRE

BROUGHTON

c. 1490 Laurence Marton, c.d. (ft miss.).

DIDDINGTON

1505 Wm. Taylard, arm., tab. (upper hf miss.).
w. Eliz., her. mant., kng., square-topped can., mut., B.V. Mary and Child, SS in side shafts.

1513 Alice Taylard, wid. dr., with 3 sons, B.V. Mary and Child.

GODMANCHESTER

c. 1520 Man, c.d.

OFFARD DARCY

c. 1440 Sir Laur. Pabenham, arm.
1st w. Eliz., c.d.
2nd w. Joan, c.d. (lower parts of effs. miss.) [1 w. pal.]

c. 1530 Wm. Taylard, rector, acad. dr., cap, kng.

SAWTRY, ALL SAINTS

1404 Sir Wm. Moyne, arm.
w. Mary, c.d., lge.

SOMERSHAM

c. 1530 Priest, mass vests., ch., wf.

STILTON

1606 Rich. Curthoyse, yeoman, c.d.
w. Anne, c.d.

1618 Thos. Curthoyse, c.d.
John Curthoyse, c.d., sons of above, sm.

STUKELEY, LITTLE

c. 1590 Man, c.d.

ISLE OF WIGHT

ARRETON

c. 1430 Harry Hawles, steward of the Isle of Wight, arm. (head miss.).

CALBORNE

c. 1380 Man, arm.

FRESHWATER

c. 1365 Man, arm., shield on jupon, scroll from hands. (Poss. of the Compton fam.)

KINGSTON

1535 Rich. Mewys, c.d., with 4 sons.

SHORWELL

1518 Rich. Bethell, vicar, surplice.

1619 Eliz. Bampfield, c.d.
Gertrude Percevall, c.d., ws. of Barnabas Leigh, rect. pl.

KENT

ACRISE

1601 Mary Heyman, c.d.

ADDINGTON

1378 Rich. Charlis, arm. (lower hf miss.), marg. inscr., mut.

1409 Wm. Snayth, sheriff of Kent, arm.
w. Alice, c.d., dble. can., mut.

c. 1415 Man, arm. (Poss. John Northwood.)

c. 1445 Man, arm., sm. (Poss. Robt. Watton.)

1446 Thos. Chaworth, rector, mass vests., hf-eff., ch., wf.

1470 Robt. Watton, arm., salade.
w. Alice, c.d.

ALDINGTON

1475 John Weddeot, arm.
w. Maud, c.d., with 3 sons.

APPLEDORE

c. 1520 Girl, flowing hair, sm.

ASH-NEXT-SANDWICH

1455 Maud Clitherow, wid. dr. (lower hf miss.), dble. can.

1455 Jane Keriell, dau. of above, c.d.

1525 Wm. Leus, c.d.
w. Anys, c.d., sm., wn.

1602 Christ. Septvans, arm.
w. Mercy, c.d., ach., marg. inscr., mut.

1642 Walter Septvans, c.d., cloak.
w. Jane, c.d., with 3 sons, 3 daus.

Ash-next-Wrotham
1465 Rich. Galon, rector, mass vests., hf-eff.
1605 Thos. Maxfield, rector.

Ashford
c.1320 Priest (head only).
1375 Eliz., Countess of Athol (arms, ft miss.), sin. can., bad. mut., marg. inscr.
1490 Sir John Fogge, arm. (head only).
1512 2 daus. of Thos. Fogg.

Aylesford
1426 John Cosyngton, arm.
w. Sarra, c.d.

Barham
1375 Roger Digges, c.d. (head miss.), lge.
c.1455 John Digges?, arm., liv. coll.
w. Joan?, wid. dr.

Bearsted
1634 Wm. Cage, c.d., with 2 sons, 1 holding skull.
w. Susanna, c.d., with 2 daus., 1 with skull, the other a chrysom, kng.

Beckenham
1552 Sir Humph. Style, arm., tab.
1st w. Brydgett, her. mant., with 6 sons, 3 daus.
2nd w. Eliz., her. mant., with 1 son, 1 dau., all kng.
1563 Dame Margt. Berney, c.d.

Bethersden
1459 Wm. Lovelace, c.d.
1591 Thos. Lovelace, c.d., sm.

Bexley
1513 Thos. Sparrow, c.d., sm.

Biddenden
c.1520 Margt. Goldwell, c.d.
2nd hus. John Goldwell, c.d., with 1 son.
1566 John Mayne, sheriff of Kent, arm.
w. Margt., c.d., with 6 sons, 8 daus., all kng., ach.
1572 Thos. Fleet, c.d. (head, ft miss.), ach. [All pal. portions of Flem. brasses, c.1360, 1525.]
1584 Wm. Boddindam, c.d.
1st w. Julian, c.d., with 1 son, 5 daus.
2nd w. Anne, c.d., with 2 daus., mut.
1593 Rich. Allarde, alderman, c.d.
1st w. Helen, c.d., with 3 sons.
2nd w. Joan, c.d., with 1 son, 2 daus.
3rd w. Thomasin, c.d.
1598 John Evrenden, c.d.
1st w, Jone, c.d., with 2 sons.
2nd w. Jane, c.d.
1609 Josiah Seyliard, c.d.
1st w. Judith, c.d., with 4 sons, 2 daus.
2nd w. Anne, c.d., with 2 sons, 1 dau.
1628 Bernard Randolphe, c.d.
w. Jane, c.d., with 5 sons, 1 dau., heads on cushions, rect. pl.
1641 Wm. Randolph, c.d.
w. Eliz., c.d., with 2 sons, 6 daus.

Birchington
1449 John Quek, c.d., anelace, with 1 son.
1454 John Feld, c.d.
1518 Alys Cryspe, c.d., with 1 dau., stg. on skirt.
1523 John Heyns, vicar, mass vests., ch., wf.
1528 Margt. Cryspe, c.d.
1533 Margt. Cryppys, with chrysom (head miss.).
1533 8 sons, 7 daus. of Agnes and John Cryspe.

Birling

1522 Walter Mylys, c.d., with 4 sons, marg. inscr.

Bobbing

c. 1420 Sir Arnold Savage, arm.
w. Dame Joan, wid. dr.

1420 Sir Arnold Savage, son of above, arm., SS coll. (head, ft miss.), trip. can., bad. mut.

1496 Joan, dau. of James Bourne, flowing hair, sm.

Borden

c. 1450 Wm. Fyge, clerk of the privy seal, c.d.

1521 Wm. Fordmell, vicar, in almuce, sm.

Boughton Malherbe

1499 Nich. Wotton, c.d., with 3 sons.
w. Eliz., c.d., with 7 daus., all kng., sm.

1529 Sir Edward Wotton, arm.
w. Dorothy, c.d., marg. inscr., mut.

Boughton-under-Blean

1508 John Best, c.d.
w. Joan, c.d., sm.

1587 Thos. Hawkins, servant to Hen. VIII, aged 101, arm., ach.

1591 Cyriac Petit, c.d.
w. Florence, c.d., with 4 daus.

Boxley

1451 Wm. Snell, vicar, acad. dr.

1576 Rich. Tomynw, arm.

Brabourne

1433 Wm. Scott, arm., sin. can., bad. mut., lge.

1450 Denis, dau. of Vincent Finch, with flowing hair.

1524 Sir Wm. Scott, arm.

1528 Dame Eliz. Pownynges, c.d.

Bredgar

1518 Thos. Coly, warden of the college, acad. dr., ch., wf.

Brenchley

1517 Thos. Robertes, mercer, c.d.
1st w. Eliz., c.d.
2nd w. Joan, c.d.
3rd w. Agnes, c.d., with 7 sons, 4 daus.

c. 1540 Man, c.d.
w., c.d.

Bromley

1600 Rich. Thornhill, c.d.
1st w. Margt., c.d. (head miss.), with 2 sons, 3 daus.
2nd w. Eliz., c.d., with 2 sons, 1 dau.

Brookland

1503 Thos. Leddes, vicar, mass vests., ch., wf.

Canterbury, St Alphege

1523 Robt. Gosebourne, rector, acad. dr.

Canterbury, Cathedral Chapter Office

1438 John Lovelle, rector, in cope, head on cushion.

Canterbury, St Gregory

c. 1522 Raff Brown, alderman, c.d., kng., rect. pl.

Canterbury, St Margaret

1470 John Wynter, mayor, c.d.

Canterbury, St Martin

1587 Mich. Fraunces, c.d.
w. Jane, c.d., with 1 son, 5 daus., ach.

1591 Thos. Stoughton, arm.

Canterbury, St Paul

1531 Geo. Wyndbourne, c.d.
w. Kath., c.d. (replaced).

Capel-le-Ferne

1526 John Gybbis, c.d.
w. Margt., c.d., with 4 sons, sm.

CHALLOCK

1504 Thos. Thorston, c.d.
w. Joan, c.d., sm.

CHART, GREAT

c. 1470 Notary, c.d., with penner and inkhorn.

1485 Wm. Goldwell, c.d.
w. Alice, c.d.

1499 Wm. Sharp, c.d.
5 ws., c.d., sm.

1500 Thos. Twesden, c.d.
w. Bennet, c.d., sm., wn.

1513 John Toke, arm.
1st w. Margt., c.d.
2nd w. Anne, c.d., marg. inscr., mut.

1565 John Toke, arm.
w. Cisley, c.d., with 7 sons, mut.

1680 Nich. Toke, arm., with 3 daus., all kng., 2 rect. pl.

CHARTHAM

1306 Sir Robt. de Setvans, arm., cross-legged, shield, bare-headed.

1416 Robt. London, rector, in cope, sm.

1454 Robt. Arthur, rector, in cope.

1508 Robt. Sheffelde, rector, in almuce.

1530 Jane Eveas, c.d., sm.

CHELSFIELD

c. 1420 Priest, mass vests., sm.

1420 Wm. Robroke, rector, mass vests., sm.

c. 1480 Woman, c.d., with 6 sons, 2 priests, acad. dr., 5 daus., wn.

1510 Alice Bray, c.d., with 4 sons.

CHERITON

1474 John Child, rector, acad. dr., sm.

1502 Thos. Fogg, rector, mass vests., sm.

1592 Joan Brodnax, c.d.

CHEVENING

1596 Griffin Lloyd, rector, in gown.
w. Anne, c.d., with 7 sons, 2 daus.

CHISLEHURST

1482 Alan Porter, rector, mass vests., hf-eff.

CLIFFE-AT-HOO

1609 Thos. Faunce, yeoman, c.d.
2nd w. Eliz., c.d., with 1 son, 2 daus. also 2 sons, 1 dau., by 1st w. Alice.

1652 Bonham Faunce, c.d.
1st w. Eliz., c.d.
2nd w. Mary, c.d.

COBHAM

1310–20 Dame Jone de Kobeham, c.d., sin. can., marg. inscr., lge.

1354 Sir John de Cobham, arm. (head rest.), sin. can., marg. inscr., rest., lge.

c. 1365 Sir John de Cobham, arm., holding a church, sin. can., marg. inscr., partly rest., lge.

1367 Sir Thos. de Cobham, arm., sin. can., marg. inscr., rest., lge.

1375 Dame Margt. de Cobham, c.d., sin. can., marg. inscr., much rest., lge.

1380 Dame Maude de Cobeham, c.d., sin. can., marg. inscr., much rest., lge.

1395 Dame Margt. de Cobeham, c.d., sin. can., marg. inscr., rest., B.V. Mary and Child above, lge.

1402 Reg. de Cobham, canon, in cope, on br. under sm. trip. can., rest.

1402 Rauf de Cobham, arm., hf-eff., holding inscr.

1405 Sir Reg. Braybrok, arm., with 2 sons, Reg. and Robt., stg. on pedestals, sin. can., Trin. above, marg. inscr., lge. (Robt., his pedestal, etc. rest.)

1407 Sir Nich. Hawberk, arm., with 1 son, John, stg. on pedestal, trip. can., marg. inscr., Trin., B.V. Mary and Child, St Geo., each under sm. can., partly rest., lge.
1418 Wm. Tannere, in almuce, hf-eff.
1433 Joan, Lady of Cobham, mant., with 6 sons, 4 daus., lge.
1447 John Gerye, priest, in head of a cross, mut.
*c.*1450 John Gladwyn, master, in cope.
1498 John Sprotte, master, in cope.
1506 Margt. Broke, c.d., with 8 sons, 10 daus., dble. can., Trin. above, marg. inscr., partly rest.
1529 Sir Thos. Brooke, arm.
w. Dorothy, with 7 sons, 6 daus., marg. inscr.

COWLING
1508 Feyth, dau. of Sir John Brook, sm.

CRANBROOK
*c.*1520 Man, c.d., with chrysom.
1627 Sir Thos. Robertes, c.d.
w. Frances, c.d., kng., marg. inscr., ach.

CRAY, ST MARY
1508 Rich. Abery, c.d.
1st w. Joan, c.d.
2nd w. Agnes, c.d.
3rd w. Elynor, c.d., sm.
1604 Rich. Manning, c.d.
w. Rachel, c.d.
*c.*1773 Philadelphia Greenwood, c.d., rect. pl.
1773 Benj. Greenwood, hus. of above, rect. pl.

CUDHAM
1503 Alys Waleys, c.d., with 6 sons, 3 daus.

DARTFORD
1402 Rich. Martyn, c.d., mant.
w., c.d., dble. can., marg. inscr., partly rest., lge.
1454 Agnes Molyngton, wid. dr.
1464 Joan Rothele, c.d.
1496 Rich. Burlton, c.d.
w. Kath., c.d.
1508 ? Wiltshire, c.d.
*c.*1590 Woman, c.d., hf-eff.
1590 Wm. Death, c.d.
1st w. Eliz., c.d., holding chrysom.
2nd w. Anne, c.d.
1612 Frances Bostocke, c.d. (head mut.).

DAVINGTON
1613 John Edwards, c.d.
w. Anne, c.d., with 1 son, 3 daus., (2 chrysoms), kng., rect. pl.
1616 Kath., dau. of Edm. Lasheford, c.d., kng., rect. pl.

DEAL, UPPER
1508 Thos. Baker, c.d.
w. Deonys, c.d., with 4 sons, 4 daus.
1562 Thos. Boys, arm., kng., ach.

DITTON
1576 Rowland Shakerley, arm. (ft only).

DOVER, ST MARY
1638 Wm. Jones, c.d.
w. Kath., c.d.

DOWNE
*c.*1400 John Petle?, c.d., anelace.
w. Julian?, c.d.
*c.*1420 Thos. Petle, c.d., sm.
1607 Jacob Verzelini, c.d.
w. Eliz., c.d., with 6 sons, 3 daus., lge.

EASTRY
1590 Thos. Nevynson, arm.
w. Anne, c.d., ach.

EDENBRIDGE
1558 John Selyard, c.d.

ELMSTED

1507 Agnes or Joan Gay, c.d.

ERITH

1425 Roger Sencler, c.d., sm.
1435 John Ailemer, c.d.
w. Margery, c.d.
1471 Emme Wode, c.d.
1496 3 sons of Rich. Walden.
1511 John Mylner, c.d.
2nd w. Bennet, c.d.
1537 Edw. Hawte, arm.
w. Eliz., c.d., with 1 dau.

FARNINGHAM

1451 Wm. Gysborne, vicar, mass vests., hf-eff.
1514 Alys Taillor, c.d., sm.
1517 Wm. Petham, c.d., kng., sm.
1519 Thos. Sibill, c.d.
w. Agnes, c.d.

FAVERSHAM

1414 Seman Tong, c.d. (upper hf miss.).
1419 Hen. Pay, arm. (ft only).
1480 Wm. Thornbury, vicar, anchorite, in cope, sin. can., bad. mut.
1504 Denis at Sole, c.d. (upper hf miss.).
1496 Roger Harrison, baker (upper hf miss.), v. wn.
c.1496 Upper hf of man. (Poss. other hf of above.)
c.1500 Woman, c.d. (lower hf miss.), v. wn.
c.1500 Man, c.d. (upper hf miss.).
c.1510 Man, c.d.
1531 John Redbourne, vicar, mass vests., ch., wf.
1533 Hen. Hatche, mcht., c.d.
w. Joan, c.d., dble can., marg. inscr., lge.
1533 Rich. Colwell, mayor, c.d.
1st w. Agnes, c.d., with 2 sons, 3 daus.
2nd w. Agnes, c.d., with 3 sons, 1 dau., marg. inscr., wn.
c.1580 Man, c.d.
1610 John Haywarde, c.d., mut., with 3 sons, 3 daus.

FORDWICH

1605 Aphra Hawkins, c.d.

GOODNESTONE-NEXT-WINGHAM

1507 Wm. Boys, c.d.
w. Isabel, c.d., with 5 sons, 3 daus., Trin.
1523 W. of Wm. Goodnestone, c.d.
1558 Vyncent Boys, c.d.
w. Mary, c.d., ach.
1558 Thos. Engeham, arm.
w. Eliz., c.d., with 2 sons, 5 daus., ach.

GOUDHURST

1424 John Bedgebury, arm., sin. can., slightly mut.
c.1490 Sir John Culpeper?, arm.
c.1520 Walter Culpeper?, arm.

GRAIN, ISLE OF, ST JAMES

c.1520 Wm. Hykkes, c.d.

GRAVENEY

c.1360 Dame Joan de Feversham, with 1 son, John, c.d., hf-effs., dble. can., bad. mut., marg. inscr., mut.
1381 Rich. de Feversham, arm., marg. inscr.
1436 John Martyn, justice of the common pleas, in robes, coif, holding heart, marg. inscr., v. lge.
w. Anne, c.d., dble. can.

HALLING, LOWER

1587 Silvester Lambarde, rect. pl. of woman in bed, with twins in cradle and child.

HALSTEAD

1444 Wm. Burys, arm.
1528 Wm. Petley, c.d.
w. Alys, c.d. (lower parts of effs. mut.).

HALSTOW, HIGH

1398 Wm. Groby, rector, c.d., tonsure, hf-eff.

1618 Wm. Palke, minister, in gown, mut.
w. Anne, c.d. (lower hf miss.), sm., ach.

HARDRES, UPPER

1405 John Strete, rector, acad. dr., cap, kng. to br. with effs. of SS Peter and Paul.

c. 1560 Man, arm. (head miss.), damaged.

HARRIETSHAM

1603 Susan Partheriche, c.d., with 1 son, 3 daus., 1 a chrysom, kng., rect. pl.

HARTY, ISLE OF SHEPPEY

1512 Habram Fare, c.d. (upper hf miss.), sm.

HAWKHURST

1499 John Roberts, c.d.
w. Alice, c.d., with 6 sons, 6 daus.

HAYES

c. 1460 John Osteler, rector, mass vests., hf-eff.

1479 John Andrew, priest, mass vests., sm.

1523 John Heygge, parson, mass vests., sm.

HEADCORN

1636 John Byrd, aged 6½, kng., rect. pl.

HERNE

c. 1430 Peter Halle, arm.
w. Eliz., c.d.

c. 1450 John Darley, B.D., vicar, acad. dr., cap, marg. inscr., mut.

1470 Dame Cristine Phelip, c.d., mant.

1539 Eliz., 2nd w. and wid. of Sir John Fyneux.

1604 John Sea, c.d.
1st w. Martha, c.d.
2nd w. Sara, c.d.

HEVER

1419 Margt. Cheyne, mant., head on cushion supported by angels.

1538 Sir Thos. Bullen, K.G., arm., with coll., mant., hood of Order, lge.

1585 Wm. Todde, schoolmaster, c.d., kng.

HOATH

c. 1430 Isabel Chakbon, c.d. (head mut.).

1532 Antony Maycot, c.d.
w. Agnes, c.d., with 2 sons, 5 daus., sm., wn. [Pal.]

HOO, ALL HALLOWS

1594 Wm. Copinger, arm., kng.

HOO, ST WERBURGH

1406 John Brown, vicar, mass vests., hf-eff.

1412 Rich. Bayly, vicar, mass vests. (head miss.), marg. inscr., mut. lge.

c. 1430 Man, c.d., anelace.

1446 Stephen Charlis, c.d.
Rich. Charlis, c.d.

1465 Thos. Cobham, arm.
w. Maud, wid. dr.

1615 Dorothy Plumley, c.d.

1640 Jas. Plumley, c.d.
w. Anne, c.d., with 3 sons, 4 daus.

HORSMONDEN

c. 1340 John de Grofhurst, priest, mass vests., sin. can., marg. inscr., rest.

1604 Joan Austen, c.d.

HORTON KIRBY

1468 Alice Drayton, mant., lge.

1595 John Browne, c.d.
w. Eliz., c.d.

HUNTON

1513 Wm. Head, alderman, c.d.

IGHTHAM

1528 Sir Rich. Clement, arm., tab. (lower hf miss.).

1626 Jane Cradock, c.d.

IWADE

1467 Symon Snelling, c.d. (head miss.).
w. Joyce, c.d.

KEMSING

1347 Thos. de Hop, rector, mass vests., hf-eff.

KINGSNORTH

1579 Humph. Clarke, arm.
w. Mary, c.d., with 6 sons, 5 daus.

LANGDON, EAST

c. 1600 1 dau., sm. (Poss. of the Master fam.)

LEEDS

1509 Wm. Merden, c.d.
w. Alice, c.d., with 1 son, 2 daus., sm.

1514 Kath. Lambe, c.d., flowing hair, sm.

LEIGH

c. 1580 Fig. in tomb with kng. eff. of woman summoned by angel, rect. pl., sm.

1591 John Stace, c.d., recumbent eff., rect. pl.

LUDDESDOWN

c. 1450 Man, arm. (legs mut.). (Poss. Jas. Montague.)

LULLINGSTONE

1487 Sir Wm. Pecche, arm.

1533 Alice Baldwyn, c.d., sm.

1544 Eliz. Cobham, c.d.

LYDD

1420 John Motesford, LL.B., vicar, acad. dr., marg. inscr., mut.

1429 John Thomas, c.d.

1430 Thos. Godefray, c.d.
w. Joan, c.d., dble. can.

1508 Robt. Cokyram, c.d., sm.

1520 Man, c.d.

1557 Thos. Harte, yeoman, c.d.
w. Malyn, c.d.

1566 Peter Godfrye, c.d.
w. Jone, c.d.

1578 Thos. Bate, jurat, c.d.

c. 1590 Man, c.d.

c. 1590 Woman, c.d.

1608 Clement Stuppeny, bailiff, c.d.

LYNSTED

1567 Eliz. Roper, c.d., with 1 son, 2 daus., ach,

1621 John Worley, c.d.
w. Alice, c.d., ach.

MAIDSTONE, ALL SAINTS

1593 Thos. Beale, mayor, c.d.
2 ws. Alice and Joan, with 6 sons, 2 daus., also his ancestors:
Wm. Beale, c.d. (1534)
w. Joan, c.d., with 4 sons, 3 daus.
Robt. Beale, c.d. (1490)
w. Agnes, c.d., with 2 sons, 1 dau.
John Beale, c.d. (1461)
2 ws. Agnes and Alice, c.d., with 2 sons.
Wm. Beale, c.d.
w. Kath., c.d., with 2 sons, 2 daus.
John Beale, c.d. (1399)
w., c.d., with 1 son, sm. kng. effs. in 6 tiers, each of 3 divisions, rect. pl.

1640 Rich. Beeston, M.A., clerk, in gown.
w. Eliz., c.d., with 4 sons, 3 daus., all kng., rect. pl.

MALLING, EAST

1479 Thos. Selby, c.d.
w. Iseult, c.d.

1522 Rich. Adams, vicar, in almuce, ch., wf.

MALLING, WEST
1497 Wm. Millys, c.d., sm.
1532 Wm. Skott, c.d., sm.
1543 Eliz. Perepoynt, c.d. (lower hf miss.).

MARGATE, ST JOHN THANET
1431 Nich. Canteys, c.d., anelace.
1441 John Parker, c.d. (recut).
w. Joan, c.d.
1442 Peter Stone, c.d., anelace (ft rest.), sm.
1445 John Daundelyon, arm.
1446 Rich. Notfelde, skeleton, partly rest.
1475 Javen Sefowle, c.d. (upper hf miss.).
1515 Thos. Cardyff, vicar, mass vests., sm.
c. 1590 Wm. Cleaybroke?, arm., ach.

MEREWORTH
1366 Sir John de Mereworth, arm. (legs miss.), lge.
1479 Wm. Shosmyth, c.d.
w. Julian, c.d., sm.
1542 Sir Thos. Nevell, c.d., kng., with sm. stg. fig. of Our Lord.

MERSHAM
c. 1420 Priest, mass vests., sm.
c. 1520 Man, c.d.
w., c.d.

MILTON-NEXT-SITTINGBOURNE
c. 1470 Man, arm.
c. 1500 Man, arm., tab. (Prob. John Northwood.)
w., c.d.
1529 Margt. Alefe, c.d., with 1 dau., kng.

MINSTER, ISLE OF SHEPPEY
c. 1330 Sir John de Northwood, arm., crossed legs, rest., with pl. of c. 1380.
c. 1335 Woman, cote-hardie, hood, head on cushion. (Poss. Eliz., 2nd w. of Roger de Northwood.) (Both effs. have been relaid on one stone but are from two separate monuments.)

MONKTON, ISLE OF THANET
c. 1460 John Spicer?, priest, mass vests.

MURSTON, OLD CHURCH
1488 John Eveas, arm.
w. Mildred, c.d., with 3 sons.

NEWINGTON-NEXT-HYTHE
c. 1480 Woman, c.d. (lower hf miss.).
1501 Thos. Chylton, in shroud.
w. Thomasin, c.d., with 2 sons, 1 dau.
1501 John Clerk, vicar, mass vests., ch., wf., sm.
1522 Rich. Ryege, c.d.
1st w. Alice, c.d.
2nd w. Joan, c.d.
3rd w. Kath., c.d.
c. 1570 Man, c.d.
1630 Hen. Brockman, arm.
w. Helen, c.d., with 2 sons, 1 arm., 5 daus., marg. inscr., ach.
1631 Hen., son of Wm. Brockman, aged 7½.

NEWINGTON-NEXT-SITTINGBOURNE
1488 Wm. Monde, c.d.
John Sayer, c.d.
1580 Alice Cobham, alias Brook, c.d., with 2 sons.
1581 Fraunces Holbrok, c.d.
1st w., c.d., with 4 sons, 6 daus.
2nd w., c.d., with 2 sons, 1 dau.
1600 Mary, wid. of Edw. Brooke, alias Cobham, wid. dr.

NORTHFLEET
1375 Peter de Lacy, prebendary, mass vests., marg. inscr., rest., lge.
1391 Wm. Lye, rector, mass vests., hf-eff.
1433 Wm. Rickhill, arm. (legs miss.).
w. Kath., c.d., marg. inscr.

ORPINGTON
1511 Thos. Wilkynson, M.A., rector, in cope.

OTHAM
1590 Thos. Hendley, c.d.
3 ws., c.d., with 2 sons, 2 daus., all kng., rect. pl.

OTTERDEN
1408 Thos. Seintlegier, arm., marg. inscr., mut.
1488 Isabel Chyrche, c.d.
1502 John Aucher, arm.
1508 Jas. Aucher, arm.
1606 Eliz. Bunce, c.d., with 3 daus.

PECKHAM, EAST
c.1525 Man, c.d.
w., c.d., sm.

PECKHAM, WEST
c.1460 Eliz. Culpepir, c.d.

PEMBURY
1607 Eliz., eldest dau. of Nich. Rowe, aged 7¾, holding book.

PENSHURST
1507 4 sons, 3 daus. of Walter Darnowll.
1514 Pawle Yden, c.d.
w. Agnes, c.d., with 1 dau.

PLUCKLEY
c.1425 John Dering, arm., marg. inscr. (whole rest. 17th cent.).
1440 Rich. Malemayns, arm., v. wn.
c.1517 John Dering, arm. (rest. 17th cent.).
c.1517 Nich. Dering, arm. (rest. 17th cent.).
w. Alice, c.d. (Orig. eff.)
1526 Julyen Deryng, c.d.
c.1545 Rich. Dering, arm., under trefoil arch, rect. pl., sm. (rest. 17th cent.).
1550 John Dering, arm., tab., kng., sm. rect. pl. (rest. 17th cent.).
1610 Rich. Dering, arm.
w. Margt., c.d., kng., rect. pl.

PRESTON-NEXT-FAVERSHAM
1442 Valentine Baret, arm.
w. Cecily, c.d.
1459 Wm. Mareys, esq. to Hen. V, arm., stg. in a marsh.
1612 Bennet Finch, c.d.

RAINHAM
1514 Wm. Aucher, arm., sm.
1529 Wm. Bloor, c.d.
c.1530 Woman, c.d., with 4 daus., sm.
c.1580 John Norden, c.d.
w., c.d.

RINGWOULD
1505 Alys or Amis, w. of Wm. Abere, c.d. (lower hf miss.), with 2 sons, 3 daus., sm.
1530 John Upton, c.d., sm.

ROCHESTER, ST MARGARET
1465 Thos. Cod, vicar, in cope, hf-eff. [Pal. of similar eff., in almuce.]

ROMNEY, NEW
1510 Thos. Lamberd, c.d.
1610 Thos. Smyth, jurat, c.d.
w. Mary, c.d.

ROMNEY, OLD
1526 John Ips, c.d.
w. Margt., c.d.

ST LAURENCE, THANET
1444 Nich. Manston, arm., with SS coll.
1493 Joan St Nicholas, c.d.

ST MARY-IN-THE-MARSH
1499 Maud Jamys, c.d.
1502 Wm. Gregory, son of above, c.d.

ST NICHOLAS-AT-WADE, THANET
1574 Valontyne Edvarod, c.d.
1st w. Agnes, c.d., with 4 sons, 2 daus.
2nd w. Joan, c.d., with 3 sons, 6 daus.

Thos. Parramore, 2nd hus. of Joan., c.d.

St Peter, Thanet

1485 Rich. Colmer, c.d. (ft mut.).
w. Margt., c.d.

1503 Nich. Esstone, c.d.
w. Alice, c.d., sm., wn.

Saltwood

1370 John Verieu, rector, mass vests., hf-eff.

1437 Thos. Brokhill, arm.
w. Joan, c.d., marg. inscr., mut.

Sandwich, St Clement

c. 1490 Man, c.d., dble. can., mut., v. wn.

Seal

1395 Sir Wm. de Bryene, arm., marg. inscr., lge.

1577 John Tebold, alias Theobauld, c.d., (L). [Pal., *c.* 1500.]

Selling

c. 1520 3 sons of Thos. Gate.

c. 1525 Man, c.d.

Sheldwich

1394 Sir Rich. Attelese, arm.
w. Dennis, c.d. (lower hf miss.), fine dble. can.

1426 John Cely, arm.
w. Isabel, c.d.

1431 Joan Mareys, in shroud, hf-eff., holding engraved heart.

Shorne

1457 John Smyth, c.d., hf-eff.
w. Marion, c.d., hf-eff.

c. 1470 Woman, c.d. (head miss.).

1583 Elynor Allen, c.d.

Snodland

1441 John Brigge, c.d. (head miss.), sm.

1486 Roger Perot, c.d., sm.

1487 Edw. Bischoptre, c.d.
w. Margt., c.d., sm.

c. 1530 Man, c.d.
2 ws., c.d.

Southfleet

1414 Joan Urban, c.d., on br.

1420 John Urban, c.d.
w. Joan, c.d., on br.

1456 John Tubney, archdeacon, in cope, hf-eff.

c. 1520 Thos. Cowrll, in shroud, v. sm.

c. 1520 John Sedley, c.d.
w. Eliz., c.d., with 4 sons, 2 daus., marg. inscr., mut.

Staple

c. 1510 Man, c.d.

Staplehurst

c. 1580 Woman, c.d. (Poss. w. of Walter Mayne.)

Stockbury

1617 John Hooper, c.d.
w. Francis, c.d., rect. pl.

1648 Dorothy Hooper, c.d., with child., rect. pl.

Stoke

1415 Wm. Cardyf, B.D., vicar, mass vests. (upper hf miss.).

Stone

1408 John Lumbarde, rector, mass vests., sm. eff. in head of floriated cross.

Stourmouth

1472 Thos. Mareys, clerk, rector, acad. dr.

Sundridge

1429 Roger Isley, arm.

c. 1460 Wm. Isley?, c.d.

1518 Thos. Isley, arm.
w. Eliz., c.d., with 10 sons, 3 daus.

Sutton, East

1629 Sir Edw. Filmer, arm.
w. Eliz., c.d., with 9 sons, 9 daus., rect. pl., marg. inscr., lge., ach.

Teynham
1444 John Frogenhall, arm., SS coll.
1509 Robt. Heyward, c.d., with 2 child., 1 a chrysom.
1533 Wm. Wreke, c.d., sm.
1639 Wm. Palmer, c.d.
w. Eliz., c.d., marg. inscr., ach.

Thanington
1485 Thos. Halle, arm.

Tilmanstone
1598 Rich. Fogg, c.d., with 1 son.
w. Anne, c.d., with 3 daus., all kng., rect. pl.

Trottescliffe
1483 Wm. Crofton, c.d.
w. Margery, c.d.

Tudeley
1457 Thos. Stydolf, c.d.
w. Marion, c.d.

Tunstall
1525 Ralph Wulf, rector, mass vests.
c. 1590 Woman, c.d., with scroll.

Ulcombe
1419 Wm. Maydestone, arm., sin. can., marg. inscr., both mut.
1442 John St Leger?, arm.
1470 Ralph St Leger, arm.
w. Anne, c.d.

Upchurch
c. 1350 Man, c.d., hf-eff.
w., c.d., hf-eff.

Westerham
1511 Rich. Potter, c.d.
2 ws., c.d.
1529 Rich. Hayward, c.d.
1531 Thos. Potter, c.d.
1533 John Stacy, c.d.
1557 Wm. Myddilton, c.d.
1st w. Eliz., c.d.
2nd w. Dorothy, c.d., with 7 sons. [Pal.]
1566 Wm. Stace, c.d., eyes closed.
1st w. Jone, c.d., eyes closed, with 2 sons, 1 dau.
2nd w. Alice, c.d., with 5 sons, 7 daus.
1567 Wm. Dye, parson, in cassock, surplice, wn.

Wickham, East
c. 1325 John de Bladigdone, c.d.
w. Maud, sm. hf-effs., in head of cross (rest. 1887).
1568 Wm. Payn, yeoman of the guard, in habit of the guard.
1st w. Eliz., c.d.
3rd w. Joan, c.d., with 2 sons, also 1 son of 2nd w. Joan.

Wickham, West
1407 Wm. de Thorp, rector, mass vests., sm.
1515 John Stockton, priest, mass vests., sm.

Wittersham
1523 Stevyn Audyan, c.d.

Woodchurch
c. 1330 Nichol de Gore, priest, mass vests., sm. eff. in head of cross, mut.
1558 Thos. Harlakynden, arm., with 6 sons.
1st w. Eliz., c.d., with 3 daus.
2nd w. Margt., c.d., with 1 dau., all kng.

Wouldham
1602 Morley Monox, aged 23, c.d.
s. Margt., aged 5, both kng., rect. pl.

Wrotham
1498 Thos. Nysell, c.d.
w. Alice, c.d., with 5 sons, 5 daus. (Child. erroneously placed.)
c. 1500 John Burgoyn, c.d.
1500 5 daus. of Jas. Pekham.

1512 Thos. Pekham, arm.
w. Dorothy, c.d., with 1 dau.
1525 Reynold Pekham, arm., tab.
w. Joyce, her. mant.
1532 Jas. Pekham, arm.
1611 Wm. Clerke, arm.
w. Anne, c.d., with 2 sons, 10 daus.
1615 Eliz. Crispe, c.d., with 5 sons, 4 daus.

WYE

c.1440 Alice Palmere, c.d., with 3 sons, 8 daus.
1st hus. John Andrew, c.d. (ft miss.).
2nd hus. Thos. Palmere, c.d.
c.1500 1 son, c.d.

LANCASHIRE

CHILDWALL

1524 Hen. Norris, arm., tab.
w. Clemence, her. mant.

ECCLESTON

c.1510 Priest, in cope.

FLIXTON

1602 Rich. Radcliffe.
1st w. Bridget, c.d.
2nd w. Margt., c.d., all kng., ach.

LANCASTER, ST MARY

1639 Thos. Covell, J.P., mayor, c.d., ach.

MANCHESTER, CATHEDRAL

1458 John Huntingdon, warden, in surplice, almuce, sin. can., marg. inscr. (rest. 1907).
1460 Sir John Byron, steward of the college, arm. (middle portion only).
w. Margt., wid. dr. (head miss.).
1515 Jas. Stanley, bp. of Ely, episcopal vests., with mitre, crosier (lower hf miss.).
c.1540 Man, arm.
w., c.d. (Poss. Alex. and Alice Radclyffe.) [W. pal., c.1450, effaced.]
1607 Anth. Mosley, mcht., c.d., with 5 sons.
w. Alice, c.d., with 3 daus., all kng., rect. pl., ach.
1630 Oswald Mosley, c.d., with 5 sons.
w. Anne, c.d., with 3 daus., all kng., rect. pl., ach.

MIDDLETON

c.1510 Sir Rich. Ashton?, arm.
w. Isabel, c.d., with 7 sons, 6 daus.
1522 Edm. Assheton, rector, mass vests., ch., wf.
1531 Alice Laurence, c.d.
1st hus. Rich. Radclyffe, arm.
2nd hus. Thos. Bothe, arm.
1618 Rich. Assheton, c.d., holding skull.
w. Mary, c.d., with 6 sons, 1 a chrysom, 2 daus.
1650 Ralph Assheton, arm.
w. Eliz., c.d., with 3 sons, Rich. arm., John in shroud, and 3 daus., Anne in shroud.

NEWCHURCH

1561 3 daus. of Wm. Ratclyff.

ORMSKIRK

c.1500 Man, arm., tab., lge.

PRESTON

1623 Seath Bushell, wool draper, c.d., rect. pl.

RIVINGTON

1627 John Shawe, rect. pl. with skeleton on mattress.

RUFFORD

1543 Sir Robt. Hesketh, arm.

SEFTON

1528 Margt. Bulcley, c.d., dble. can.

1570? Sir Wm. Molineux, arm., SS coll.
1st w. Jane, c.d.
2nd w. Eliz., c.d., 2 ach.
1568 Sir Rich. Molyneux, arm., son of above.
1st w. Eleanor, c.d., with 5 sons, 8 daus.
2nd w. Eleanor, c.d.

ULVESTON
1606 Myles Dodding, c.d.
w. Margt., c.d.

WALTON-ON-THE-HILL
1586 Thos. Beri, c.d., rect. pl.

WHALLEY
1515 Raffe Catterall, arm., with 9 sons, eldest a priest.
w. Eliz., c.d., with 11 daus., all kng.

WINWICK
1492 Peers Gerard, arm., tab., with 1 son, trip. can., mut., lge., wn.
1527 Sir Peter Legh, knight and priest, arm., with chasuble, holding shield of arms.
w. Ellen, her. mant., marg. inscr., wn., ach.

LEICESTERSHIRE

AYLESTONE
1594 Wm. Heathcott, parson, in gown, holding book, lge.

BARWELL
1614 John Torksey, B.D., rector, in pulpit.
w., c.d., kng., with 5 daus., 1 chrysom, rect. pl.
1659 Rich. Breton, c.d.
w. Eliz., c.d., with 3 sons, 4 daus., rect. pl., ach.

BOTTESFORD
1404 Hen. de Codyngtoun, rector, in cope, trip. can., B.V. Mary and Child, marg. inscr., mut., lge.
c. 1440 John Freman, rector, in cope (head miss.).

CASTLE DONINGTON
1458 Robt. Staunton, arm., salade, with 4 sons.
w. Agnes, c.d., with 3 daus., dble. can., mut., marg. inscr., mut., ach.

HINCKLEY
c. 1490 Woman, c.d., extremely wn.

HOBY
c. 1480 Man, arm. (head miss.).

LEICESTER, WIGSTON'S HOSPITAL
c. 1540 Wm. Fyssher, master of the hospital, mcht., in shroud, marg. inscr.

LOUGHBOROUGH
1445? Giles Jorden, c.d. (middle portion only).
w. Margt., c.d., effaced and mut.
1480 Thos. Marshall, mcht., c.d.
w. Agnes, c.d., with 6 sons, 6 daus., mut.

LUTTERWORTH
1418 John Fildyng, c.d.
w. Joan, c.d.
c. 1470 Man, c.d., anelace.
w., c.d. (Poss. John Renolds, mcht.)

QUEENIBOROUGH
1634 Margt. Bury, with recumbent eff. on tomb, rect. pl.

SAXELBY
1523 Woman, c.d., one of the ws. of Wm. Brokysbi.

SCALFORD
c. 1520 Man, c.d., kng.

Sheepshed
1592 Thos. Duport, arm.
w. Cornelia, c.d., rect. pl.

Sibstone
1532 John Moore, M.A., rector, in almuce, scrolls from hands to eff. of Our Lord, seated on rainbow above.

Stapleford
1492 Geoffrey Sherard, arm.
w. Joyce, c.d., with 7 sons, 7 daus.

Stokerston
1467 John Boville, arm. (head miss.).
w. Isabel, mant., holding hands, lge.
1493 John Southill, arm.
w. Eliz., wid. dr.

Swithland
*c.*1455 Agnes Scot, c.d., wn.

Thurcaston
1425 John Mershden, rector, canon, in cope (lower hf miss.), sin. can., mut., marg. inscr., mut.

Wanlip
1393 Sir Thos. Walsch, arm.
w. Dame Kath., c.d., marg. inscr.

Wymondham
1521 Margery Barkeley, c.d., marg. inscr.

LINCOLNSHIRE

Algarkirk
1498 Nich. Robertson, mcht., c.d.
1st w. Isabel, c.d.
2nd w. Alice, c.d., with hf-eff. of B.V. Mary and Child.

Althorpe
*c.*1365 Wm. de Lound, rector, mass vests., hf-eff.

Ashby Puerorum
*c.*1560 Rich. Lytleburye, arm.
w. Eliz., c.d., with 6 sons, 4 daus.
*c.*1560 Man, arm.

Barrowby
1479 Nich. Deen, c.d.
w. Kath., c.d., with 9 sons.
1508 Jas. Deen, arm. (ft only).
w. Margt., her. mant., with 3 daus.

Barton-on-Humber, St Mary
*c.*1380 Woman, c.d., holding heart, hf-eff., effaced.
1433 Simon Seman, vintner, c.d., stg. on wine casks, marg. inscr., lge.

Barton-on-Humber, St Peter
1440 Robt. Barnetby, arm. (ft only).

Bigby
*c.*1520 Eliz. Skypwith, c.d.
1632 Edw. Naylor, rector, in gown, with 2 sons.
w., c.d., with 5 daus., all kng., rect. pl.

Boston, St Botolph
1398 Walter Pescod, mcht., c.d., with mant. (lower hf miss.), trip. can., with apostles, lge.
*c.*1400 John Strangill?, priest, in cope, lge., wn.
*c.*1400 Man, c.d. (ft only).
1st w., c.d. (upper hf miss.).
2nd w., c.d., trip. can. on mut. br., sm., v. wn.
*c.*1460 Woman, c.d. (head, ft miss.).
[Pal., *c.*1390.]
*c.*1470 Man, c.d.
w., c.d., wn.
*c.*1500 9 sons.
1659 Thos. Lawe, mayor, c.d., hf-eff.

Broughton
*c.*1390 Man, arm.

w., c.d., holding hearts, lge. (Poss. of Redford fam.)

BURTON COGGLES

c.1590 Robt. Cholmeley, c.d.

c.1620 Sir Hen. Cholmeley, arm.
w. Alice, c.d.

BURTON PEDWARDINE

1631 Mary Horsman, c.d.

BUSLINGTHORPE

c.1310 Sir Rich. de Boselyngthorpe, in mail, with ailettes, surcoat, holding heart, hf-eff.

COATES, GREAT

c.1420 Isabel Barnardston, mant.

1503 Sir Thos. Barnardiston, c.d.
w. Eliz., c.d., with 8 sons, 2nd a priest, acad. dr., 7 daus., 3rd a nun, all kng., marg. inscr., mut., wn.

COATES-BY-STOW

1590 Wm. Butler, arm.
w. Eliz., c.d., with 1 dau., Priscilla, a chrysom.

1602 Chas. Butler, arm.
w. Douglas, c.d., with 5 sons, 3 daus., all kng., rect. pl.

CONISHOLME

1515 John Langholme, arm.
w. Anne, c.d., with 5 sons, 9 daus., marg. inscr.

CORRINGHAM

1628 Hen. Clifford, S.T.B., vicar, in gown.
w. Elinor, c.d., with 3 sons, rect. pl.

COVENHAM, ST BARTHOLOMEW

1415 John Skypwyth, arm.

CROFT

c.1300 Man, arm., in mail, surcoat, hf-eff.

DRIBY

1583 Jas. Prescott, c.d. (head miss.), with 5 sons.
w. Alice, c.d., with 1 dau., all kng., ach.

EDENHAM

c.1500 St Thos. of Canterbury, full vests., with mitre and cross, sm.

EVEDON

1630 Dan. Hardeby, J.P., c.d., with 5 sons.
w. Anne, c.d., with 8 daus., all kng., rect. pl.

FISKERTON

c.1490 Priest, in cope.

GEDNEY

c.1390 Woman, mant., lge. (Poss. of the Roos fam.)

GLENTHAM

1452 Eliz. Tournay, c.d., hf-eff., v. wn.

GUNBY

c.1400 Man, arm., SS coll. (Of the Massingberd fam.)
w., mant., SS coll., dble. can., mut., *appropriated to*

1552 Sir Thos. Massyngberde, arm.
w. Joan, mant., SS coll.

1419 Wm. de Lodyngton, justice of the common pleas to Hen. V, in robes, coif, anelace, leopard at ft, sin. can., mut.

HAINTON

1435 John Henege, c.d.
w. Alice, c.d.

1553 Sir Thos. Henneage, arm., tab. (upper hf renewed).
w. Kath., her. mant., with 1 dau., Eliz., her. mant. (both rest.).

HALTON HOLGATE

1658 Bridget Rugeley, c.d.

HARPSWELL

c.1480 John Whichcote?, arm.
w. Eliz., c.d.

HARRINGTON

1480 Margt. Copuldyk, mant., hands apart.

1585 John Copledike, arm.
w. Anne, c.d., kng., ach.

HOLBEACH

c.1410 Man, arm. (head miss.), wn.

1488 Joan, wid. of Thos. Welby, mant.

HORNCASTLE

1519 Sir Lionel Dymoke, arm., kng., with 3 daus.
Sir Lionel Dymoke, in shroud (head miss.), v. wn.

INGOLDMELLS

1520 Wm. Palmer, c.d., with crutch.

IRNHAM

1390 Sir Andrew Loutterell, arm., sin. can., mut., lge.

c.1440 Man, arm. (legs miss.).

KELSEY, SOUTH

c.1410 Rich. Hansard, arm.
w. Joan, mant., with head on cushion.

LAUGHTON, NR GAINSBOROUGH

c.1400 Man, arm., trip. can., lge. (Of the Dalison fam.) *Repaired and appropriated to*

1549 Wm. Dalison, sheriff, J.P., arm.

LEADENHAM

1624 Lady Eliz. Beresforde, c.d.

LINCOLN, ST BENEDICT

1620 John Becke, twice mayor, c.d., with 7 sons.
w. Mary, c.d., with 3 daus., all kng., rect. pl.

LINWOOD

1419 John Lyndewode, woolman, c.d., mant., stg. on woolpack.
w. Alice, c.d., mant., dble. can., entab., with 4 sons, 3 daus., also under can., lge.

1421 John Lyndewode, woolman, son of above, c.d., anelace, stg. on woolpack, sin. can., mut., lge.

MABLETHORPE

1522 Eliz. Fitzwilliam, c.d., flowing hair.

NORTHORPE

1595 Francis Yerburgh, c.d.
1st w., c.d.
2nd w., c.d. (lower hf miss.), with 1 child.

NORTON DISNEY

1578 Wm. Disney, arm.
w. Margt., c.d., with 4 sons, 5 daus.
Rich. Disney, arm.
1st w. Nele, c.d., with 7 sons, 5 daus.
2nd w. Jane, c.d., all hf-effs., rect. pl. [Pal. Flem., c.1518.]

ORMSBY, SOUTH

c.1410 Woman, mant.

1482 Sir Wm. Skypwyth, arm.
w. Agnes, wid., c.d., with 1 son, 2 daus., dble. can.

PINCHBECK

1608 Margt. Lambart, c.d., kng., rect. pl.

RAND

c.1500 Man, arm. (legs and ft only).

1590 Woman, c.d.
Woman, c.d. (upper hf only), ws. of Wm. Metham, ach.

RAUCEBY

1536 Wm. Styrlay, vicar, canon, in mass vests., ch., wf., sm.

SCOTTER

1599 Marmaduke Tirwhit, c.d., with 5 sons, eldest arm.

w. Ellen, c.d., with 6 daus., 1 a chrysom, all kng., rect. pl., 2 achs.

SCRIVELSBY

1545 Sir Robt. Demoke, arm.

SLEAFORD

1521 Geo. Carre, c.d.
w. Anne, c.d., with 7 sons, 3 daus.

SOMERSBY

1612 Geo. Littlebury, c.d., kng., rect. pl.

SPALDING, JOHNSON HOSPITAL

1597 Thos. Lovell, c.d., with 4 sons.
w. Margt., c.d., with 5 daus., all kng., rect. pl.

SPILSBY

1391 Margery de Wylughby, c.d., mant., head on cushion, marg. inscr., mut., lge.

*c.*1400 Wm., 5th Baron Willoughby d'Eresby, arm.
1st w. Lucy, c.d., each under trip. can., bad. mut.

STALLINGBOROUGH

1509 Sir Wm. Ayscough, arm., tab.
1st w. Margery, her. mant.

1610 Kath. Ayscough, c.d., with 2 sons, 2 daus.

STAMFORD, ALL SAINTS

1460 John Browne, mcht., c.d., mant., stg. on woolpacks.
w. Margery, c.d.

*c.*1465 Wm. Browne, son of above, c.d., mant., stg. on woolpacks.
w. Margt., c.d., dble. can. (hf miss.), lge.

1471 Margt. Elmes, c.d., sm.

1475 John Browne, son of no. 1 (1460), c.d., mant.
w. Agnes, wid. dr.

*c.*1500 Man, c.d. (Poss. Christ. Browne.)
w., c.d.

1508 Hen. Wykes, vicar, in cope (head miss.), wn.

STAMFORD, ST JOHN

1489 Nich. Byldysdon, alderman, c.d.
w. Kath., c.d., with 4 sons, 5 daus.

1497 Hen. Sargeaunt, rector, mass vests., mut., wn.

STAMFORD, ST MARY

1684 Rich. Warwick, alderman, c.d.

STOKE ROCHEFORD

1470 Hen. Rochforth, arm., salade.

1503 Oliver St John, arm.
w. Dame Eliz. Bygod, with 5 sons, 3 daus.

TATTERSHALL

1411 Hugh de Gondeby, c.d., anelace, wn.

1456 Wm. Moor, provost, mass vests.

*c.*1470 Ralph, Baron Cromwell, arm., mant. (head and r. shoulder miss.), lge.

*c.*1470 Joan, Lady Cromwell, wid. of Sir Humph. Bourchier, mant., flowing hair, sin. can., SS, B.V. Mary, lge.

*c.*1470 Lady Maud, wid. of Robt., Lord Willoughby, sister of above, trip. can., mut., entab., SS, lge.

*c.*1510 Priest, in cope, cap, lge. (Poss. John Gygur.)

1519? Wm. Symson, chaplain, mass vests. (eff. engraved *c.*1490?).

THEDDLETHORPE, ALL SAINTS

1424 Robt. Hayton, arm.

WALTHAM

1420 Joan Waltham, c.d., with 1 son and 1 dau., 3 hf-effs.

WINTERTON

1504 2 ws. of John Rudd. c.d., v. wn., marg. inscr., mut.

WINTHORPE

1505 Rich. Barowe, mcht., c.d.
w. Baterich, c.d., with 4 daus.

1515 Robt. Palmer, c.d.

WITHAM, NORTH

1425 Wm. Misterton, c.d. (upper hf miss.), sm., wn.

WRANGLE

1503 John Reed, mcht., c.d.
w. Margt., c.d., with 8 sons, 5 daus., marg. inscr., mut.

At Frieston the brass to

1608 Symon Clarke and w. *has been renewed.*

In Lincoln Cathedral Church of B.V. Mary is a modern replica of the lost brass to

c. 1495 Wm. Smyth, bp.

LONDON

(postal area only, not area covered by Greater London Council)

ACTON, ST MARY

1558 Humf. Cavell, c.d., kng.

BARNES

1508 Edith and Eliz., c.d., flowing hair, unmarried daus. of John and Ann Wylde, sm.

CAMBERWELL, ST GILES

1497 Mighell Skinner, c.d., sm., wn.

1499 Rich. Skynner, c.d., kng., sm. (head miss.).

1532 John Scott, baron of the exchequer, arm.
w. Eliz., c.d., kng., with 4 sons.

1538 Edw. Scott, arm. (an appropriated fig. of *c.*1465.)

1570 John Bowyar, c.d., with 8 sons.
w. Eliz., c.d., with 3 daus., all kng., ach.

1577 Mathye Draper, c.d.
w. Sence, c.d., kng., ach.

CHELSEA, ALL SAINTS

1555 Lady Jane Guyldeford, her. mant., kng., with 5 daus., also kng.

1625 Sir Arthur Gorges, arm.
2nd w. Eliz., c.d., with 6 sons, eldest arm., 5 daus., all kng., rect. pl., ach.

CLAPHAM, ST PETER

c. 1740 Priest, in cope.

CLERKENWELL, ST JAMES

1556 John Bell, Bp. of Worcester, episcopal vests., mitre, crosier (lower hf miss.). (Repaired 1884.)

EALING, ST MARY

c. 1490 Rich. Amondesham, mercer, c.d.
w. Kath., c.d., with 3 sons, 6 daus., all kng.

EAST HAM

1610 Hester Neve, c.d.

1622 Eliz. Heigham, c.d.

EDMONTON, ALL SAINTS

c. 1500 Eliz., c.d.
1st hus. John Asplyn, c.d.
2nd hus. Godfrey Askew, c.d., sm.

1523 Nich. Boone, c.d.
w. Eliz., c.d.

1616 Edw. Nowell, c.d.
w. Mary, c.d., with 3 sons, 1 dau., wn.

FINCHLEY, ST MARY

c. 1480 Woman, c.d., mut., wn.

1487 Joan Prate, c.d., v. sm.

1609 Simon Skudemore, c.d.
w. Jeane, c.d., ach.

1609 Eliz. Luke, dau. of above, c.d., with 3 daus.

1610 Thos. White, grocer, c.d.
1st w. Mary, c.d., with 3 sons, 2 daus.
2nd w. Mary, c.d., with 1 son, 3 daus.

3rd w. Honnor, c.d., with 3 sons, 1 dau., all kng., rect. pl.

FULHAM, ALL SAINTS

1529 Margt. Horenbault, hf-eff. in shroud, rect. pl., Flem.

HACKNEY, ST JOHN

1521 Christ. Urswick, D.C.L., rector, archdeacon, in cope, cap.

1545 John Lymsey, arm. (Eff. is a re-used fig., *c.*1510–20.)

1562 Arthur Dericote, arm.
1st w. Marie, c.d.
2nd w. Eme, c.d.
3rd w. Margt., c.d.
4th w. Jane, c.d., with 2 sons, all kng.

1618 Hugh Johnson, vicar, in gown, hf-eff., in pulpit.

HENDON, ST MARY

1515 John Downer, c.d., sm.

1615 Rich. Marsh, yeoman, c.d.

HORNSEY, ST MARY

*c.*1615 Rect. pl., with lower portions of 3 civilians. (In frame.) [Pal., *c.* same date.]

ISLINGTON, ST MARY

1540 Robt. Fowler, arm.
w. Alice, both on 1 plate under sin. can. [Pal. 15th cent.] French?

1546 Hen. Savill, arm. [Pal., *c.*1370]
w. Margt. c.d. [Pal., *c.*1520]

KILBURN, ST MARY

14th cent. Head of a nun.

KINGSBURY, ST ANDREW

1520 John Shepard, c.d.
1st w. Anne, c.d., with 7 sons, 3 daus.
2nd w. Mawde, c.d., with 5 sons, 3 daus., sm., wn.

LAMBETH, ST MARY

1535 Lady Kath. Howard, her. mant.

1545 Thos. Clere, arm.

LEE, ST MARGARET

1513 Eliz. Couhyll, c.d., flowing hair, sm.

1582 Isabel Annesley, c.d.

1593 Nich. Annesley, servant to Eliz. I, arm., kng., ach.

LONDON, ALL HALLOWS, BARKING

1437 John Bacon, woolman, c.d., stg. on woolpack.
w. Joan, c.d., with scrolls round heart.

1477 John Croke, skinner, alderman, c.d., mant., with 7 sons.
w. Margt., wid. dr., with 5 daus., all kng., wn., bad cond.

1498 John Rusche, c.d.

1518 Christ. Rawson, mercer, mcht., c.d.
1st w. Margt., c.d.
2nd w. Agnes, c.d.

1533 Andrew Evyngar, salter, c.d.
w. Ellyn, c.d., with 1 son, 6 daus., rect. pl., dble. can. with fig. of B.V. Mary. Flem.

1546 Wm. Thynne, master of the household to Hen. VIII, arm.
w. Anne, c.d., marg. inscr. [All pal., *c.*1530, *c.*1510.]

1560 Wm. Armar, servant to Hen. VIII, Edw. VI, Mary, Eliz. I, arm., with 3 sons,
w. Eliz., c.d., with 2 daus., all kng., rect. pl., bad cond.

1591 Roger James, brewer, c.d.

LONDON, HOLY TRINITY, MINORIES

1596 Constance, eldest dau. of Sir Thos. Lucy, aged 11, sm., v. wn.

LONDON, ST ANDREW UNDERSHAFT

1539 Nich. Leveson, mercer, sheriff, c.d., mant., with 8 sons.
w. Denys, c.d., with 10 daus,. all kng.

1593 Simon Burton, wax-chandler, c.d.
1st w. Eliz., c.d., with 1 son, 3 daus.
2nd w. Ann, c.d., all kng., rect. pl.

LONDON, ST BARTHOLOMEW-THE-LESS
1439 Wm. Markeby, c.d.
w. Alice, c.d., wn.

LONDON, ST DUNSTAN-IN-THE-WEST
1530 Hen. Dacres, mcht. tailor, c.d. mant.
w. Eliz., c.d., kng.

LONDON, ST HELEN, BISHOPSGATE
c.1465 Man, c.d. (ft miss.).
w., c.d.
1482 Nich. Wotton, LL.B., rector, acad. dr.
1495 Thos. Wylliams, c.d.
w. Margt., c.d.
1500 7 sons of Hugh Pemberton.
c.1500 Priest, acad. dr., cap.
1510 John Leventhorp, usher of the chamber to Hen. VII, arm.
1514 Robt. Rochester, serjeant of the pantry to Hen. VIII, arm., SS coll.
1535 Woman, her. mant.

LONDON, ST MARTIN, LUDGATE HILL
1586 Thos. Beri, c.d., rect. pl.

LONDON, ST OLAVE, HART ST.
1516 —?, c.d., with 3 daus.
Kath., c.d., ws. of Sir Rich. Haddon with 2 sons, Wm. and John, all kng.
1584 John Orgone, c.d.
w. Ellyne, c.d., sm.

LONDON, TEMPLE CHURCH
1597 Roger Bishop, of the Inner Temple, c.d., kng., rect. pl.

MORTLAKE
1608 Ann, dau. of Lewis Jeames, aged 6.

PUTNEY
1478 John Welbek, arm.
c.1585 Eleanor Agar?, c.d., mut., wn.

ROTHERHITHE
1614 Peter Hills, mariner, c.d.
2 ws., c.d., rect. pl., v. wn.

STEPNEY, ST KATHERINE, RATCLIFF
1599 Wm. Cutinge, c.d.
w., c.d., kng., rect. pl., 2 achs.

STREATHAM, ST LEONARD
1513 Wm. Mowfurth, rector, mass vests.

TOOTING GRAVENEY
1597 Wm. Fitzwilliam, c.d.
w. Eliz., c.d., kng., rect. pl., ach.

TOTTENHAM, ALL HALLOWS
1616 John Burrough, c.d.
w. Eliz., c.d., with 2 sons, 1 dau.
1640 Lady Margt. Irby, c.d., with 3 daus., all kng., rect. pl.

WALTHAMSTOW
1543 Sir Geo. Monox, lord mayor of London, c.d.
w. Dame Ann, c.d., kng.
1588 Thos. Hale, c.d.
w. Anne, c.d. (upper hf miss.).
[Pal., c.1450.]

WANDSWORTH, ALL SAINTS
1420 Nich. Maudyt, serjeant-at-arms to Hen. V, arm., with mace (head miss.), marg. inscr., mut., v. wn.

WEST HAM
1592 Thos. Staples, tanner, c.d.
1st w. Anne, c.d.
2nd w. Margt., c.d.
3rd w. Denis, c.d.
4th w. Alice, c.d., rect. pl.

Westminster Abbey

1395 John de Waltham, bp. of Salisbury, lord high treasurer, episcopal vests., mitre, crosier (lower hf miss.), lge., wn.

1397 Robt. de Waldeby, S.T.D., archbp. of Dublin and York, episcopal vests., mitre, crosier, sin. can., royal arms, marg. inscr., mut., wn.

1399 Eleanor Woodstock, wid. dr., fine trip. can., chamfer inscr., lge.

1438 Sir John Harpenden, arm.

1471 Sir Humf. Bourgchier, arm. (only helmet crest, 4 shields, 6 badges remaining).

1483 Sir Thos. Vaughan, private treasurer to Edw. IV and Prince Edw., arm. (ft miss.).

1498 John Estney, abbot of Westminster, full vests., mitre, crosier, trip. can.

1505 Sir Humph. Stanley, bodyguard to Hen. VII, arm.

1561 Wm. Bill, S.T.D., dean of Westminster, provost of Eton, almoner to Eliz. I, in gown, hood, chamfer inscr., mut.

Westminster, St Margaret

1597 Thos. Cole, burgess in parliament, c.d.
w. Margt., c.d., with 1 son, 2 daus., all kng., rect. pl.

Willesden, St Mary

1492 Barth. Willesden, c.d.
w. Margt., c.d.

1505 Margt. Roberts, c.d.

1517 Wm. Lichefeld, LL.D., vicar, in cope, cap.

c. 1555 Woman, c.d., kng., with 2 sons, 4 daus.

1585 Edm. Roberts, arm.
1st w. Frauncys, c.d., with 2 sons, 4 daus.
2nd w. Fayth, c.d., with 2 sons, 1 dau.

1609 Jane Barne, c.d., with 1 dau.

MIDDLESEX

Ashford

1522 Edw. Goode, c.d.
w. Agnes, c.d., with 6 sons, 2 daus.

Bedfont

1631 Math. Page, c.d.
m. Isabel, c.d., kng.

Brentford, New

1528 Hen. Redman, chief mason to the king's works, c.d.
w. Joan, c.d., with 2 daus., kng.

Cowley

1502 Walter Pope, yeoman, c.d.
w. Joan or Alice, c.d.

Drayton, West

c. 1520 Man, c.d., sm.

1529 Margt. Birnell, c.d., with 2 sons, 1 dau.

1581 Jas. Good, M.D., c.d.
w. Joan, c.d., with 6 sons, mut., 5 daus., ach.

Enfield

c. 1470? Joyce Tiptoft, her. mant., coronet, trip. can., marg. inscr., lge.

1592 Wm. Smith, served Hen. VIII, Edw. VI, Q. Mary and Eliz. I, c.d.
w. Joan, c.d.

Greenford, Great

c. 1450 Simon Hert?, rector, mass vests., hf-eff.

c. 1480 Woman, c.d.

1521 Thos. Symons, rector, mass vests.

HADLEY (MONKEN HADLEY)
1442 Margt., dau. of Walter Grene, c.d.
Margt. Somercotes, c.d., sm.
1500 Wm. Turnour, c.d.
w. Joan, c.d., with 4 daus.
1504 Joan Goodeyere, c.d.
1518 Thos. Goodeyere, c.d.
w. Joan, c.d.
1610 5 sons, 8 daus. of Wm. Gale.
1614 Wm. Gale, M.A., c.d.
w. Anne, c.d., with 2 sons.

HAREFIELD
1444 Edith Neudegate, c.d., sm.
1528 John Newdegate, serjeant-at-law, in robes, coif, holding scroll.
w. Amphelice, her. mant., with 10 sons, 7 daus.
c. 1537 Geo. Assheby, clerk of the signet to Hen. VIII, arm.
w. Rose, c.d., with 4 sons, 3 daus. [Pal., *c.* 1380, *c.* 1480, *c.* 1470, *c.* 1500.]
c. 1537 Wm. Assheby, arm.
w. Jane, c.d., with 1 son, 7 daus. [Pal. various dates.]
1545 John Newdegate, c.d.
w. Ann, c.d., with 8 sons, (head of 1 miss.), 5 daus., all kng.

HARLINGTON
1419 John Monemouthe, rector, mass vests., hf-eff.
1545 Gregory Lovell, arm.
w. Anne, c.d. [All pal., 15th cent.]

HARROW
c. 1370 Edm. Flambard, arm., sm.
c. 1390 John Flambard, arm., lge., wn.
1442 Simon Marcheford, canon, in cope (head miss.).
c. 1460 Priest, acad. dr., hf-eff.
1468 John Byrkhed, rector, in cope, with SS, B.V. Mary, sin. can., mut., marg. inscr., mut.
1488 Geo. Aynesworth, c.d.
1st w. Agnes, c.d., with 1 son, a priest, acad. dr.
2nd w. Isabel, c.d., with 5 sons, 6 daus.
3rd w. Joan, c.d., with 2 sons.
1579 Wm. Wightman, arm.
w. Audrey, c.d., marg. inscr., mut., ach.
1592 John Lyon, c.d.
w., c.d., both mut.
c. 1600 Man, c.d.
w., c.d., lge.
1603 John Sonkey, c.d.
w. Alice, c.d.

HAYES
c. 1370 Robt. Levee, rector, mass vests., hf-eff.
1456 Walter Grene, arm., marg. inscr., mut.
1576 Thos. Higate, arm.
w. Eliz., c.d., mut., with 5 sons, 4 daus.

HESTON
1581 Constance Bownell, in bed with dead infant, angel at side, Our Lord above.

HILLINGDON
1509 John le Strange, arm.
w. Jacquette, c.d., with only child, Joan, dble. can.
1528 Hen. Stanley, arm.
c. 1560 6 sons, 3 daus.
1579 Drew Saunders, mcht., c.d.
w., c.d., with 1 dau., mut.
1599 John Atlee, high constable of Elthorne, c.d.

ICKENHAM
c. 1580 Robt. Say?, c.d.
1582 Wm. Say, c.d.
w. Isabel, c.d., with 7 sons, 9 daus.

1584 Edm. Shorditche, arm.
w. Ellen, c.d., with 2 sons, 1 dau.

ISLEWORTH

c. 1450 Geoff. Goodluck?, arm.
1561 Margt. Dely, nun, v. sm.
c. 1590 Laur. Manley?, yeoman, c.d.
1598 2 sons of Rich. Cox, mcht. tailor.

MIMMS, SOUTH

1448 Eliz. Frowyk, wid. dr., with 6 sons, 13 daus., bad. mut.

NORTHOLT

1452 Hen. Rowdell, arm., liv. coll., sm.
1560 John Gyfforde, arm.
w. Susan, c.d., with 9 sons, 3 daus. [Part pal., *c.* 1480, 15th cent.]
1610 Isiah Bures, M.A., vicar, in gown, kng., ach.

NORWOOD

1618 Math. Housley, c.d.
1624 Francis Awsiter, c.d.

PERIVALE

1500 Hen. Myllet, c.d.
1st w. Alice, c.d., with 3 sons, 6 daus.
2nd w. Joan, c.d., with 3 sons, 3 daus., v. sm.

RUISLIP

1574 Ralph Hawtrey, c.d., with 6 sons.
w. Winifred, c.d., with 6 daus., all stg. under dble. arch, rect. pl.
1593 John Hawtrey, J.P., c.d.
w. Bregget, c.d., ach.
c. 1600 Man, c.d., 4 daus.

SHEPPERTON

c. 1520 2 daus.

STANWELL

1408 Rich. de Thorp, rector, mass vests., hf-eff.

1506 TEDDINGTON, ST MARY
John Goodyere, c.d.
w. Thomasyn, c.d., sm.

MONMOUTHSHIRE

ABERGAVENNY

1579 Wm. Herbert, with 3 ws. and 13 child. (Under floor.)
1631 Maurice Hughes, vicar, in gown. (Under wooden floor.)
1637 Margt. Robertes, c.d., with chrysom, rect. pl., sm.

LLANGATTOCK-NIGH-USK

1625 Zirophaeniza Powell, c.d., kng., rect. pl.

LLANOVER

1610 Wm. Pritchard, arm., with 1 son, Math., arm., rect. pl., ach.

MATHERNE

1590 Philip Williams, c.d.
w. Alice, c.d., kng., rect. pl.

NORFOLK

ACLE

1533 John Swanne, c.d., sm. (head miss.).
1627 Thos. Stones, minister, in gown, cap, hf-eff., sm.

ALDBOROUGH

1481 Robt. Herward, arm.
1485 w. Anne, c.d.
c. 1490 Robt. Farnham, mcht., c.d.

ANTINGHAM

1562 Rich. Calthorp, arm., with 19 child., all named.

AYLSHAM

c. 1490 Thos. Tylson, B.C.L., vicar, in surplice.

c. 1490 Robt. Farman, c.d.
w. Kath., c.d., sm.

1499 Rich. Howard, sheriff, in shroud.
w. Cecily, in shroud, both skeletons.

c. 1500 Man, c.d.
w., c.d., wn.

1507 Thos. Wymer, "worsted wever", in shroud.

BACONSTHORPE

1561 Anne Heydon, her. dr., kng., sm.

BARNHAM BROOM

1467 Edm. Bryghtye, c.d., ¾-eff., with scroll.

1514 John Dorant, c.d.
w. Ellen, c.d., wn.

BARNINGHAM NORTHWOOD

1516 Hen. Pagrave, arm.
w. Anne, c.d., with 5 sons, 7 daus.

BARNINGHAM WINTER

c. 1410 John Wynter, arm., lge., partly rest.

BAWBURGH

1500 Robt. Grote, c.d., sm.

1505 Thos. Tyard, S.T.B., vicar, in shroud.

1660 Philip Tenison, S.T.P., rector, archdeacon, in shroud, sm.

BEECHAMWELL

c. 1385 John Chervill, rector, mass vests.

1430 John Grymston, rector, mass vests., hf-eff.

BEESTON REGIS

1527 John Deynes, c.d., with whistle from neck.
w. Kath, c.d., Death's head.

BINHAM

c. 1530 Man, c.d., ¾-eff.
w., c.d., ¾-eff., bad. wn.

BLICKLING

c. 1360 Man, c.d., bust.

1401 Sir Nich. Dagworth, arm., marg. inscr., mut., lge.

1454 Roger Felthorp, c.d.,
w. Cecilie, c.d., with 11 sons, 5 daus., stg. before their parents.

1458 Cecilie Boleyn, c.d., flowing hair, "aged L years".

1479 Anne Boleyn, c.d., aged 3 years, 11 months, 13 days.

1485 Isabel (Boleyn) Cheyne, c.d.

1512 Anne a Wode, 2nd w. of Thos. Asteley, c.d., holding chrysoms in arms.

BRAMPTON

1468 Robt. Brampton, in shroud.
w. Isabel, in shroud, B.V. Mary and child above, sm.

1535 John Brampton, arm.
1st w. Tomasseyng, c.d.
2nd w. Anne, c.d., with 4 sons.

1622 Edw. Brampton, c.d.
w. Jone, c.d., with 6 sons, mut.

BRISLEY

1531 John Athowe, rector, mass. vests., ch., wf. (head miss.).

BURGH ST MARGARET

1608 John Burton, rector, in gown, kng., sm.

BURNHAM THORPE

1420 Sir Wm. Calthorpe, arm., SS coll., sin. can., entab., marg. inscr., lge.

BURNHAM WESTGATE

1523 Mary or Anne Hunteley, c.d., with 1 son, 2 daus.

BYLAUGH (EYNESFORD)

1471 Sir John Curson, arm.
w. Joan, c.d., lge.

CLEY

1450 Man, c.d. (ft miss.).

c. 1460 Man, c.d. with 6 sons.

1512 John Symondes, mcht., in shroud.

w. Agnes, in shroud, with 4 sons, 4 daus., all named, lge.
c. 1520 John Yslyngton, S.T.P., in cassock, cap, ch.

CLIPPESBY
1503 Thos Pallyng, c.d.
w. Emme, c.d.
1594 John Clippesby, arm.
w. Julian, c.d., with 1 son, Wm., in shroud, 3 daus.

CREAKE, NORTH
c. 1500 Man, c.d., holding church, trip. can., lge. (Poss. Sir Wm. Calthorpe.)

CREAKE, SOUTH
c. 1400 Priest, in cope, hf-eff.
1509 John Norton, clerk, cassock, surplice, almuce, cope with crosier, with f. Rich., c.d. (both heads miss.). (Re-used brasses?, engraved *c.* 1470?)

CRESSINGHAM, GREAT
1497 Rich. Rysle, arm.
w. Thomasine, c.d.
1509 Wm. Eyre, J.P., c.d., monogram.
1518 John Abarfeld, rector, in gown, almuce.
1588 Eliz. Fludd, c.d. (upper hf miss.).

CROMER
1518 Margt. Counforth, c.d., sm., wn., mut.

DEREHAM, EAST
1479 Edm. Kelyng, vicar, mass vests., hf-eff., v. sm.
1486 Audrey Castell, c.d., sm.

DITCHINGHAM
1490 Philip Bosard, c.d.
w. Margery, c.d., with 4 sons, 5 daus., stg. before parents.
1505 Roger Bozard, c.d., with 1 son, Wm., c.d.

DUNSTON
1649 Clere Talbot, LL.D., c.d.
1st w. ? , in shroud.
2nd w. Anne, in shroud.

ELLINGHAM, GREAT
c. 1500 Woman, c.d. (Poss. Anne Wyllugby.)

ELSING
1347 Sir Hugh Hastyngs, arm., jupon, shield, head on cushion (legs miss.), sin. can., mut., St George, coronation of the Virgin, 8 weepers in side shafts, lge.

ERPINGHAM
c. 1415 Sir John de Erpingham, arm., lge.

FAKENHAM
1428 Hen, Keys, archdeacon, in cope (lower hf miss.), v. wn.
c. 1470 Man, c.d. (head miss.).
1st w., c.d. (head miss.).
2nd w., c.d.
c. 1510 Audrie Narborow, c.d.

FELBRIGG
c. 1380 Symond de Felbrig, c.d., anelace.
w. Alice, c.d. (lower hf miss.).
c. 1380 Roger de Felbrig, son of above, arm.
w. Eliz., c.d.
1416 Sir Symon Felbrygge, K.G., banner-bearer to Rich. II, arm., banner.
1st w. Margt., lady-in-waiting to Anne of Bohemia., c.d., mant., dble. can., v. lge.
c. 1480 Woman, c.d., flowing hair, sm. (Poss. Francis Windham.)
1612 Thos. Windham, arm.
1612 Jane Coningsby, c.d.

FELTWELL ST MARY
1479 Francis Heṫht, arm., sm.
1520 Margt. Mundford, c.d.

FINCHAM

c. 1520 Woman, in shroud.

FRANSHAM, GREAT

1414 Geoff. Fransham, arm.
sin. can., marg. inscr., lge.

c. 1500 Cecily Legge, in shroud.

FRENZE

1475 Ralph Blenerhaysett, arm.

1510 John Blenerhayset, arm.

1519 Dame Joan Braham, wid. dr.

c. 1520 Thos. Hobson, in shroud, sm.

1521 Jane Blenerhaysett, c.d.

1551 Anne Duke, c.d., head on cushion (lower hf miss.).

FRETTENHAM

c. 1420 Alys Thorndon, c.d., wn.

c. 1460 Woman, c.d.

GUESTWICK

1505 Rich. at Hyll, c.d., sm.

c. 1520 Jas. at Hylle, c.d., sm.

HALVERGATE

c. 1440 Frater Wm. Jernemu, bust in cassock, and hood. [Pal. on reverse:

1540 Alice Swane, hf-eff. in turban.] (Mounted in frame.)

HARLING, WEST

1479 Ralph Fuloflove, rector, mass vests.

c. 1490 Wm. Berdewell, arm.
w. Eliz., c.d.

1508 Wm. Berdewell, arm.
w. Margt.

HEACHAM

c. 1485 Man, arm., wn.

HELLESDON

c. 1370 Rich. de Heylesdone, c.d.
w. Beatrice, c.d., hf-effs.

1389 Rich. Thaseburgh, rector, mass vests.

HINDOLVESTONE

1568 Edm. Hunt, c.d., with 10 sons.
w. Margt., c.d., with 4 daus., all kng., ach.

HOLME-NEXT-THE-SEA

1405 Herry Notingham, judge, c.d., liv. coll., anelace.
w., c.d.

HONING

1496 Nich. Parker, arm.

HUNSTANTON, OLD

c. 1480 Edm. Grene, c.d., with long scarf.
w. Agnes, c.d.

1506 Sir Roger le Strange, bodyguard to Hen. VII, arm., tab., hands uplifted, stg. on br. under trip. can. with sm. effs. of himself and 7 ancestors, arm., tab., marg. inscr., lge., fine ach.

INGOLDISTHORPE

1608 Agnes Bigge, c.d., with parents, Thos. Rogerson, parson, in gown, cap, holding book.
w. Agnes, c.d., mut.

KENNINGHALL

c. 1500 5 sons, 5 daus.

KETTERINGHAM

c. 1470 Emma Grey, c.d.

1499 Thos. Hevenyngham, arm., tab., with 5 sons.
w. Anne, her. dr., with 5 daus., all kng., coloured.

KIMBERLEY

c. 1530 John Wodehows, arm.
w. Constance, c.d.

KIRBY BEDON

1505 Wm. Dussyng, in shroud.
w. Kath., in shroud, both sm.

LANGLEY

1628 Robt. Berney, c.d.

LODDON

1546 Dame Kath. Sampson, in shroud, with previous hus., John Blomeville, in shroud.

1561 Hen. Hobart, arm., tab. (head rest.).
1609 Jas. Hobart, c.d.
w. Francis, c.d., ach.

LYNN, ST MARGARET
1349 Adam de Walsokne, burgess of Lynn, c.d.
w. Margt., c.d., both under rich can., souls etc. above, 12 apostles, attendant prophets beside, between effs., rustic scene below, royal arms, marg. inscr., rect. pl., v. lge. (118″×68″), upper hf wn., Flem.
1364 Robt. Braunche, c.d.
2 ws. Letice, c.d., Margt., c.d., under rich can. with souls, etc. above, 8 weepers at sides, peacock feast below, royal arms, marg. inscr., rect. pl., v. lge. (107″×61″), Flem.

LYNN, WEST
1503 Adam Owtlawe, chaplain, mass vests.

MATTISHALL
c. 1480 Man, c.d., sm.
c. 1510 Geoff. Dene, c.d.
c. 1510 Robt. Foster, woolman, c.d.
w., c.d.

MERTON
1495 Wm. de Grey, arm., tab., with 5 sons.
1st w. Mary, c.d., with 3 daus.
2nd w. Grace, c.d., with 2 daus., all kng.
1562 Thos. de Grey, arm. (legs miss.).

METHWOLD
1367 Sir Adam de Clyfton, arm., v. mut., sin. can., mut., lge. (Brass stolen in 1680 and broken up into pieces. These are now fastened to a board.)

METTON
1493 Robt. Doughty, c.d., ¾-eff.
w. Maud, c.d., ¾-eff.

MILEHAM
1526 Christ. Crowe, c.d.
w. Christian, c.d., with 5 daus.

MORSTON
1596 Rich. Makynges, clerk, rector, in gown.

MOULTON, NR ACLE
1544 Thomasine Palmer, c.d., kng., sm.

NARBOROUGH
1496 Hen. Spelman, recorder, c.d., mant.
w. Ele, c.d.
1545 John Spelman, arm.
1545 Sir John Spelman, justice of the king's bench, in robes, coif.
w. Eliz., her. mant., kng., sm.
1561 John Eyer, receiver general to Eliz. I, arm.
w. Margt., c.d., kng., sm., ach.
1581 John Spelman, arm. [Pal., 15th cent.]

NECTON
1372 Ismayne de Wynston, c.d.
1383 Phelippe de Beauchampe, wid. dr., lge.
1499 Wm. Curteys, notary, c.d., penner and inkhorn.
w. Alice, c.d.
1528 John Bacon, c.d., sm.
1532 Robt. Goodwyn, c.d.
w. Sabine, c.d., with 7 sons.
1596 Mary Rust, c.d.

NEWTON FLOTMAN
1571 Rich. Blondevyle, arm.
Ralph Blondevyle, arm.
Edw. Blondevyle, arm., 3 sm. effs., kng., rect. pl.

Norwich, St Andrews
c.1500 Robt. Gardiner, mayor, c.d.
w., c.d.

Norwich, St Clement
1514 Margt. Pettwode, wid., c.d.

Norwich, St George Colegate
1472 Wm. Norwiche, c.d., mant.
w. Alice, c.d., with 1 son, c.d., all on br.

Norwich, St Giles
1432 Robt. Baxter, mayor, c.d., mant.
w. Cristine, wid. dr., lge.
1436 Rich. Purdaunce, mayor, c.d., mant. (head rest.).
w. Margt., wid. dr.

Norwich, St John Maddermarket
1412 Walter Moneslee, c.d., anelace.
w. Isabel, c.d., v. wn.
c.1450 John Todenham, c.d., long scroll from hands.
1472 Ralph Segrym, mayor, c.d., mant.
w. Agnes, c.d.
1476 Wm. Pepyr, alderman, c.d.
w. Joan, c.d.
1506? Joan Caus, c.d.
1524 John Terry, mayor, c.d., mant.
w. Lettys, c.d., with 2 sons, 2 daus, all stg. on br. springing from tree trunk, rect. pl., lge.
1525 John Marsham, mayor, c.d., mant.
w. Eliz., c.d., crucifix on rosary, stg. on br.
1558 Robt. Rugge, alderman, c.d., mant.
w. Eliz., c.d., with 5 sons, on br.

Norwich, St John Sepulchre
c.1535 Man, c.d.
w., c.d. [Both pal., wife reversed to show eff. of monk behind grille, under can. English, 15th cent.]

Norwich, St Laurence
1436 John Asger, mayor, c.d., mant. (ft miss.), lge.
1436 John Asger jun., c.d.
1437 Geoff. Langeley, prior of Horsham St Faith, Norwich, monastic dr., on br. under sin. can., mut., marg. inscr., mut.
1452 Thos. Childes, priest, skeleton.
1483 John Stylle, chaplain, mass vests.
1495 John Wellys, mayor, c.d., mant.

Norwich, St Margaret
1577 Anne Rede, c.d. [Pal., 13th, 14th, 15th cents.]

Norwich, St Michael-at-Plea
1588 Skeleton rising from tomb holding scyth, to Barbara Ferrer, v. sm.

Norwich, St Michael Coslany
1515 Hen. Scolows, alderman, in shroud.
w. Alice, in shroud.

Norwich, St Peter Mancroft
1512 Four groups of child. to Rich. Aylmer, bad. effaced.
1568 Peter Rede, arm., salade. (Copy of an earlier brass, c.1470.) [Pal. Flem., 16th cent.[

Norwich, St Stephen
c.1410 Woman, c.d., *appropriated by addition of sm. pl. bearing inscr. and 2 bedesmen to* Eel Buttry, prioress of Campsey. (Brass under floorboards.)
1460 Thos. Bokenham, c.d., wn. (Under floorboards.)
c.1513 Robt. Brasyer, mayor, c.d., mant.
w. Cristian, c.d.
c.1513 Rich. Brasyer sen., mayor, c.d., mant., with 1 son, Rich. jun., mayor, c.d., mant.

1545 Thos. Capp, D.C.L., vicar, in cope.

ORMESBY, GREAT

c.1440 Woman, c.d., holding heart, hf-eff., *altered by shading and inscr. to*

1538 Dame Alice Boleyn, 2nd w. of Sir Robt. Clere.

1529 Sir Robt. Clere, arm., marg. inscr.

OUTWELL

1511 Rich. Quadryng, arm.

PASTON

c.1570 Erasmus Paston, c.d.

PLUMSTEAD, LITTLE

c.1480 Man, c.d. (ft miss.).
w., c.d.

1565 Sir Edw. Warner, arm., lge., ach.

RAINHAM, EAST

c.1500 Geo. Townsend, c.d.

1522 Robt. Godfrey, LL.B., rector, in cassock, sm.

RAVENINGHAM

1483 Margt. Wyllughby, c.d., suns and roses on coll., stg. on dragon, lge.

REEDHAM

1474 Eliz. Berney, c.d.

REEPHAM

1391 Sir Wm. de Kerdeston, arm. (legs mut.).
w. Cecily, c.d., mant., dble. can., marg. inscr., bad. mut., lge.

RINGSTEAD, GREAT

1482 Rich. Kegall, rector, mass vests.

ROUGHAM

1472 Sir Wm. Yelverton, justice of the king's bench, arm., judicial mant., coif, suns and roses on coll.
2nd w. Agnes, c.d., mant.

c.1510 Wm. Yelverton, esq. to Edw. IV, arm.
w. Kath, c.d., with 7 sons.

1586 Wm. Yelverton, c.d.
1st w. Anne, c.d., with 6 sons, 4 daus., ach.
2nd w. Jane, c.d., with 4 sons, 2 daus.

SALL

c.1420 Man, c.d., sm. (lower hf miss.).

1440 Geoff. Boleyn, c.d.
w. Alice, c.d.

1441 Thos. Roose, sheep farmer, c.d.
w. Kath, c.d., with 8 sons, 4 daus., stg. beside parents, on br., mut.

1453 2 ws. of John Funteyn, either Alice, Joan or Agnes., sm.

1454 John Brigge, in shroud.

SCULTHORPE

1470 Hen. Unton, arm., kng.

1521 John Humpton, c.d.
w. Eliz., c.d., with 7 sons, 1 dau.

SHARRINGTON

c.1445 Man, arm., lge.

1486 John Botolff, rector, mass vests wn., sm.

c.1520 Woman, c.d., wn.

1593 Christ. Dawbeney, arm. (head miss.), with 5 sons.
w. Phillipa, c.d., with 3 daus., all kng.

SHERNBOURNE

1458 Thos. Shernbourne, chamberlain to Q. Margt. of Anjou, arm.
w. Jamon, maid of honour to the Q., c.d., mant., lge.

SHERRINGHAM

1513 John Hook, c.d.
w. Magdalen, c.d.

SHOTESHAM ST MARY

1528 Edw. White, arm.
w. Eliz., c.d.

SNETTISHAM

c.1560 Woman, c.d., mut. [Pal. on

reverse, woman, child, c.d., mut. in frame.]
1610 John Cremer, c.d.
w. Anne, c.d., with 6 sons, 1 dau., all separate.

SNORING, GREAT
1424 Sir Ralph Shelton, arm., tab. (head only).
w. Alice, c.d., mant., with arms mut. (Part engraved in lead.)

SOUTHACRE
1384 Sir John Harsick, arm., arms on jupon.
w. Kath., c.d., mant., arms on kirtle, holding hands, marg. inscr., mut., lge., ach.
1534 Thos. Leman, rector, cassock, surplice, kng.

SPARHAM
c. 1490 Wm. Mustarder, rector, mass vests.

SPROWSTON
1559 John Corbet, arm. (upper hf miss.), with 4 sons.
w. Jane, c.d., with 6 daus., all kng., sm., ach.

STALHAM
c. 1460 Man, c.d.
w., c.d.

STOKESBY
1488 Edm. Clere, arm., salade.
w. Eliz., c.d.
1506 Thos. Gerard, rector, acad. dr. (lower hf miss.).
1570 Ann Clere, c.d. (upper hf miss.). [Pal. Flem., 16th cent.]
1614 Anne Clere, c.d., with 5 sons, 6 daus.

STRADSETT
1418 Thos. Lathe, arm., liv. coll.

SURLINGHAM
1460 John Alnwik, vicar, acad. dr.

SWAFFHAM
c. 1480 Man, arm., wn.

SWANTON ABBOTT
1477 Stephan Multon, rector, mass vests.

THEMELTHORPE
1505 Wm. Pescod, c.d., sm.

THWAITE (SOUTH ERPINGHAM)
1469 John Puttock, c.d.
w. Alice, c.d.

TOTTINGTON
1598 Margt. Pory, c.d., with 1 son, kng.

TROWSE
1585 Eliz. Dalyson, c.d.

TUDDENHAM, EAST
c. 1500 Man, c.d. (head rest.).
2 ws., c.d.

UPWELL
c. 1430 Priest in cope, trip. can., entab., lge. (Poss. Wm. Mowbray.)
1435 Hen. Martyn, rector, mass vests., crossed stole.
1621 Sinolphus Bell, c.d., with 7 sons.
w. Jane, c.d., with 4 daus., all kng., rect. pl., wn.

WALSINGHAM, NEW
c. 1460 Margt. Stoke, c.d., hf-eff., sm.
1485 Geof. Porter, c.d. (head miss.).
w. Beatrice, c.d.
c. 1490 Man, c.d. (head miss.), sm.
1509 Hen. Clederow, c.d.
w. Joan, c.d.
1540 Man, c.d.
w., c.d. [Pal. Flem., *c.* 1340.]

WARHAM, ALL SAINTS
1474 Wm. Rokewood, arm.

WESTON
1533 Eliz. Rokewoode, c.d., with 2 sons, kng.

WHISSONSETT

c. 1484 Wm. Bozon, arm.

1484 Thos. Gybon, arm.

WITTON

c. 1500 Dame Julian Anyell, vowess.

WIVETON

1512 Wm. Bisshop, clerk, rector, mass vests., ch., wf., sm.

c. 1540 Man, skeleton, in shroud. (Poss. Thos. Brigges.)

1597 Geo. Brigge, c.d.
w. Anne, c.d.

WOOD DALLING

1465 Robt. Dockyng, chaplain, mass vests., sm.

1504 Simon Bolwar, c.d.

1507 John Crane, c.d.

1518 John Bulwer, c.d.
b. Thos. Bulwer, c.d., $\frac{3}{4}$-effs., v. sm.

WOODTON

1532 Cristian Bacon, c.d., sm.

WORSTEAD

1404? John Yop, rector, mass vests., hf-eff., sm.

c. 1500 Man, c.d.

1520 John Alblastyr, c.d., $\frac{3}{4}$-eff., sm.

YELVERTON

1525 Margt., dau. of Thos. Aldriche, c.d., $\frac{3}{4}$-eff., sm.

In the Society of Antiquaries, London, is a sm. pl. of 8 daus. from the brass to John Marsham at St John Maddermarket, Norwich.

The following brasses are in the care of Norwich Museums, either on show in St Peter Hungate church Museum, or in the reserve collection at Strangers Hall.

c. 1450 Head only. (From St Mary Coslany, Norwich.)

c. 1460 4 daus. (From Cley, Norfolk.)

1467 ? Gilbert, a boy, c.d., wn. (From St Andrew, Norwich.)

1474 John Berney, head only, (From Reedham, Norfolk.)

1487 Roger Clerk, priest, mass vests., sm., wn. (From St Peter, Southgate, then St Etheldreda, Norwich.)

1495 John Horslee, c.d.
w. Agnes, c.d. (From St Swithin, Norwich.)

1523 Anne Hawte or Haste, c.d., sm., wn.

c. 1575 Woman with child, sm. (Poss. from Norwich Cathedral.)

1630 Thos. Holl, c.d., sm., wn. (From St Bartholomew, Heigham, Norwich.)

At St Margaret, Kings Lynn, the brass to

1376 Robt. Attelath, burgess, lge., Flem. *is a modern restoration. (The original was sold for 5s. by a churchwarden.)*

NORTHAMPTONSHIRE

ABINGTON

1557 3 daus. of Wm. Nayle, sm.

ADDINGTON, GREAT

1519 John Bloxham, chaplain, mass vests., ch., wf., marg. inscr.

ALDWINKLE, ALL SAINTS

1463 Wm. Aldewyncle, c.d.

ASHBY, CANONS

1584 John Dryden, c.d., ach.

ASHBY, CASTLE

1401 Wm. Ermyn, rector, in cope, lge.

ASHBY ST LEGERS

1416 Thos. Stokes, c.d.
w. Ellen, c.d., with 4 sons, 12 daus., kng., sin. can., sm. super can.

1471 Sir Wm. Catesby, in shroud (lower hf miss.).
2nd w. Joan, in shroud.
1494 Wm. Catisby, arm., tab.
w. Margt., her. mant., with 3 sons, 2 daus. (dble. can., ach., appropriated, *c.* 1430).
c. 1500 Geo. Catesby, arm., tab., kng.
1553 Sir Rich. Catesby, arm., tab., lge.
1510 Wm. Smyght, rector, in cassock, scarf.

Ashton
1584 Robt. Mariott, yeoman, c.d.
w., c.d., with 9 sons, 6 daus.

Aston-le-Walls
1609 Alban Butler, c.d.
1st w. Sybil, c.d., with 5 sons, 7 daus.
2nd w. Isabel, c.d., with 2 daus., all kng., rect. pl.

Barnwell St Andrew
1610 Christ. Freeman, c.d., with 4 sons.
w., c.d., with 4 daus., all kng., rect. pl., sm.

Barton, Earl's
1512 John Muscote, c.d.
w. Alice, c.d., with 4 sons, 2 daus.

Barton Segrave
1616 Jane Floyde, c.d., kng., with 1 son, 1 dau., infant in cot, 2 deceased on tomb, rect. pl.

Blakesley
1416 Matt. Swetenham, esq. for the body to Hen. IV, arm., SS coll.

Blatherwyck
1548 Sir Humf. Stafford, esq. for the body to Hen. VIII, arm.
w. Margt., c.d. (upper hf miss.), with 6 sons.

Blisworth
1503 Roger Wake, arm.
w. Eliz., c.d., with 7 sons, 3 daus., marg. inscr., mut.

Boddington
1627 Wm. Procter, rector, in gown, cap.

Brampton, Church
1585 Jone Furnace, skeleton, rect. pl., sm., wn.

Brampton-by-Dingley
c. 1420 Sir John Holt?, arm.
w., mant. (head miss.), dble. can. bad. mut.
1476 Simon Norwiche, arm., B.V. Mary and Child, inscr., mut.

Brington, Great
c. 1340 Priest, mass vests., hf-eff., on br., mut.

Burton Latimer
c. 1510 9 sons of Rich. Boyvill.
1626 Margt. Bacon, c.d., with chrysom.

Charwelton
1490 Thos. Andrewe, arm.
w. Emme, c.d., with 4 sons, 7 daus., under sm. cans., marg. inscr., ach.
c. 1490 Thos. Andrewe, mcht., c.d.
w. Margery, c.d., dble. can. with 4 pediments, with 5 sons, 3 daus., under sm. can., marg. inscr., lge., ach. (rest. 1904).
1541 Thos. Andrewes, arm. [Pal. re-used, *c.* 1510.]
w. Agnes, c.d. [Pal. *c.* 1510.]

Chipping Warden
1468 Wm. Smarte, rector, mass vests., sm.
1584 Rich. Makepeace, yeoman, c.d.
w. Dorothy, c.d., bad. mut., with 9 daus.

COLLYWESTON
1508 Eliz. Follett, c.d., sm.

COTTERSTOCK
1420 Robt. Wyntryngham, canon, prebendary, provost, in cope, sin. can., on br., marg. inscr.

CRANFORD ST ANDREW
1418 John Fossebrok, arm.
w. Maud, c.d., SS coll.
1602 John Fosbroke, c.d.
2 ws., c.d., sm.

CRANSLEY
1515 Edw. Dalyson, c.d.
w. Eliz., c.d.
1589 Edw. Dallison, arm.
w. Anne, c.d., kng., rect. pl., ach.

DEENE
1584 Sir Edm. Brudenell, arm.
1st w. Agnes, c.d.
2nd w. Aubrey, c.d., with 1 dau., Aubrey, all kng., rect. pl.
1586 Sir Thos. Brudenell, arm.
w. Eliz., c.d., ach.
1606 John Brudenell, arm.
w., c.d.

DINGLEY
1577 Anne Boroeghe, wid, dr., kng., rect. pl.

DODFORD
1414 John Cressy, arm.
w. Cristine, c.d.
1422 Wm. Wylde, arm.
w. Cecily, wid. dr.
1637 Bridget Wyrley, c.d., holding book, sm.

EASTON NESTON
1552 Rich. Fermer, mcht., arm.
w. Anne, c.d., marg. inscr.

FARNDON, EAST
1622 Daniel Halford, rector, in gown, rect. pl.

FAWSLEY
1516 Thos. Knyghtley, arm., tab., heart, scrolls above head.
1557 Sir Edm. Knyghtleye, arm.
w. Ursula, c.d., with 6 daus., marg. inscr.

FLOORE
1498 Thos. Knaresburght, arm.
w. Agnes, c.d.
1510 Hen. Michell, arm.
w. Phillipe, c.d., Trin., wn.

GEDDINGTON
c. 1480 Hen. Jarmon, c.d.
w. Anne, c.d., mut.

GRENDON
c. 1480 Man, arm.
Woman, wid. dr.
Man, arm., slightly mut.

HARRINGTON
1545 Laur. Saunders, arm., with 4 sons, eldest arm.
w. Alice, c.d., with 5 daus., all kng.

HARROWDEN, GREAT
1433 Wm. Harwedon, arm.
w. Margery, wid. dr., both on br., marg. inscr., mut.

HEMINGTON
1517 Thos. Mountagu, c.d.
w. Agnes, c.d.

HEYFORD, NETHER
1487 Sir Walter Mauntell, arm.
w. Eliz., c.d., holding hands, chamfer inscr., lge.

HIGHAM FERRERS
1337 Laur. de St Maur, rector, mass vests., sin. can., with SS, mut.
1425 Wm. Chichele, sheriff, alderman, c.d., mant.
w. Beatrice, c.d., mant., dble. can., marg. inscr., lge.

c.1435 Dame Edith Chaunceler, wid. dr. (head mut.).
1498 Hen. Denton, chaplain, mass vests., ch., wf.
1504 Wm. Thorpe, mercer, c.d.
w. Marion, wid. dr., with 6 sons, 6 daus.
1518 Arthur Sotheryn, c.d., sm.
1523? Rich. Wylleys, warden of the college, in cope.
c.1540 Man, c.d., wn.
c.1540 Man, c.d.

HORTON
1491 Roger Salusbury, arm.
1st w. Emme, c.d.
2nd w. Anne, c.d.

IRCHESTER
1506 w. of John Glynton, mcht., c.d.

KELMARSH
c.1534 Morris Osberne, c.d., bad. mut.

KETTERING
1630 Edm. Sawyer, arm.
w. Anne, c.d., kng., rect. pl., ach.

LOWICK
1467 Hen. Grene, arm., tab.
w. Margt., wid. dr., head on cushion.

MARHOLM
1534 Sir Wm. Fitzwilliams, arm., tab.
1st w. Anne, her. mant., kng. (upper hf of man renewed).

NASEBY
1446 John Olyver, c.d. (head miss.).
w. Agnes, wid. dr.

NEWBOTTLE
1555 Peter Dormer, c.d., stg. (ft miss.).
1st w., c.d., kng., with 8 sons, 11 daus.
2nd w., c.d., kng.

NEWNHAM
1467 Lettice Catesby, c.d., mant., was holding husband's hand.

NEWTON BROMSHOLD
1426 Wm. Hewet, rector, mass vests., sm.
1487 Roger Hewet, chaplain, mass vests.

NEWTON-BY-GEDDINGTON
1400 John Mulsho, c.d.
w. Joan, c.d., sm. effs. kng. to a cross with St Faith in the head, marg. inscr. (rest. 1858).
1604 Margt. Tresham, c.d., rect. pl.

NORTHAMPTON, ST SEPULCHRE
1640 Geo. Coles, c.d.
1st w. Sarah, c.d., with 2 sons, 1 dau.
2nd w. Eleanor, c.d., with 7 sons, 2 daus., marg. inscr., lge.

NORTON
1504 Wm. Knyght, c.d.
w. Kath., c.d.

NORTON, GREEN'S
1462 Sir Thos. Grene, arm.
w. Maud, wid. dr., with 1 dau., marg. inscr., lge.
c.1490 Woman, c.d.

ORLINGBURY
1502 Wm. Lane, c.d.
w. Eliz., c.d., sm.

POTTERSPURY
1616 Agnes Ogle, c.d., sm., ach.

PRESTON DEANERY
1622 Sir Clement Edmonds, secretary to Jas. I, arm.
w. Mary, c.d., sm.

RAUNDS
c.1510 John Tawyer, c.d.
w. Margt., c.d., with 4 daus.
c.1510 Woman, c.d., with 4 sons.

ROTHWELL
1361 Wm. de Rothewelle, archdeacon of Essex, in cope, head on cushion supported by angels.

1514 Edw. Saunders, c.d.
w. Joan, c.d.
1591 Owen Ragesdale, c.d., kng., rect. pl., ach.

SPRATTON
1474 Robt. Parnell, c.d. (head miss.).
w. Jone, c.d., with 5 sons (head of 1 miss.), 4 daus., wn.

STAVERTON
1580 Thos. Wylmer, c.d., with 6 sons.
w. Eliz., c.d., with 4 daus., all kng., ach.

STOKE BRUERNE
1625 Rich. Lightfoot, rector, in gown, kng., rect. pl.

SUDBOROUGH
1415 Wm. West, c.d.
w. Joan, c.d., with below on 1 pl. their child., John West, chaplain, in mass vests., Wm. West, marbler, c.d., Alice, c.d. (head miss.), with 5 sons, 3 daus.

SULGRAVE
1564 Laur. Wasshington, c.d. (head miss.), with 4 sons, 7 daus.

TANSOR
1440 John Colt, rector, mass vests.

WAPPENHAM
c.1460 Man, arm., salade (lower hf miss.).
1479 Sir Thos. Billyng, chief justice of the common pleas, in robes, coif.
w. Kath., c.d. (lower parts of effs. miss.), with 1 dau.
1499 Constance Butler, c.d., sm.
c.1500 Thos. Lovett?, arm.
2nd w. Anne?, c.d., sm.
c.1500 Thos. Lovett, arm.
w. Eliz., c.d.

WARKWORTH
1412 Sir John Chetwode, arm. (head, legs miss.).
1420 John Chetewode, arm., son of above.
1420 Margery Brounyng, c.d.
1430 Amabel Straunge, c.d.
1454 Wm. Ludsthorp, arm.

WELFORD
1585 Francis Saunders, arm.
1st w., c.d., with 2 sons, 1 dau.
2nd w., c.d., with infant in cradle.
3rd w., c.d., with 1 son, 4 daus., all kng., rect. pl.

WOODFORD-CUM-MEMBRIS
c.1420 Nich. Stafford, vicar, mass vests.

WOODFORD, NR THRAPSTONE
1580 Simon Malory, arm., ach.

At Islip, the brass to
1467 John Nicoll, c.d.
w. Anne, cd.
was completely renewed in 1911.

NORTHUMBERLAND

NEWCASTLE-UPON-TYNE, ALL SAINTS
1411 Roger Thornton, mcht., c.d.
w. Agnes, c.d., mant., with 7 sons, 7 daus., fine trip. can. with Deity, souls, 12 apostles, SS, etc., marg. inscr., lge. rect. pl. Flem. (Covered with glass.)

In the Keep Museum, Newcastle-upon-Tyne, is a fragment of the ft of
1387 Sir Aymer de Athol, arm. (From St Andrew, Newcastle.)

NOTTINGHAMSHIRE

ANNESLEY
1595 Wm. Breton, hunting dress, bow, arrows, hound, sm. rect. pl.

Clifton
1478 Sir Robt. Clyfton, arm.
1491 Sir Gervis Clifton, arm., son of above.
1587 Geo. Clifton, c.d.
w. Winifred, c.d.

Darlton
c. 1510 Man, arm.
w., c.d.

Hickling
1521 Ralph Babyngton, rector, mass vests., ch., wf.

Holme Pierrepont
c. 1390 Woman, c.d., lge.

Markham, East
1419 Dame Millicent Meryng, c.d., marg. inscr.

Newark
1361 Alan Fleming, mcht., c.d., fine groined trip. can., with Deity, souls, etc. (39 figs.), marg. inscr., v. lge. rect. pl., wn. Flem.
c. 1540 John Boston?, mercer, c.d.
1557 Wm. Phyllypott, mcht., c.d.

Ossington
1551 Reynold Peckham, arm.
w. Eliz., c.d., marg. inscr., mut.
[All pal. eff. Flem., 14th cent.]

Radcliffe-on-Trent
1626 Anne Ballard, c.d., kng., rect. pl.

Stanford-on-Soar
c. 1400 Priest, mass vests., ch. (ft miss.).

Strelley
1487 Sir Robt. Strelley, arm.
w. Isabel, mant., ach., mut.

Wollaton
1471 Rich. Wylloughby, arm., stg. on lge. whelk shell.
w. Anne, mant., chamfer inscr., mut.

OXFORDSHIRE

Adderbury
c. 1460 Man, arm., liv. coll.
w., c.d.
1508 Jane Smith, c.d.

Alvescot
1579 ? Malorye, c.d., with 1 son.
w. Alice, c.d., with 1 dau.

Aston Rowant
1445 Ralph Coppyn, c.d.
w. Isabel, c.d., sm.
c. 1470 Man (covered ?).
w., c.d., with 5 daus. (upper hf miss.).
1508 Eleanor Eggerley, c.d. (lower hf miss.), sm.

Bampton
c. 1420 Thos. Plymmyswode, vicar, in surplice, almuce, hf-eff.
1500 Robt. Halcot, M.A., vicar, in cope, sm.
1633 Frances Hord, c.d.

Barford, Great
1495 Wm. Foxe, c.d.
w. Jone, c.d., mut., sm.

Beckley
1619 Anne Croke, c.d., kng., rect. pl.

Bicester
c. 1510 Man, c.d.
w., c.d.

Brightwell Baldwin
1439 John Cottusmore, chief justice of the common pleas, in robes, coif.
w. Amice, c.d., kng., v. sm., both also represented stg. under fine dble. can., with kng. figs. of 5 sons, 13 daus., below, lge.

Brightwell Salome
1492 Morris Jones, rector, mass vests., sm.

BROUGHTON

1414 Dame Philippe Byschoppesdon, marg. inscr., lge.

BURFORD

1437 John Spycer, c.d.
w. Alys, c.d., kng. to br., marg. inscr., mut.

1609 John Huntt, mercer, c.d., kng., sm., rect. pl. (In churchyard ?)

1614 John Osbaldeston, c.d.
w. Grace, c.d., with 10 sons, 2 daus., all kng., rect. pl.

CASSINGTON

1590 Thos. Nele, prof. of Hebrew at Oxford, in shroud, rect. pl.

CAVERSFIELD

1435 John Langstone, c.d., anelace.

1506 Amice Langston, c.d., with 12 sons, 10 daus.

CHALGROVE

1441 Reginald Barantyn, arm.

1446 Drew Barantyn, arm.
1st w. Joan, c.d.
2nd w. Dame Beatrix, c.d.

CHARLTON-UPON-OTMOOR

1476 Thos. Key, rector, canon, chaplain, in cope, marg. inscr., mut.

CHASTLETON

1592 Kath. Throckmorton, c.d., with 5 sons, 5 daus., sm., ach.

1613 Edm. Ansley, c.d.
w., c.d., mut., with 7 sons, 3 daus., sm.

CHECKENDON

1404 John Rede, c.d., trip. can., marg. inscr.

1490 Anne Bowett, c.d.

CHESTERTON

1612 Wm. Maunde, c.d.
w. Anne, c.d.

CHINNOR

1361 John Hotham, rector, provost, acad. dr., cap, hf-eff., lge.

1385 Reynald de Malyns, arm.
2 ws., c.d., lge.

c. 1385 Esmoun de Malyns, arm.
w. Isabel, c.d., hf-effs.

1388 Alex. Chelseye, rector, mass vests., ch., wf., hf-eff., lge.

c. 1390 Woman, c.d., hf-eff. (Poss. of the Malyns fam.)

1392 John Cray, esq. to Rich. II, arm., lge.

c. 1410 Robt. atte Heelde, c.d. (ft only).
w. Kath., c.d. (head miss.).

c. 1410 Nich. atte Heelde, c.d., son of above (onto whose ft he has now been fitted).

1430 Reginald Malyns, arm. (head, legs miss.).

1514 Folke Poffe, c.d.
w., c.d.

CHIPPING NORTON

c. 1450 John Stokes, mercer, c.d.
w. Alice, c.d., sm., wn.

1451 John Yonge, woolman, c.d., stg. on woolpack.
w. Isabel, c.d., lge.

c. 1460 Thos. Grene ?, c.d. (legs miss., head mut.).

1484 John Pergetter, ironmonger, c.d. (ft miss.).
w. Agnes, c.d., with 7 daus.

1503 Agnes Tanner, c.d.

1507 Margt. Ashefyld, c.d.

1530 Eliz. Tante, c.d.

COTTISFORD

c. 1500 John Samwell, arm., with 8 sons.
w., c.d., with 5 daus., all kng.

CROWELL

1469 John Payne, parson, mass vests., hf-eff. [Pal., *c.* same date.]

CUXHAM

1506 John Gregory, c.d.
1st w. Parnel, c.d., with 5 sons, 1 dau.
2nd w. Agnes, c.d., sm.

DEDDINGTON

c.1370 Man, c.d., hf-eff.

DORCHESTER

1417 Sir John Drayton, arm., SS coll. (legs mut.), lge.

c.1490 Jenit Sherrey?, c.d., sm.

c.1510 Rich. Bewfforeste, abbot, in surplice, almuce, mant. of Austin canon, crosier.

1513 Margt. Beweforest, c.d. (head miss.).
2nd hus. Rich. Beweforest, c.d. sm.

EWELME

1436 Thos. Chaucer, arm.
w. Maud, wid. dr., chamfer inscr., rest.

1458 John Bradstane, rector, mass vests., hf-eff.

1467 Hen. Morecote, rector, mass vests., hf-eff.

1498? Wm. Branwhait, master of the hospital, mass vests., hf-eff. (engraved *c.*1470).

1517 John Spence, S.T.B., master of the hospital, acad. dr.

1518 Thos. Broke, serjeant-at-arms to Hen. VIII, arm.
w. Anne, c.d.

1599 Thos. Palmer, c.d., with 6 sons.
w. Kath. c.d., with 1 dau., all kng., rect. pl., ach.

FIFIELD

1620 Mary Bray, c.d., with 3 sons, 6 daus., all kng., rect. pl.

GARSINGTON

1484 Thos. Radley, c.d.
w. Eliz., c.d., with 5 sons, 5 daus., sm., wn.

GLYMPTON

1610 Thos. Tesdale, c.d.

GORING

1401 Eliz. ? , c.d., sin. can., marg. inscr., mut.

c.1600 Man, c.d.
w., c.d., with 3 sons, 5 daus. [Pal., 1594.]

HAMPTON POYLE

1424 John Poyle, arm.
w. Eliz., c.d.

HANDBOROUGH

c.1500 Christ. Ford, c.d.
w. Joan, c.d., with her 1st hus. Thos. Wheeler, c.d., sm., wn.

1567 Alex. Belsyre, first president of St John's College, Oxford, recumbent in shroud, rect. pl.

HARPSDEN

c.1460 ? Forster, wid. dr.

c.1480 Man, arm.
w., c.d.

1511 Walter Elmes, rector, mass vests., sm.

1620 Sarah Webb, c.d., with 1 son, 1 dau.

HASELEY, GREAT

1494 Thos. Buttler, rector, almuce.

1497 Wm. Leynthall, in shroud.

1581 Mary Huddleston, c.d., with 2 sons, 3 daus.

HEYTHROP

1521 John Aschefeld, arm.
w. Elenor, with 4 sons, 4 daus.

HOLTON

1461 Wm. Brome, arm., salade.

1599 Wm. Brome, aged 10, c.d.

HORLEY

c.1520 6 daus. (Poss. child. of Thos. Light.)

HORNTON

1586 Thos. Sharman, yeoman, c.d., with 1 son.

IPSDEN

1525 Thos. Englysshe, arm.
w. Isabel, c.d. [Both pal., c. 1420.]

ISLIP

1637 Susanna Norrys, c.d.
1st hus. Robt. Bancks, c.d., with 8 sons, 10 daus.
2nd hus. Hen. Norrys, c.d., with 1 son, all kng., rect. pl., ach.

KIDDINGTON

1513 Walter Goodere, rector, acad. dr., sm.

KINGHAM

1588 Kath. James, c.d., with 3 sons, all kng., rect. pl.

LEWKNOR

c. 1380 John Aldebourne, rector, mass vests., hf-eff.

MAPLEDURHAM

1395 Sir Robt. Bardolf, arm., sin. can., mut.

MIDDLETON STONEY

1607 Eliz. Harman, c.d., ach.

MILTON, GREAT

c. 1510 John and Eliz., child. of Kath. and Robt. Eggerley, c.d., v. sm.

NEWNHAM MURREN

1593 Lettice Barnade, c.d., with 2 sons, 2 daus., all kng., rect. pl.

NOKE

1598 Joan Bradshawe, c.d.
1st hus. Wm. Manwayringe, c.d.
2nd hus. Hen. Bradshawe, chief baron of the exchequer, in judicial robes, with 4 sons, 4 daus., all kng., rect. pl.

NORTHLEIGH

1431 Thos. Bekingham, arm., liv. coll., lge.

NUFFIELD

c. 1360 Beneit Engliss, c.d., hf-eff.

ODDINGTON

c. 1510 Ralph Hamsterley, rector, fellow of Merton College, Oxford, skeleton, in shroud, eaten by worms.

OXFORD, ALL SOULS COLLEGE

1461 Philip Polton, B.C.L., archdeacon, in cope, kng., sm. (head miss.).

1490 Rich. Spekynton, LL.B., fellow, acad. dr.

1510 David Lloyde, LL.B., acad. dr., hf-eff.
Thos. Baker, scholar, c.d., in gown, hf-eff.

OXFORD, CHRIST CHURCH CATHEDRAL

c. 1450 Edw. Courtenay, c.d., anelace, sm.

1452 John Fitzaleyn, c.d., sm.

1557 Jas. Coorthopp, canon, dean, in almuce, marg. inscr., mut.

1578 Hen. Dow, B.A., in gown, hood, kng., ach.

1584 Thos. Morrey, M.A., in gown, kng.

1587 Stephen Lence, M.A., in gown, hood, cap, ¾-eff.

1588 John Bisshop, c.d., kng., rect. pl.

1602 John Walrond, c.d., kng., rect. pl.

1613 Thos. Thornton, M.A., in gown, hood, kng., rect. pl.

OXFORD, CORPUS CHRISTI COLLEGE

c. 1530 John Claimond, first president, emac. eff. in shroud, marg. inscr., mut.

1602 Francis Colthurst, mcht., c.d. (covered).

OXFORD, MAGDALEN COLLEGE

1478 Ralph Vawdrey, M.A., chaplain, acad. dr., hf-eff., with scroll.

1478 Thos. Sondes, scholar, acad. dr., marg. inscr., mut., scroll.

1480 Wm. Tibarde, S.T.B., first president, in cope, marg. inscr. (rest. 1911).
c.1480 Priest, acad. dr. (Poss. Geo. Epworth, M.A.)
c.1480 John Bentley ?, M.A., priest, in acad. dr., hf-eff.
c.1485 Thos. Freer ?, M.A., priest, in acad. dr., mut.
1487 John Perch, M.A., chaplain, in cope, marg. inscr. (rest. 1911).
c.1500 Geo. Lassy, acad. dr., hf-eff.
c.1500 Thos. Dyke ?, M.A., acad. dr. (ft miss.).
1501 Thos. Mason, M.A., fellow, acad. dr.
1502 Walter Charyls, M.A., fellow, acad. dr. (head miss.), ¾-eff.
1515 Wm. Goberd, B.A., archdeacon, in almuce.
1523 Nich. Goldwell, M.A., fellow, acad. dr., sm.
1558 Arthur Cole, S.T.B., canon, president, in almuce, garter mant. [Pal., c.1460, c.1520.]

OXFORD, MERTON COLLEGE

c.1311 Rich. de Hakeborne, rector, mass vests., hf-eff., in head of floriated cross (cross miss.), lge.
c.1370 Wm. de Durant ?, priest, acad. dr., in head of cross, bad. mut., sm.
c.1420 John Bloxham, warden, in gown, hood (died 1387).
John Whytton, rector, in cassock, hood, under sm. dble. can., supported on br., long shaft with Holy Lamb at base.
1445 John Kyllyngworth, M.A., acad. dr., hf-eff.
1471 Hen. Sever, S.T.P., warden, in cope, with bp. in cope, trip. can. (Poss. the founder, Walter of Merton, bp. of Rochester, to whom Hen. Sever was related.)
1519 John Bowke, M.A., acad. dr., hf-eff., ch., wf.

OXFORD, NEW COLLEGE

1403 Rich. Malford, warden, in cope.
1417 Thos. Cranley, warden, archbp. of Dublin, in archiepiscopal vests., with mitre, cross, trip. can., embattled entab., lge.
1419 John Desford, canon, in cope, hf-eff.
1427 John Lowthe, fellow, acad. dr., cap.
1441 Wm. Hautryve, fellow, acad. dr., cap.
1447 Geoff. Hargreve, fellow, acad. dr.
1451 Walter Wake, fellow, acad. dr., hf-eff.
1468 Thos. Hylle, D.D., fellow, acad. dr., holding cross with 5 wounds.
1472 Thos. Flemyng, fellow, emac. eff. in shroud, sm.
1478 Rich. Wyard, fellow, acad. dr., holding sm. cross (lower hf miss.).
1479 John Palmer, B.A., acad. dr.
1494 Walter Hyll, M.A., warden, in cope.
1507 John Frye, fellow, mass vests., ch., wf., hf-eff.
1508 John London, M.A., scribe of the university, acad. dr.
c.1510 Notary, c.d., inkhorn and penner, sm.
1521 John Rede, S.T.B., warden, in cope.
c.1525 John Young, warden, bp. of Callipolis, episcopal vests., mitre (head miss.), lge.
1592 Walter Bailey, physician to Eliz. I, c.d., marg. inscr., mut., ach.

1601 Hugh Lloyd, D.C.L., fellow, master, in gown, hood, kng., rect. pl.
1619 Anth. Aylworth, prof. of medicine, fellow, in gown, hood, marg. inscr., mut.

OXFORD, QUEEN'S COLLEGE
1477 Nich. Hyenson, fellow, acad. dr., effaced.
c.1518 Robt. Langton, D.C.L., fellow, in cope, cap.
1616 Hen. Robinson, provost, bp. of Carlisle, in rochet, cap, crosier, kng., rect. pl.
1616 Hen. Airay, S.T.D., provost, in gown, hood, cap, kng., rect. pl.

OXFORD, ST JOHN'S COLLEGE
1571 Robt. Harte, scholar, in gown, hood, kng.
1573 Hen. Huchenson, fellow, in gown, hood, kng.
1577 Robt. Shingleton, M.A., fellow, in gown, hood, kng.
1578 John Glover, M.A., fellow, sen. proctor, in gown, hood, kng.

OXFORD, ST ALDGATE
1607 Lewis and Griffin Owen, both M.A.s, bs., Lewis in gown and hood, kng., Griffin, c.d., with cloak, kng.
1612 Arthur Strode, c.d., kng., rect. pl.
1637 Nich. Roope, B.A., gown, hood, kng., rect. pl.

OXFORD, ST CROSS, HOLYWELL
1622 Eliza Franklin, in bed, with 3 child. in shrouds, and 1 chrysom on coverlet, rect. pl.
1625 Agnes Hopper, c.d., with 1 dau., Jane, both kng., rect. pl.

OXFORD, ST MARY MAGDALEN
1580 Wm. Smith, M.A., fellow, physician, in gown, hood, kng.

OXFORD, ST MARY THE VIRGIN
1507 Edm. Croston, in almuce, kng., fig. of St Kath.
1581 Edw. Chernock, c.d., kng., rect. pl.
1584 Malin Boys, c.d., with 7 sons, 5 daus., all kng.

OXFORD, ST MICHAEL
1578 Ralph Flexney, alderman, c.d. 2nd. w. Cath., c.d., kng., rect. pl., ach.
1617 John Pendarves, commoner of Exeter College, in gown, holding book, stg. in pew, rect. pl.

OXFORD, ST PETER IN THE EAST
1478 Wm. Robertson, butler of Queen's College, c.d.
w. Joan, c.d., sm., wn.
1572 Simon Parret, M.A., fellow, proctor, c.d., with 9 sons.
w. Eliz., c.d., with 10 daus., all kng., rect. pl., ach.
1574 Rich. Atkinson, J.P., alderman, five times mayor, c.d., mant., with 5 sons, 6 daus.
w. Annes ?, c.d. [All pal., 16th cent. Flem.]
1599 Rich. Ratcliff, M.D., c.d.
w., c.d., kng., rect. pl.

OXFORD, ST PETER-LE-BAILEY
1419 John Sprunt, mayor, c.d. (head miss.), wn.
c.1420 Woman, c.d.
c.1650 G. Box, c.d.
w. M. Box, c.d., kng. [Pal.]

PYRTON
1522 Thos. Symeon, c.d.
w. Margt., c.d., sm.

ROLLRIGHT, GREAT
1522 Jas. Batersby, rector, mass vests., ch., wf.

ROTHERFIELD GREYS
1387 Sir Robt. de Grey, arm., sin. can., marg. inscr., lge.

SHIPLAKE

c.1540 John Symondes, c.d.
w. Joan, c.d., with 3 sons, 6 daus.

SHIPTON-UNDER-WYCHWOOD

1548 Eliz. Horne, recumbent in shroud, rect. pl. [Pal., c.1494.]

SHIRBURN

1496 Rich. Chamburleyn, arm., with 4 sons.
w. Sybyll, c.d., with 3 daus., all kng.

SOMERTON

1552 Wm. Fermoure, "clerke of the crowne", arm.
w. Eliz., c.d. [Pal., late 15th cent.]

SOULDERN

1514 Thos. Warner, parson, in almuce, sm.

c.1580 John Throckmorton, c.d.

SOUTHLEIGH

1557 Wm. Secoll, c.d.

STADHAMPTON

1498 John Wylmot, c.d.
w. Anne, c.d., with 5 sons, 7 daus.

1508 John Wylmot, c.d.
w. Alys, c.d.

STANTON HARCOURT

1460 Thos. Harecourt, c.d., sm.
Nich. Atherton, c.d., sm., 3 v. sm. effs. of Geo, Alys and Isobel Harcourt below.

1516 Elen Camby, c.d., with 1 son, 1 dau.

1519 Hen. Dodschone, vicar, mass vests.

STEEPLE ASTON

1522 John Foxe, c.d.
w. Joan, c.d., with 5 sons, 5 daus.

STOKE LYNE

1535 Edw. Love, c.d., with 5 sons.
1st w. Alys, c.d., with 3 daus., all kng., fig. of Our Lord in Pity.

1582 Wm. Holt, c.d., with 2 sons.
w. Kath., c.d., with 8 daus., all kng., rect. pl.

STOKE, NORTH

1363? Roger Parkers, rector, canon, in garter mant. (head miss.), hf-eff.

STOKE TALMAGE

1504 John Adene, c.d.
w. Joan, c.d., sm., wn.

1589 John Pettie, arm.
w. Eliz., c.d.

SWINBROOK

c.1470 John Croston, arm.
3 ws., c.d., with 2 sons, 2 daus. by 1st w.

1510 Anth. Fetyplace, arm., tab.

TEW, GREAT

1410 John Wylcotes, arm., liv. coll.
w. Alice, mant., marg. inscr., dble. can., lge, wn.

1513 Wm. Bosby, c.d.
w. Agnes, c.d.

THAME

c.1420 Thos. Quatremayn, arm.
w. Kath., c.d. (both died 1342), with 1 son,
Thos. Quatremayn, arm. (lower hf miss.).
w. Joan, wid. dr., on br., mut.

c.1460 Rich. Quatremayns, councillor to Edw. IV, arm.
w. Sibil, mant. (head miss.), with 1 son, arm., chamfer inscr.

c.1500 Man, c.d.
w., c.d., with 3 sons, 6 daus., wn.

1502 Geoff. Dormer, mcht., c.d.
1st w. Margery, c.d., with 8 daus.
2nd w. Alice, c.d., with 7 sons, 5 daus., chamfer inscr.

1503 Christ. Bridgeman, c.d.
w. Mawde, c.d.
1508 Walter Pratt, c.d.
w. Isabel, c.d., with 3 sons, 3 daus., wn.
1539 Sir John Clerk, arm., tab., kng.
1543 John Galey, c.d. (head miss.).
1597 Edw. Harris, M.A., fellow of New College, c.d., kng.

WATERPERRY
*c.*1370 Isabel Beaufo, c.d., sm., mut.
*c.*1540 Walter Curson, arm.
w. Isabel, c.d., with 8 sons, 7 daus., lge. [Effs. pal., *c.*1440, altered by shading etc.]
*c.*1530 Man, arm., mut.

WATLINGTON
1485 Wm. Frankeleyn, c.d.
w. Sibill, c.d.
1501 Wm. Gibson, in shroud.
w. Maud, in shroud.
1588 Jerem Ewstes, yeoman, c.d.

WHITCHURCH
*c.*1420 Thos. Walysch, arm.
w., c.d.
*c.*1455 Roger Gery, vicar, mass vests., ch., wf.
1610 Peter Winder, curate, in gown, kng.

WITNEY
1500 Rich. Wenman, c.d.
1st w. Anne, c.d., with 3 daus.
2nd w. Cristian, c.d., with 2 daus.
1606 Rich. Ayshcome, c.d.

WOODSTOCK
1441 Rich. Bailly, haberdasher, c.d., sm.
1631 Jerome Keyt, LL.B, fellow of St John's College, in gown, hood, kng., rect. pl.

RUTLAND

BRAUNSTON
1596 Kenelme Cheseldyn, c.d.
w. Winefrid, c.d., both mut., ach.

CASTERTON, LITTLE
*c.*1410 Sir Thos. Burton, arm., SS coll.
w. Margery, mant., marg. inscr., mut.

LYDDINGTON
1486 Helyn Hardy, c.d.
1530 Edw. Watson, J.P., c.d.
w. Emme, c.d., with 5 sons (heads miss.), 10 daus.

SHROPSHIRE

ACTON BURNELL
1382 Sir Nich. Burnell, arm., sin. can., lge.

ACTON SCOTT
1571 Thos. Mytton, c.d., with 9 sons.
w. Eliz., c.d., with 2 daus., all kng.

ADDERLEY
*c.*1390 Abbot or bp., full vests., holding book and crosier (head miss.), lge.
1560 Sir Robt. Nedeham, arm.
w. Agnes, c.d., with 7 sons, 2 daus.

ALVELEY
1616 John Grove, c.d.

BURFORD
*c.*1370 Dame Eliz. de Cornewaylle, c.d. (lower hf repaired), marg. inscr., mut., lge.

DRAYTON
*c.*1580 Rowland Corbet, c.d., kng., rect. pl.

EDGEMOND
1533 Francis Yonge, in shroud.
w. Anne, c.d., with 9 sons, 5 daus.

GLAZELEY
1599 Thos. Wylde, c.d.
w. Eliz., c.d., with 4 sons, 2 daus., ach.

HARLEY
c. 1475 Man, arm.
w., c.d., with 8 sons (3 heads miss.), 5 daus. (1 head miss.). (Poss. of the Lacon fam.)

IGHTFIELD
c. 1495 Dame Margery Calveley, c.d., with 4 sons, 4 daus., trip. can., with St J.B., mut., marg. inscr., lge.
1497 Wm. Maynwaryng, c.d. (head rest.), lge.

MYDDLE
1564 Arthur Chambre, c.d.
w. Margt., c.d., with 1 son, 1 dau.

PLOWDEN HALL, PRIVATE CHAPEL
1557 Humph. Plowden, c.d.
w. Eliz., c.d., with 7 daus. (From Bishop's Castle church.)

SHREWSBURY, ST ALKMUND
c. 1500 Margery Humphreston, c.d.
1st hus. John Hervy, c.d.
2nd hus. John Humphreston, c.d.

TONG
1467 Sir Wm. Vernon, knight constable of England, arm.
w. Margt., wid. dr., with 7 sons, 3 daus., marg. inscr.
1510 Ralph Elcok, a brother of the College, in surplice, almuce, wn.
1517 Arthur Vernon, M.A., acad. dr., ch. above head.

UPTON CRESSETT
1640 Rich. Cressett, c.d.
w. Jane, c.d., with 2 sons, 3 daus., all kng., rect. pl.

WENLOCK, MUCH
1592 Rich. Ridley, c.d.
w. Eleanor, c.d., kng.

WITHINGTON
1512 John Onley, arm., mut.
w. Joan, c.d., with 7 sons.
1530 Adam Graffton, chaplain to Edw. V, archdeacon, warden, rector, in cope.

SOMERSETSHIRE

AXBRIDGE
1493 Roger Harper, mcht., c.d.
w. Joan, c.d., kng.

BACKWELL
1604 Rice Davis, c.d.
w. Dorothy, c.d., with 3 sons, 3 daus., all kng., rect. pl., ach.

BANWELL
c. 1480 Man, c.d.
w., c.d., sm.
1503 John Martok, physician, in cope.
1554 John Blandon, c.d. (head miss.), sm.

BATCOMBE
1613 Philip Biss, D.D., pastor, archdeacon, in gown, hood, rect. pl.

BATH ABBEY
1639 Sir Geo. Ivy, arm.
w. Susanna, with 4 sons, 4 daus., all kng., rect. pl.

BECKINGTON
1485 John Seyntmour, arm.
w. Eliz., c.d.
1505 John Compton, c.d.
w. Edith, c.d., with 5 sons.

BROOMFIELD
c. 1443 Rich. Silverton, chaplain, mass vests. (head miss.), wn.

BURNETT

1575 John Cutte, mayor of Bristol, c.d., with 8 sons.
w. Joan, with 4 daus., all kng.

CHEDDAR

1442 Sir Thos. Chedder, arm.
c.1475 Dame Isabel Chedder, wid. dr.

CHEDZOY

c.1490 Man, arm., crest of a ram on helmet above head, lge.

CHURCHILL

1572 Raphe Jenyns, arm.
w. Jane, c.d., 3 achs.

COMBE FLOREY

1485 Florence Fraunceys, c.d.
1526 Nich. Fraunceys, arm.

COSSINGTON

1524 John Brent, arm.
w. Maud, c.d., marg. inscr.

CREWKERNE

1525 Thos. Golde, arm., kng., sm.

CROSCOMBE

1606 Jas. Biss, c.d., with 6 sons.
w., c.d., with 6 daus., all kng., rect. pl.
1625 Wm. Bisse, c.d., with 9 sons.
w. c.d., with 9 daus., all kng., rect. pl.

DOWLISH WAKE

1528 Sir Geo. Speke, arm., marg. inscr., mut.

DUNSTER

c.1520 John Wyther, c.d.
w. Agnes, c.d.

FIVEHEAD

c.1565 Jane Seymour, c.d. [Pal., 14th cent. Flem.]

HINTON ST GEORGE

c.1590 Adam Martin, c.d.
w. Eliz., c.d. with 6 sons, 5 daus., rect. pl.

HUTTON

1496 John Payne, arm., liv. coll.
w. Eliz., c.d., with 4 sons, 7 daus.
1528 Thos. Payne, arm.
w. Eliz., c.d., with 8 sons, 3 daus., all kng.

ILMINSTER

c.1440 Sir Wm. Wadham, arm.
m. Joan, wid. dr., each under trip. can. with super can., lge.
1618 Nich. Wadham, founder of the college, arm.
w. Dorothy, c.d., v. lge., ach.

KITTISFORD

1524 Rich Bluett, arm.
w. Agnes, c.d.

LANGRIDGE

1441 Eliz. Walsshe, wid. dr.

LUCCOMBE

1615 Wm. Harrison, c.d.

LYDIARD, BISHOP'S

1594 Nich. Grobham, c.d., with 3 sons.
w. Eleanor, c.d., with 2 daus., all kng., rect. pl.

MINEHEAD

1440 Joan ? , mant. (lower hf miss.), sin. can., marg. inscr., both bad. mut.

MONKTON, WEST

c.1440 Hen., Abyndon, S.T.P., acad. dr., hf-eff., mut., sm.

MUDFORD

1617 Wm. Whitbye, c.d.
w. Annis, c.d., sm. (On table tomb, S.E. of churchyard.)

PETHERTON, NORTH

1652 Kath. Morley, kng., rect. pl.

PETHERTON, SOUTH

c.1430 Sir Giles Daubeney ?, arm.
1st w. Joan, mant., dble. can., marg. inscr. (rest. 1883).

1442 Dame Mary Daubeney, mant., wn.

PORTBURY

1621 Sara Kemish, with 2 daus., kng., and 2 infant sons, rect. pl., sm.

ST DECUMANS

1571 Sir John Wyndham, arm.
w. Eliz., c.d.

1596 John Windham, son of above, arm.
w. Florence, c.d., lge., ach.

1616 Edm. Windham, arm.

SHEPTON MALLET

1649 Wm. Strode, arm., with 6 sons.
w. Joan, c.d., with 3 daus., all kng., rect. pl. with fig. of Death, etc., lge.

STOGUMBER

1585 Margery Windham, c.d.

SWAINSWICK

1439 Edm. Forde, c.d.

THORNE ST MARGARET

c. 1600 John Worthe, c.d.

TINTINHULL

1464 John Heth, rector, canon, in cope, ¾-eff.

WEARE

c. 1500 John Bedbere, c.d.

WEDMORE

c. 1630 Geo. Hodges, buff-coat, pike and sword, rect. pl.

WELLS CATHEDRAL

c. 1460 Priest, in cope, hf-eff.

1618 Humph. Willis, c.d., kng., rect. pl.

WELLS, ST CUTHBERT

1623 Frauncis Hayes, c.d., kng., rect. pl., v. sm.

YEOVIL

c. 1460 Martin Forester, friar, in gown, hood, hf-eff. (On lectern, 2 effs.)

1519 Giles Penne, c.d.
w. Isabel, c.d.

STAFFORDSHIRE

AUDLEY

1385 Sir Thos. de Audeley, arm., lge. (new head engraved 1914).

1628 Wm. Abnet, c.d.

BIDDULPH

1603 Wm. Bowyer, c.d.
w. Anne, c.d., with 8 sons, 7 daus., also 2 sons, by Anne's 1st hus., rect. pl., ach.

BLORE-RAY

1498 Wm. Basset, c.d. (head miss.).
w. Joan, wid. dr., marg. inscr., mut.

BROMLEY, ABBOT'S

1463 John Draycote, burgess, c.d., ¾-eff.

CLIFTON CAMPVILLE

c. 1360 Woman, c.d., hf-eff. on br., bad. mut. [Pal. man in arm., *c.* 1300.]

ECCLESHALL

1672 Kath. Yong, kng., rect. pl., sm., ach.

HANBURY

c. 1480 Priest, in cope, wn.

HORTON

1589 John Wedgwood, c.d.
w. Mary, c.d., with 3 sons, 5 daus., all kng., rect. pl.

KINVER

1528 Sir Edw. Grey, arm.
2 ws., c.d., with 7 sons, 10 daus., marg. inscr., mut.

LEEK

1597 John Ashenhurst, c.d.
1st w. Joyce, c.d., with 2 sons, 5 daus.
2nd w. Alice, c.d., with 2 sons.
3rd w. Kath., c.d.
4th w. Mary, c.d., with 1 dau., all kng., rect. pl., ach.

MADELEY
1518 John Egerton, c.d.
w. Ellen, c.d.
1586 Robt. Hawkins, c.d., aged 14½, kng., sm.

NORBURY
1360 Hawise Botiller, wid. dr.

OKEOVER
1447 Wm., 5th Lord Zouch of Harringworth, arm.
1st w. Alice, mant.
2nd w. Eliz., flowing hair., trip. can., marg. inscr., *then altered as memorial to*
1538 Humph. Oker,
w. Isabel, with 13 child. (The brass was stolen in 1857 and broken up into 55 pieces; these are all now mounted on a board.)

RUGELEY, OLD CHURCH
1566 John Weston, c.d., marg. inscr.

STONE
1619 Thos. Crompton, arm.
w. Ethelred, c.d., with 4 sons, 2 daus., rect. pl., ach.

TRENTHAM
1591 Sir Rich. Leveson, arm.
w. Mary, with 1 son, arm., 2 daus., all kng., ach.
At Elford, the brass to
1621 John Hill, rector, *is a modern restoration.*

SUFFOLK

ACTON
1302 Sir Robt. de Bures, cross-legged, mail surcoat, shield on arm, lge.
1435 Alice Bryan, wid. dr., trip. can., bad mut., lge.
1528 Hen. Bures, arm.
1589 Edm. Daniel, c.d.
w. Margt., c.d., with 5 sons, mut., sm.
1598 John Daniel, c.d., sm.

ALDEBURGH
1519 Benet ? , c.d. (head miss.), with 3 sons.
*c.*1520 Woman, c.d.
*c.*1570 Emme Fox, c.d., with 7 sons, 7 daus.
1601 John James, c.d.
w. Joan, c.d., with 2 sons, 3 daus., rect. pl.
1606 Wm. Bence, chief burgess, c.d., w. Mary, c.d.
1612 Alexander Bence, bailiff, c.d., with 9 sons, 2 daus.
1635 John Bence, bailiff, c.d.
1st w. Mary, c.d. with 4 sons, 2 daus.
2nd w. Eliz., c.d.

AMPTON
*c.*1480 Man, c.d.
w., c.d., with 7 daus., all kng. (Of the Coket fam.)
*c.*1480 Woman, c.d.
*c.*1490 Woman, c.d. [Pal., *c.*1470.]
*c.*1490 2 sons.

ASH BOCKING
1585 Edm. Bockinge, arm.
1st w. Frances, c.d., with 1 dau.
2nd w. Mary, c.d., with 1 dau.

ASSINGTON
*c.*1500 Man, arm.
w., c.d.

BARHAM
1514 Robt. Southwell, J.P., c.d.
w. Cecily, c.d., marg inscr.

BARNINGHAM
1499 Wm. Goche, rector, acad. dr., sm.

BARROW
1570 Sir Clement Heigham, chief baron of the exchequer to Q.

Mary, arm., with 1 son, in shroud.
1st w. Anne, c.d., with 5 daus.
2nd w. Anne, c.d., with 2 daus., all kng., ach.

BARSHAM

c. 1415 Man, arm., SS coll., lge.

BELSTEAD

1518 John Goldingham, arm.
1st w. Joan, c.d.
2nd w. Thomasin, c.d.

BENHALL

1598 Edw. Duke, c.d.
w. Dorothy, c.d., with 10 sons, 6 daus.
1611 Ambrose Duke, arm.
w. Eliz., c.d.

BERGHOLT, EAST

1639 Robt. Alfounder, c.d.

BILDESTON

1599 Alice Wade, c.d., with 2 sons, 4 daus.

BRADLEY, LITTLE

c. 1510 Thos. Underhill ?, c.d., kng.
w., c.d., kng.
c. 1530 Thos Knighton, arm. (head miss.), with 2 sons, 1 dau.
1584 John Daye, printer, c.d., with 6 sons.
2nd w. Als, c.d., with 5 daus., all kng., also 2 chrysoms, ach.
1605 John le Hunt, c.d.
w. Jane, c.d.
1612 Thos. Soame, arm., with 5 sons.
w. Eliz., c.d., with 2 daus., all kng., rect. pl.

BRAISEWORTH, OLD CHURCH

1569 Alex. Newton, arm.

BREDFIELD

1611 Leonard Farrington, c.d.
w. Eliz., c.d., with 6 sons, 2 daus., sm.

BRUISYARD

1611 Eliz. Hobert, c.d.
Mary Brudenell, c.d., ws. of Michiel Hare.

BRUNDISH

c. 1360 Esmound de Burnedisshe, parson, mass vests.
1559 John Colby, arm., ach.
1560 John Colby, arm.
w. Alice, c.d., with 4 sons, 9 daus., ach.
c. 1570 Margt. Colby, c.d. (head miss.).
1571? Thos. Glemham, c.d., kng., ach.

BURGATE

1409 Sir Wm. de Burgate, arm.
w. Eleanor, mant., dble. can., marg. inscr., lge.

BURY ST EDMUNDS, ST MARY

c. 1480 Man., c.d.
w., c.d., kng.
1514 John Fynexs, archdeacon, in almuce.

CAMPSEY ASH

1504 Alex. Inglisshe, parish priest, mass vests., ch., wf.

CARLTON

c. 1480 Man, c.d.
c. 1490 Man, c.d.

CHATTISHAM

1592 Marie Revers, c.d., with 3 sons, 7 daus.

COOKLEY

1595 Wm. Browne, c.d.
w. Margery, c.d., with 4 sons, 4 daus. [Daus. pal.]

COWLINGE

1599 Robt. Higham, c.d.
w. Margt., c.d., with 5 sons, 5 daus.

DARSHAM

1641 Anne Bedingfield, c.d.

DEBENHAM

c.1425 John Framlingham ?, arm.
w. Margt ?, c.d., hf-effs.

DENHAM, NR EYE

1574 Anth. Bedingfield, c.d. [Pal., c.1500, Flem.]

DENSTONE

1524 Hen. Everard, arm., tab.
w. Margt., her. mant.

c.1530 Woman, c.d. (Of the Drury fam.)

DEPDEN

1572 Anne Drewry, c.d.
1st hus. Geo. Waldegrave, arm., with 5 sons, 2 daus.
Anne Drewry (same), with 2nd hus., Sir Thos. Jermyn, arm., with 2 sons, all kng.

EASTON

c.1425 John Brook ?, arm.

1584 John Wingfield, arm.

1601 Radclif Wingfield, c.d.

EDWARDSTONE

1636 Benj. Brand, c.d.
w. Eliz., c.d., with 6 sons, 6 daus., ach.

ELLOUGH

c.1520 Woman, c.d., sm.

1607 Margt. Chewt, c.d., sm.

ELMHAM, SOUTH, ST JAMES

c.1500 Man, c.d.
w., c.d.

EUSTON

c.1480 Man, c.d.
w., c.d.

c.1520 Man, c.d. (lower hf miss.).
w., c.d. (head miss.).

c.1520 Woman, c.d., sm.

c.1530 ? Rokewood, arm. (lower hf miss.).
w., c.d.

EYKE

c.1430 John Staverton, baron of the exchequer, in robes (head miss.).
w., c.d. (head mut.).

1619 Hen. Mason, M.A., minister, in gown.

FORNHAM, ALL SAINTS

1599 Thos. Barwick, prof. of medicine, c.d., with staff (lower hf miss.).

FRESSINGFIELD

1489 Wm. Brewes, arm.
w. Eliz., c.d.

GORLESTON

c.1320 Man, arm. (legs miss.). (Of the Bacon fam.)

HADLEIGH

1592 Thos. Alabaster, clothier, c.d., kng. beneath arch, rect. pl.

1593 Anne Still, c.d.

1637 John Alabaster, clothier, mayor, c.d., kng. beneath arch.

1637 Rich. Glanfield, c.d., ¾-eff.
w. Eliz., c.d., ¾-eff., clasping hands, rect. pl.

HALESWORTH

1476 John Everard, c.d., hf-eff.

1581 w. of John Browne, c.d. (lower hf miss.), with 6 sons, 10 daus., all mut. (These effs. were retrieved from the river Waveney, 1825.)

HAWKEDON

c.1510 Man, c.d.
w., c.d., with 2 sons, 5 daus., wn.

HAWSTEAD

c.1500 Boy, c.d.

c.1500 Girl, flowing hair.

c.1530 Ursula Alington, c.d., sm.

1557 Sir Wm. Drury, arm., eyes closed.

1st w. Jane, c.d., eyes closed.
2nd w. Eliz., c.d., with 13 daus., ach.

HOLBROOK

c.1480 Man, arm., with 6 sons.

HONINGTON

1594 Geo. Duke, c.d.

IPSWICH, ST CLEMENT

1583 John Tye, mcht. portman, c.d.
1st w. Ales, c.d., with 2 sons, 3 daus.
2nd w. Julyan, c.d., with 3 sons, 6 daus., wn.
1607 Wm. Cocke, c.d., wn.

IPSWICH, ST MARY TOWER

c.1475 Notary, c.d., penner and ink-horn, lge.
c.1500 Man, c.d.
2 ws., c.d.
1506 Alys Baldry, c.d.
1st hus. Robt. Wymbyll, notary, c.d., penner and inkhorn.
2nd hus. Thos. Baldry, c.d., with 4 sons, 5 daus.
c.1520 Man, c.d.
2 ws. (head of 1 miss.), with 2 sons, 3 daus., on br., mut.

IPSWICH, ST NICHOLAS

1475 Wm. Style, c.d.
w. Isabel, c.d.
c.1490 Wm. Stiles ?, c.d.
c.1600 Man, c.d.
w., c.d.

IPSWICH, ST PETER

1604 John Knapp, mcht. portman, c.d.
w. Martha, c.d., with 4 sons, 8 daus., ach.

IXWORTH

1567 Rich. Codington, c.d.
w. Eliz., c.d., with 1 son, 1 dau. by her 1st hus. Thos. Bucknham, all kng.

KENTON

1524 John Garneys, arm., tab., with 6 sons.
w. Eliz., her mant., with 9 daus., all kng., rect. pl. with crucifix, ach.

KETTLEBURGH

1593 Arthur Pennyng, c.d.
2 ws., c.d., both mut.

KNODISHALL

1460 John Jenney, arm.
1st w. Maude, c.d.

LAKENHEATH

c.1530 Man, c.d.
w., c.d., sm.

LAVENHAM

1486 Thos. Spryng, with 4 sons.
w. Margt., with 6 daus., all in shrouds rising from tombs.
c.1560 Allaine Dister, clothier, c.d., with 3 sons.
w. Agnes, c.d., with 3 daus., all kng., rect. pl. (See this woman's brass at St Peters, Colchester, Essex.)

LETHERINGHAM

1389 Sir John de Wyngefeld, arm. arms on jupon, lge.
c.1490 Man, arm.

LIDGATE

c.1380 Priest, mass vests., sm. (Once in head of cross.)

LOWESTOFT

c.1500 2 skeletons, in shrouds (heads miss.).
c.1540 Man, c.d.
w., c.d. (head miss.).

MELFORD, LONG

c.1420 Woman, c.d. (Poss. Margery or Anne Clopton.)
c.1420 Thos. Clopton ?, c.d.
c.1480 Margery Clopton ?, her. mant., sin. can., mut.

c.1480 Alice Harleston, her. dr., with arms on kirtle and mant.
1577 Francis Clopton, arm.
1615 Roger Martin, c.d.
1st w. Ursula, c.d., with 4 sons, 2 daus.
2nd w. Margt., c.d., with 2 sons, 2 daus.
1624 Rich. Martin, c.d.
1st w. Eleanor, c.d., with 2 sons, 1 chrysom.
2nd w., c.d., with chrysom.
3rd w., c.d., sm.

MELTON, OLD CHURCH

c.1430 Man, c.d. (ft miss.).
w., c.d., with 1 son, a priest, acad. dr., trip. can., bad. mut.

MENDHAM

1615 Cecily Freston, c.d.
1616 Rich. Freston, c.d.
1634 Rich. Freston, c.d., ach.

MENDLESHAM

c.1420 John Knyvet ?, arm.

MICKFIELD

1617 Peter Preston, c.d.
w. Thomasin, c.d., sm., rect. pl.

MIDDLETON

c.1500 Man, c.d.
w., c.d., sm., wn.
1610 Anth. Pettow, yeoman, c.d.

MILDENHALL

1618 Sir Hen. Warner, arm.

MONEWDEN

1595 Thos. Reve, fellow of Caius College, in gown, hood, kng., rect. pl., ach.

NAYLAND

c.1485 w. of John Hacche, c.d., with book under arm. (lower hf miss.).
c.1500 Man, c.d.
w., c.d., dble. can., marg. inscr., both mut.
1516 Rich. Davy, c.d.
w. Joan, c.d., v. wn.

NETTLESTEAD

c.1500 Man, arm., sm.

OCCOLD

c.1490 Wm. Corbald, c.d.
w. Joan, c.d.

ORFORD

c.1480 Man, c.d., sm.
c.1490 Woman, c.d., with 3 sons, 7 daus., sm.
c.1500 Woman, c.d.
2 hus., c.d., sm.
c.1510 Man, c.d., sm.
c.1510 Man, c.d., sm.
c.1510 Woman, c.d., with 6 sons, 6 daus., sm.
c.1520 Man, c.d.
w., c.d., sm.
1580 Jas. Coo, mayor, c.d., with 3 sons.
1591 Jas. Coe, mayor, c.d.
w. Eliz., c.d., with 6 sons, 6 daus.
1605 Bridgett Bence, c.d., with 1 dau., Jone Wheatley, with 1 son, 3 daus., marg. inscr.
1640 John Coggeshall, mayor, c.d., with 5 sons.
w. Eliz., c.d., with 2 daus., all kng., rect. pl., ach.

PAKEFIELD

1417? John Bowf, c.d.
w. Augnes, c.d., with 2 sons, 9 daus., marg. inscr., mut., wn.
1451 Rich. Folcard, rector, acad. dr., hf-eff.

PETISTREE

1580 Frances Bacon, c.d.
1st w. Eliz., c.d.
2nd w. Mary, c.d.

PETTAUGH

c.1530 Man, c.d. (Of the Fastolfe fam.)
w., c.d., with 4 daus., sm.

PLAYFORD
1400 Sir Geo. Felbrigg, arm., arms on jupon, marg. inscr., bad. mut., lge.

POLSTEAD
c. 1430 Nich. Blundell ?, priest, mass vests.
c. 1490 Man, c.d.
w., c.d., with 5 sons.

RAYDON
1479 Eliz., dau. of Thos. Reydon, c.d. (head miss.), sm.

REDGRAVE
1609 Anne Butts, wid. dr., marg. inscr.

RINGSFIELD
c. 1595 Nich. Garneys, arm., tab., with 6 sons.
w. Anne, her mant., with 5 daus., all kng., rect. pl., ach.

ROUGHAM
1405 Sir Roger Drury, arm.
w. Margery, mant., lge.

SAXHAM, GREAT
1632 John Eldred, alderman, c.d., 2 achs.

SIBTON
1574 Edm. Chapman, c.d., with 8 sons.
w. Margt., c.d., with 5 daus., all kng.
1582 John Chapman, c.d. (head miss.).
w. Julyan, c.d., mut., with 3 sons, 3 daus.
1626 Edm. Chapman, c.d., with 8 sons.
w. Marryan, c.d., with 5 daus., all kng., rect. pl.

SOTTERLEY
1479 Thos. Playters, arm.
w. Anne, c.d.
c. 1480 John Bomsted ?, arm., sm.
1572 Thos. Playters, arm.
1578 Thomazine Playters, c.d., with 1 dau., Susan.
c. 1630 Jane Playters, c.d., kng., chamfer inscr.
c. 1630 Christ. Playters, arm.

SOUTHOLT
1585 Margt. Armiger, c.d.

SPEXHALL
1593 Silvester Browne, c.d., with 6 sons.

STOKE-BY-CLARE
c. 1530 Woman, c.d.
1597 Edw. Talkarne, c.d., ach.
1605 Alice Talkarne, wid. dr.

STOKE-BY-NAYLAND
c. 1400 Woman, mant. (Poss. Kath., w. of Sir Wm. Tendring.)
1408 Sir Wm. Tendring, arm., bare-headed, with beard, lge.
c. 1535 Lady Kath., w. of John Howard, Duke of Norfolk, her. mant. (died 1452).
1590 Two groups of child. of Francis Mannock,
1 son, 5 daus. by 1st w.
1 son, 3 daus. by 2nd w.
1632 Dorothy Mannock, c.d.

STONHAM ASPALL
1606 John Metcalfe, rector, in gown.

STOWMARKET
1638 Ann Tyrell, aged 8½, in shroud.

STRATFORD ST MARY
1558 Edw. Crane, c.d.
w. Eliz., c.d.

TANNINGTON
1612 Ann Dade, c.d.

THURLOW, GREAT
c. 1460 Man, arm., with salade.
w., wid. dr.

c.1460 Woman, wid. dr. (head miss.).
c.1530 Thos. Underhill, arm. (lower hf miss.).
w. Anne, c.d., with 9 sons.

THURLOW, LITTLE
c.1520 Man, arm.
w., c.d., wn.

UFFORD
1488 Symon Brooke, c.d. (upper hf miss.).
1st w. Emot, c.d.
2nd w. Margt., c.d.
3rd w. Alice, c.d.
1598 Rich. Ballett, goldsmith, skeleton on tomb, rect. pl.

WALDINGFIELD, LITTLE
1506 John Colman, c.d., with 6 sons, 7 daus.
1526 Robt. Appleton, arm.
w. Mary, c.d.
c.1530 Woman, c.d., sm. (Poss. of the Brewse fam.)
1544 John Wyncoll, clothier, c.d.

WALTON
1459 Wm. Tabard, c.d.
w. Agnes, c.d.
1612 Wm. Simond, aged 11, c.d., kng., rect. pl., sm., wn.

WENHAM, LITTLE
1514 Thos. Brewse, arm.
w. Jane, c.d., with 2 sons, 3 daus., dble. can., marg. inscr., mut.

WICKHAMBROOK
1597 Thos. Burrough, c.d.
1st w. Eliz., c.d., with 2 sons, 1 dau.
2nd w. Brigett, c.d., with 3 sons, 3 daus., rect. pl., ach.

WICKHAM SKEITH
c.1530 Woman, wid. dr., kng., with 3 daus.

WILBY
c.1530 Man, c.d., also design of sheep running.

WOODBRIDGE
1601 John Shorland, aged 7, c.d.

WORLINGHAM
1511 Nich. Wrenne, c.d.
w. Mary, c.d.

WORLINGWORTH
c.1520 4 sons, 1 a priest, acad. dr., and 7 daus.

WRENTHAM
1400 Ele Bowet, c.d.
1593 Humph. Brewster, arm., ach.

YAXLEY
1598 Andrew Felgate, c.d.

YOXFORD
1428 John Norwiche, arm.
w. Maud, c.d.
1485 Tomesin Tendryng, in shroud, with 3 sons, 2 daus., in shrouds, and 2 daus., c.d., flowing hair, lge.
1613 Anth. Cooke, c.d.
1618 Christian Foxe, c.d., and sm. bust of 1 son.
1618 Joan Brooke, c.d.

The following brasses from St Mary Quay, Ipswich, are now in the care of Ipswich Museum, Suffolk.
1525 Thos. Pownder, mcht. c.d.
w. Emme, c.d., stg. with 2 sons, 6 daus., kng., marg. inscr., rect. pl., Flem.
1565 Hen. Toolye, portman, c.d.
w. Alice, c.d., with 1 son, 2 daus., all kng.
1583 w. of Christ. Merell, c.d.

SURREY

ADDINGTON

1540 Thos. Hatteclyff, master of the household to Hen. VIII, arm.

1544 John Leigh, c.d.
w. Isabel, c.d., with 2 sons, 3 daus., marg. inscr., ach.

ALBURY, OLD CHURCH

1440 John Weston, arm., wn. (head rest. 1920).

BEDDINGTON

1414 Philipe, dau. of Nich. Carrew, and sm. hf-effs. of 7 b., 6 s., marg. inscr.

1432 Nich. Carrew, c.d.
1st w. Isabel, c.d., fine dble. can., marg. inscr., lge.

*c.*1430 Man, c.d.
Woman, c.d. (Poss. Thos. Carew and s. Isabel.)

1437 Roger Elmebrygge, arm.

1507 Kath. Berecroft, c.d.
s. Eliz., wid. dr., w. of Wm. Barton, sm.

1520 Sir Rich. Carew, arm., tab.
w. Malyn, her. mant., chamfer inscr. (nearly all completely restored).

BETCHWORTH

1533 Wm. Wardysworth, vicar, mass vests., ch., wf.

BLETCHINGLEY

*c.*1470 Woman, c.d., flowing hair, sm.

*c.*1510 Priest, mass vests.

*c.*1520 5 daus., 6 sons, 6 daus.

1541 Thos. Warde, c.d.
w. Joan, c.d., Trin.

BOOKHAM, GREAT

1433 Eliz. Slyfeld, c.d., sm., wn.

1597 Eliz. Slyfeld, c.d.

1598 Hen. Slyfeld, c.d.
w. Eliz., c.d., with 6 sons, 4 daus.

1668 Robt. Shiers, of the Inner Temple, c.d., holding book.

BYFLEET

*c.*1480 Thos. Teylar, rector, canon, in almuce.

CARSHALTON

*c.*1485 Nich. Gaynesford, esq. for the body to Edw. IV, Hen. VII, arm., with 4 sons, the eldest arm., the 2nd a priest, acad. dr.
w. Margt., c.d., suns and roses on coll.

1493 Walter Gaynesford, chaplain, mass vests., ch., wf. (lower hf miss.).

1497 Thos. Elynbrigge, J.P., arm. (lower hf miss.), dble. can., mut., with Our Lady of Pity.

1524 Joan Burton, c.d.

CHARLWOOD

1553 Nich. Saunder, arm., kng., with 4 sons, stg.
w. Alys, c.d., kng., with 6 daus., stg.

CHEAM

*c.*1390 Man, c.d. (centre part miss.).

*c.*1390 Man, c.d., hf-eff.

1458 John Compton, c.d.
w. Joan, c.d., hf-effs.

1459 Wm. Wodeward, c.d., hf-eff.

*c.*1475 John Yerde, arm., liv. coll., v. sm., wn.

1542 Thos. Fromond, c.d., with 6 sons.
w. Eliz., with 4 daus. All kng., Trin. [All pal., various dates.]

CHIPSTEAD

1614 Lucy, dau. of Lactansius Roper, c.d., sm.

COBHAM

*c.*1550 Man, arm., slightly mut. [Pal., *c.*1510, a priest, mass vests., ch., wf., on pivot.]

COMPTON
1508 Thos. Gennyn, c.d.
w. Margt., c.d., with 2 sons, wn.

CRANLEY
c.1510 Rich. Carington ?, priest, mass vests., scrolls from mouth, hf-eff, sm.

CROWHURST
1450 John Gaynesford, sen., arm.
1460 John Gaynesford, arm.

CROYDON, ST JOHN
1512 Gabriel Silvester, rector, prebendary, in cope.
1544 7 daus. of Thos. Heron.
1562 Wm. Heron, J.P., arm.
w. Alse, c.d. (lower hf miss.).

DITTON, LONG
1527 Robt. Castleton, J.P., c.d.
w. Eliz., c.d., with 6 daus.
1616 Rich. Hatton, c.d.
w. Mary, c.d.

DITTON, THAMES
1559 Erasmus Forde, arm.
w. Julyan, c.d., with 6 sons, 12 daus., all kng., rect. pl., ach.
1580 Julyan Boothe, c.d.
1st hus. Cuthbert Blakedon, serjeant of the confectionery to Hen. VIII, c.d., with 6 child.
2nd hus. John Boothe, gentleman usher to Hen. VIII, Edw. VI, c.d., with 5 child.
1582 John Polstead, c.d.
w. Anne, c.d., with 4 daus., all kng.
1587 Robt. Smythe, c.d.
w. Kath., c.d., with 4 sons, 3 daus., all kng.
Wm. Notte, c.d.
w. Eliz., dau. of R. Smythe, c.d., with 14 sons, 5 daus., all kng., ach.

1590 John Cheke, c.d.
w. Isabel, c.d., with 6 sons.

EGHAM
1576 Anth. Bond, scrivener, c.d.
1st w., c.d., with 1 son.
2nd w., c.d., all kng., rect. pl.

EWELL
1519 Lady Jane Iwarby, her. mant.
1521 Margery Treghstin, c.d., wn.
1577 Lady Dorothy, c.d., w. of Sir Laur. Taylare, with 5 sons, 5 daus. by her 1st hus. Allen Horde, also 2nd son, Edm. Horde, c.d., and his w. with 3 sons, 3 daus. (renewed 1912). [Pal., various dates.]

FARLEY
1495 John Brook, poulterer, c.d.
w. Ame, c.d., with 4 sons, 1 dau., sm.

FARNHAM
1594 Benet Jay, c.d.
w. Eliz., c.d., with 3 sons, 3 daus., all kng., rect. pl., ach.
1597 Sibil Jay, c.d., with 6 child., 1 son and 2 daus. by each hus., Thos. Lloide and Francis Jay, all kng., rect. pl.

GODALMING
1509 Thos. Purvoche, c.d.
w. Joan, c.d.
1595 John Barker, arm.

GODALMING, WYATT'S ALMSHOUSES
1619 Rich. Wyatt, carpenter, founder of the almshouses, c.d.
w. Margt., c.d., with 3 sons, 3 daus., all kng., rect. pl.

GUILDFORD, HOLY TRINITY
c.1500 John Wheeler ?, c.d.
1607 Maurice Abbot, c.d.
w. Alice, c.d., with 6 sons, all kng., rect. pl.

GUILDFORD, ST MARY

c. 1500 Man, c.d.
w., c.d., sm.

HORLEY

c. 1420 Woman, c.d., SS coll., sin. can., (Of the Salman fam.) *Appropriated by inscr. to*

1516 Joan, w. of John Fenner.

c. 1510 Man, c.d.

HORSELL

1603 John Sutton, c.d., with 2 sons, 1 dau.

1603 Thos. Sutton, bachelor, c.d., eldest son of above.

1619 Thos. Edmunds, carpenter, c.d.
w. Anne, c.d., with 5 sons, 2 daus.

HORSLEY, EAST

c. 1390 Robt. de Brantyngham, c.d., hf-eff.

1478 John Bowthe, bp. of Exeter, episcopal vests., mitre, crosier, kng.

1498 John Snellyng, c.d.
w. Alys, c.d., with 6 sons, 5 daus., sm.

1504 8 sons, 5 daus. of Thos. Snelling.

KINGSTON-UPON-THAMES

1437 Robt. Skern, c.d.
w. Joan, mant.

1488 John Hertcombe, c.d. (head miss.).
w. Kath., c.d., kng., sm.

LEATHERHEAD

c. 1470 Man, c.d. (ft miss.), with 3 sons, 3 daus., wn.

LEIGH

1449 John Arderne, c.d.
w. Eliz., mant., with 3 sons, mut., 3 daus.

c. 1450 Susan Arderne, dau. of above, c.d., sm.

LINGFIELD

1375 Lady Eliz. Cobham, mant., lge., partly rest.

1403 Sir Reginald Cobham, arm., marg. inscr., lge.

1417 John Hadresham, arm.

1420 Dame Eleanor Cobham, mant. (head rest.), sin. can., marg. inscr.

c. 1420 Kath. Stoket, c.d., hf-eff., sm.

c. 1440 Priest, mass vests. (head miss.), effaced.

1445 John Wyche, master of the college, mass vests., hf-eff.

c. 1450 Woman, c.d., flowing hair, sm.

1458 Jas. Veldon, priest of the college, mass vests., hf-eff., sm.

1469 John Swetecok, master of the college, mass vests.

1503 John Knoyll, master of the college, mass vests.

MERSTHAM

1463 John Ballard, c.d.
w. Margt., c.d., sm.

1473 Isabel, c.d., with 7 daus.
Anne, c.d., ws. of John Elmebrygge, sm.

1498 John Newdegate, arm., liv. coll.

1507 Thos. Elmerugge, arm.
w. Joan, c.d.

1587 Rich., son of Nich. Best, c.d., sm. (A chrysom stolen in 1860 was renewed in 1911 to another son, Peter.)

MICKLEHAM

1513 Wm. Wyddowsoun, mercer, c.d.
w. Jone, c.d., kng.

NUTFIELD

c. 1465 Wm. Graffton, c.d.
w. Joan, c.d., sm.

OAKWOOD

1431 Edw. de la Hale, arm., SS coll., sm.

OCKHAM

1376 Walter Frilende, rector, mass vests., hf-eff.

1483 John Weston, arm.
w. Margt., c.d.

OXTED

1428 John Ynge, rector, mass vests. (upper hf miss.), sm.

1480 Joan Haselden, c.d., with 1 son, mut.

1611 Thos. Hoskins, aged 5, c.d. (head miss.) and b. Thos., aged 6 months, c.d., sm.

1613 John Hoskins, aged 5, c.d., sm.

PEPER HAROW

1487 Joan, wid. of Wm. Brokes, wid. dr., kng., Trin., rest.

1621 Eliz., dau. of Robt. Woodes, rector, sm.

PUTTENHAM

1431 Edw. Cranford, rector, mass vests.

RICHMOND

1591 Robt. Cotton, yeoman of the wardrobe to Eliz. I, c.d., with 4 sons.
w. Grace, c.d., with 4 daus., all kng., rect. pl., ach.

SANDERSTEAD

1525 John Awodde, c.d.
w. Dyones, c.d., with 10 sons, sm. [Sons pal.]

SEND

1521 Laur. Slyffeld, c.d.
w. Alys, c.d., with 3 sons, sm.

SHALFORD

1509 3 sons of Roger Elyott.

SHERE

1412 Robt. Scarclyf, rector, mass vests.

1512 Olever Sandes, c.d.

1516 John Redfford, c.d.
w., c.d., with 4 sons, 2 daus.

c.1520 Woman, c.d., flowing hair.

c.1525 Sir John Towchet, Lord Audley, arm. (Legs and marg. inscr. rest.)

STOKE D'ABERNON

1277 Sir John D'Aubernoun, chain mail, enamelled shield on arm, holding lance, marg. inscr., lge.

1327 Sir John D'Abernon, son of above, arm., marg. inscr., bad. mut., lge.

1464 Dame Anne Norbury, wid. dr., with 4 sons, 4 daus., stg. on skirt, sm.

1592 Thos. Lyfelde, c.d.
w. Fraunces, c.d., with 1 dau., Jane, all kng., rect. pl.

THORPE

1578 John Bonde, clerk of the household to Hen. VIII, c.d. [Pal.]
w. Joan, c.d., with 7 sons, 7 daus.

1583 Wm. Denham, goldsmith, c.d.
w., c.d., with 5 sons, 10 daus., all kng., rect. pl.

TITSEY

1579 Wm. Gresham, c.d., with 4 sons.
w. Beatrys, c.d., with 3 daus., all kng., 2 achs.

WALTON-UPON-THAMES

1587 John Selwyn, hunting dress with horn.
w. Susan, c.d., with 5 sons, 6 daus., also device above effs. of John Selwyn performing feat of agility at a stag hunt, in the presence of Eliz. I. [Pal.]

WEYBRIDGE

15th cent. Man and 2 ws., skeletons (head of 1 w. miss.).

1586 Thos. Inwood, yeoman, c.d.
1st w., c.d., with 2 daus.
2nd w., c.d., with 2 sons, 1 dau.
3rd w., c.d., all kng., rect. pl.

1598 John Woulde, c.d.
1st w. Adrye, c.d., with 4 sons, 4 daus.
2nd w. Eliz., c.d., with 5 sons, 3 daus.

WITLEY

c.1530 Thos. Jonys, sewer of the chamber to Hen. VIII, c.d.
w. Jane, c.d., with 3 sons, 3 daus.

WOKING

1523 Joan Purdan, c.d., with 4 daus.
1527 John Shadet, c.d.
w. Isabel, c.d.

WONERSH

1467 Thos. Elyot, c.d.
w. Alice, c.d.
1503 Hen. Elyot, c.d.
w. Joan, c.d., with 12 sons, 11 daus.

In the possession of Surrey Archaeological Society:

c.1500 Man, arm.
w. mant., kng. (From Netley Abbey church.)

SUSSEX

AMBERLEY

1424 John Wantele, arm., tab.

ANGMERING

1598 Eden Baker, aged 23, c.d.

ARDINGLY

c.1500 Rich. Wakeherst, c.d.
w. Eliz., c.d., dble. can.
1504 Rich. Culpepyr, arm.
w. Margt., c.d. (upper hf rest.), dble. can., rest.
1510 Nich. Culpeper, arm.
w. Eliz., c.d., with 10 sons, 8 daus.
1633 Eliz. Culpeper, c.d.
1634 Eliz. Culpeper, aged 7.

ARUNDEL

1382? Adam Ertham, 1st master of the college, in choir cope, hf-eff.
1419 Wm. Whyte, 2nd master of the college, in almuce.
1430 Thos. Salmon, usher of the chamber to Hen. V, arm. (centre part only).
w. Agnes, c.d., SS coll., dble. can., entab., both bad. mut., lge.
c.1450 Esperaunce Blondell, rector, mass vests., hf-eff.
1455 John Baker, fellow of the college, mass vests.
1465 John Threel, marshal to the Earl of Arundel, arm., salade, liv. coll., staff of office.
1474 Robt. Warde, priest, mass vests., ¾-eff.

BATTLE

1426 John Lowe, arm., lge.
c.1430 Robt. Clere, dean, mass vests., dog at ft, scroll from mouth.
1435 Wm. Arnold, arm., hf-eff.
1590 Eliz. Alfraye, c.d.
1615 John Wythines, S.T.D., dean, vice-chancellor of Oxford, in gown, cap, holding book, ach.

BILLINGSHURST

1499 Thos. Bartlet, c.d.
w. Eliz., c.d.

BODYHAM

c.1360 John Wardedieu, arm. (legs, head miss.).
1513 Wm. Wetherden, vicar, in shroud, sm.

BREDE

1493 Robt. Oxenbrigg, arm. (ft only).

BRIGHTLING

c.1490 Man, c.d.
w., c.d.
1592 Thos. Pye, c.d., kng.

BROADWATER

1432 John Mapilton, rector, chancellor to Joan, w. of Hen. IV, in cope, sin. can.

BURTON

1520 John Goring, arm., kng.
1558 Eliz. Goringe, tab., kng., rect. pl.

BURWASH

c. 1440 Man, c.d., v. wn.

BUXTED

1408 Britell Avenel, rector, canon, mass vests., hf eff. in diapered head of floriated cross, mut., marg. inscr., mut.
c. 1460 Man, arm. (part of legs only).
1485 Denis Slon, priest, mass vests. ch., wn., sm.

CHICHESTER CATHEDRAL

1592 Wm. Bradbridge, mayor, c.d., with 6 sons.
w. Alice, c.d., with 8 daus., all kng., rect. pl.

CLAPHAM

1526 John Shelley, arm., tab.
w. Eliz., her. mant., Trin.
1550 John Shelley, arm., with 4 sons.
w. Mary, c.d., with 8 daus., all kng.
1592 John Shellee, arm., with 1 son.
w. Elinor, c.d., with 1 dau., all kng., rect. pl.

CLAYTON

1523 Rich. Idon, parson, mass vests., ch., wf.

COWFOLD

1433 Thos. Nelond, prior of the Cluniac monastery of Lewes, in monastic habit, trip. can., B. V. Mary and Child, SS Pancras and Thos. of Cant., marg. inscr., v. lge.
c. 1500 John a Gate, c.d.

CRAWLEY

c. 1520 Woman, c.d.

CUCKFIELD

1589 Hen. Bowyer, arm.
1601 Hen. Bowyer, arm, with 3 sons.
w. Eliz., c.d., with 2 daus., all kng., rect. pl.

ETCHINGHAM

1388 Sir Wm. de Echingham, arm. (head miss.), lge.
1444 Sir Wm. Echyngham, arm.
w. Joan, mant., with 1 son, Sir Thos., arm., trip. can., lge.
1480 Eliz., eld. dau. of Thos. Echyngham, c.d., flowing hair.
Agnes, dau. of Robt. Oxenbrigg, c.d.

EWHURST

1520 Wm. Crysford, c.d., kng., sm.

FIRLE, WEST

1476 Barth. Bolne, arm.
w. Eleanor, c.d.
c. 1595 Sir Edw. Gage, arm.
w. Eliz., c.d., ach.
c. 1595 Thos. Gage, arm.
w. Eliz., c.d., with 2 daus., ach.
c. 1595 George Gage, arm., ach.
1595 John Gage, arm.
1st w. Eliz., c.d.
2nd w. Margt., c.d., ach.
1638 Mary Howard, in shroud.

FLETCHING

c. 1380 Sir ? Dallingridge, arm., jupon.
w., mant., dble. can., entab., both mut., lge.

FRAMFIELD

1595 Edw. Gage, c.d., with 1 son.
w. Margt., c.d., with 5 daus., all kng., rect. pl.

FRISTON

1542 Thos. Selwyn, c.d.
w. Margery, c.d., sm.

GORING

c. 1490 Man, arm.
w., c.d.

GRINSTEAD, EAST

1505 Sir Thos. Grey, arm.
Rich. Lewkenor, arm., both hus. of Dame Kath., dau. of Thos., Lord Scales.

c. 1520 Man, c.d., sm.

GRINSTEAD, WEST

c. 1440 Philippe Halsham, mant., sin. can.

1441 Sir Hugh Halsham, arm.
w. Joyce, mant., dble. can.

HASTINGS, ALL SAINTS

c. 1520 Thos. Goodenouth, burgess, c.d.
w. Margt., c.d.

HASTINGS, ST CLEMENT

1563 Thos. Wekes, c.d.

1601 John Barley, mercer, c.d.
dau. Alyce, aged 7.

HELLINGLY

c. 1440 Woman, mant., lge.

HENFIELD

1559 Thos. Bysshopp, c.d., sm., ach.

1633 Ann Kenwellmersh, c.d., with 1 grandson, Meneleb, aged 9.

HORSHAM

1411 Thos. Clerke, in cope, crossed stole, initials on orphreys (head miss.).

1513 Eliz. Foys, c.d., sm.

HORSTED KEYNES

c. 1420 Woman, mant. (head miss.), mut.

HERSTMONCEUX

1402 Sir Wm. Fienlez, arm., sin. can., marg. inscr., lge.

IDEN

1427 Walter Seller, rector, mass vests.

ISFIELD

1558 Edw. Shurley, arm.
w. Joan, c.d., with 1 son, 1 dau.

1579 Thos. Shurley, son of above, arm.
w. Anne, c.d., ach.

LEWES, ST MICHAEL

c. 1430 ? Warrene, arm. (head miss.).

1457 John Braydforde, rector, mass vests., hf-eff.

NORTHIAM

1518 Robt. Beuford, parson, mass vests.

1538 Nich. Tufton, c.d., tonsure.

ORE

c. 1400 Man, c.d., anelace, dble. can., mut.
w., c.d.

POLING

c. 1460 Walter Davy, vicar, mass vests., hf-eff.

PULBOROUGH

1423 Thos. Harlyng, canon, in cope, sin. can., marg. inscr.

1452 Edm. Mille, c.d.
w. Maud, c.d.

1478 Rich. Mille, c.d.

RUSPER

c. 1370 John de Kyggesfolde, c.d.
w. Agneys, c.d., hf-effs.

1532 Thos. Challoner, c.d.
w. Margt., c.d., with 1 son.

RYE

c. 1490 Man, c.d. (head miss.).
w., c.d., mut.

1607 Thos. Hamon, burgess, mayor, captain of the band, c.d.

SHOREHAM, NEW

c. 1450 Man, c.d.
w., c.d.

SLAUGHAM

1503 John Covert, arm., sin. can. (engraved much earlier).

c. 1525 Rich. Covert, arm., kng.
1st w. Eliz., c.d., kng.
2nd w. Eliz., c.d., kng.

1527 3rd w. Jane, c.d., stg., marg. inscr. (added 1547).
1586 Jane Fetyplace, c.d., kng.

SLINFOLD
1533 Rich. Bradbrydge, c.d.
w. Denys, c.d.
*c.*1600 Woman, c.d. (upper hf miss.).

STOPHAM
*c.*1460 John Bartelot, c.d.
w. Joan, c.d., with 2 sons (added *c.*1630).
(New head added to man, both effs. partly recut, *c.*1675.)
*c.*1460? John Bartelot, arm.
w. Joan, c.d., with 3 sons, 2 daus. (added *c.*1630).
(New head added to man, both effs. partly recut, *c.*1675.)
1482? Rich. Bertlot, c.d., liv. coll., staff of office.
w. Parnell, c.d., with 1 son, 1 dau. (added *c.*1630).
1493 John Bartellot, c.d., kng. (rest. *c.*1630).
1601 Wm. Bartelot, c.d.
w. Anne, c.d. (Ft of man and upper hf of w. rest. *c.*1675.)
*c.*1630 Rich. Barttelot, arm.
1st w. Mary, c.d., with 4 sons, 1 dau.
2nd w. Rose, c.d., with 2 sons, 2 daus.
1626 6 daus. of Mary and Walter Barttelot.
*c.*1630 Fragments of 3 sons, 1 dau.

STORRINGTON
1591 Hen. Wilsha, S.T.B., priest, chaplain, in gown, scroll and text.

THAKEHAM
1515 Beatrix Apsley, c.d.
1517 Thos. Apsley, son of above, c.d.

TICEHURST
*c.*1370 Man, arm., lge., *to which have been added sm. effs. of 2 women and inscr. to*
1503 John Wybarne.
1st w. Edith, c.d.
2nd w. Agnes, c.d.

TROTTON
*c.*1310 Margarete de Camoys, kirtle, cote-hardie, wimple, veil, lge.
1421 Thos., Baron Camoys, arm., garter.
w. Eliz., mant., both with SS colls., holding hands, her son, Rich., stg. by her side on skirt, dble. can., embattled entab., v. lge.

UCKFIELD
1610 John Fuller, c.d., rect. pl.

WARBLETON
1436 Wm. Prestwyck, dean, in cope, sin. can., mut., marg., inscr., mut., lge.

WARMINGHURST
1554 Edw. Shelley, master of the household to Hen. VIII, Edw. VI, and Q. Mary, c.d.
w. Joan, c.d., with 7 sons, 3 daus.

WILLINGDON
1558 John Parker, arm.

WINCHELSEA
*c.*1440 Man, c.d. (ft miss.).

WISTON
1426 Sir John de Brewys, arm., marg. inscr., lge.

WARWICKSHIRE

ASTLEY
*c.*1400 Woman, mant. (head and lower hf miss.). (Of the Astley fam.)

ASTON

1545 Thos. Holte, justice of North Wales, in robes (head miss.), holding scroll.
w. Margt., c.d., with 1 son, 2 daus.

BADDESLEY-CLINTON HALL, PRIVATE CHAPEL

c. 1520 Woman, her. mant., kng., sm.

BAGINTON

1407 Sir Wm. Bagot, arm., jupon.
w. Margt., mant., both with SS colls., lge., rest.

BARCHESTON

1530 Hugh Humfray, M.A., S.T.B., rector, acad. dr.

BARTON

1608 Edm. Bury, c.d., with 2 sons, 1 dau.

CHADSHUNT

1613 Wm. Askell, c.d., kng., rect. pl.

COLESHILL

1500 Wm. Abell, vicar, mass vests., ch., wf., sm.

1506 Alice Clifton, c.d., marg. inscr., mut.

1566 John Fenton, LL.B., vicar, in gown, holding book.

COMPTON VERNEY

1523 Anne Odyngsale, c.d.

1526 Rich. Verney, arm.
w. Anne, c.d., with 9 sons, 5 daus., marg. inscr., mut.

c. 1630 Geo. Verney, arm.

COUGHTON

c. 1535 Sir Geo. Throkmerton, arm.
w. Kath., mant., with 8 sons, 11 daus., marg. inscr.

COVENTRY, HOLY TRINITY

1600 John Whithead, mayor, c.d., stg.
1st w., c.d., with 1 son, 3 daus.
2nd w., c.d., with 3 sons, 2 daus., all kng., rect. pl.

EATINGTON, LOWER

c. 1490 4 daus., mut.

1603 Thos. Underhill, c.d.
w. Eliz., c.d.

EXHALL, NR ALCESTER

c. 1590 John Walsingham, arm.
w. Elenor, c.d.

HAMPTON-IN-ARDEN

c. 1500 Rich. Brokes ?, bailiff, c.d., sm.

HARBURY

1563 1 dau. of Alice Wagstaff., v. sm.

HASELEY

1573 Clement Throkmorton, arm.
w. Kath., c.d., with 6 sons, 7 daus., marg. inscr. [Sons pal., 14th cent.]

HILLMORTON

c. 1410 Woman, mant.

HUNNINGHAM

15th cent. 7 daus. (Found in churchyard.)

ITCHINGTON, LONG

1674 John Bosworth, yeoman, c.d.
1st w. Ellinor, c.d.
2nd w. Isabel, c.d., kng., rect. pl.

MEREVALE

1413 Robt., Lord Ferrers, arm.
w. Margt., mant., lge.

MERIDEN

1638 Eliz., dau. of Thos. Rotton, c.d.

MIDDLETON

1476 Sir Rich. Byngham, justice of the king's bench, in judicial robes, coif.
w. Dame Margt., wid. dr.

PRESTON BAGOT

1637 Eliz. Randoll, c.d. (head miss.).

SHUCKBURGH, UPPER

c. 1500 Margt. Cotes, c.d. (upper hf miss., but eff. incised on the stone).

1549 Thos. Shukburghe, arm.
w. Eliz., c.d.

1594 Anth. Shukburgh, arm. (head only).
w. Anne, c.d., with 3 sons, 5 daus., ach.

SOLIHULL

1549 Wm. Hyll, c.d.
1st w. Isabel, c.d., with 4 sons, 11 daus.
2nd w. Agnes, c.d., with 1 son, 2 daus.

1610 Wm. Hawes, c.d., with 4 sons.
w. Ursula, c.d., with 4 daus., all kng., rect. pl.

SUTTON COLDFIELD

1606 Barbara Eliot, c.d., with 1 son, 1 dau.

1621 Josiah Bull, c.d., with 4 sons, 1 dau., corroded.

TANWORTH

1531 10 daus. of Robt. Fulwode.

1614 Margt. Archer, c.d., kng., rect. pl., ach.

TYSOE

1463 Thos. Mastrupe, chaplain, mass vests., ch., sm.

1598 Jane Browne, c.d., hf-eff., sm.

UFTON

1587 Rich. Woddomes, parson, in gown, with 3 sons.
w. Margery, c.d., with 4 daus., all kng., rect. pl.

WARWICK, ST MARY

1406 Thos. de Beauchamp, Earl of Warwick, arm., jupon.
w. Margt., her. dr., lge.

1573 Thos. Oken, c.d.
w. Jone, c.d.

WARWICK, ST NICHOLAS

1424 Robt. Willardsey, vicar, mass vests.

WELLESBOURNE-HASTINGS

1426 Sir Thos. le Strange, constable of Ireland, arm., SS coll., marg. inscr., rest.

WHATCOTE

1511 Wm. Auldington, parson, mass vests. (head miss.), ch., sm.

WHICHFORD

1582 Nich. Asheton, S.T.B., chaplain, rector, in gown.

WHITNASH

c. 1500 Benedict Medley ?, clerk of the signet to Hen. VII, c.d.,
w., c.d.

1531 Rich. Bennet, pastor, mass vests., ch., wf.

WITHYBROOK

c. 1500 Rich Wright ?, c.d.

WIXFORD

1411 Thos. de Cruwe, arm.
w. Julian, mant., dble. can., chamfer inscr., partly rest., lge.

1597 Rise, son of Rise Griffyn, aged 9 months, c.d., kng., rect. pl.

WOOTTON-WAWEN

1505 John Harewell, arm.
w. Dame Anne, c.d., with 5 sons, 5 daus., chamfer inscr.

WROXALL

c. 1430 Woman, c.d.

WESTMORLAND

KENDAL

1577 Alan Bellingham, arm., ach.

MUSGRAVE, GREAT

c. 1500 Thos. Ouds, rector, mass vests., scroll.

WILTSHIRE

Aldbourne

1492 Rich. Goddard, c.d.
w. Eliz., c.d.

1508 Hen. Frekylton, chaplain, mass vests., sm.

Alton Priors

1528 Agnes Button, c.d.

c. 1620 Wm. Button, rect. pl. with eff. rising from tomb.

Barford, St Martin

1584 Alis Walker, c.d., with 7 sons, 4 daus., all kng.

Bedwyn, Great

1510 John Seymoure, c.d.

Berwick Basset

1427 Wm. Bayly, c.d., hf-eff.

Blunsden, Broad

1608 w. of Thos. Heydock, c.d., with 2 daus.

1612 Thos. Heydock, arm., with 2 daus., Margt. and Sibil.

Bradford-on-Avon

c. 1520 Thos. Horton, c.d.
w. Mary, c.d., Trin., sm.

1601 Anne Longe, c.d., with 2 daus.

Bromham

c. 1490 Eliz. Beauchamp, mant., chamfer inscr., mut.

1516 John Baynton, arm., marg. inscr.

1578 Sir Edw. Baynton, arm.
1st w. Agnes, c.d., with 1 son, 1 dau.
2nd w. Anne, c.d., all kng., ach.

Charlton

1524 Wm. Chaucey, c.d.
w. Marion, c.d.

Chisleden

1592 Fraunсis Rutland, c.d.
w. Mary, c.d., sm.

Cliffe-Pypard

c. 1380 Man, arm. (Of the Quinton fam.)

Collingbourne Ducis

1631 Edw. Saintmaur, c.d., sm.

Collingbourne Kingston

1495 Joan Darell, mant.

Dauntsey

1514 Sir John Danvers, arm.
w. Anne, c.d., marg. inscr.

1539 Dame Anne Danvers, kng., sin. can., rect. pl., Trin.

Dean, West

1641 Geo., son of Sir John Evelyn, aged 6, sm.

Devizes, St John

1630 John Kent, c.d.
w. Mary, c.d., ach.

Draycot Cerne

1393 Sir Edw. Cerne, arm.
w. Elyne, wid. dr., holding hands.

Durnford, Great

1607 Edw. Younge, c.d., with 6 sons.
w. Joan, c.d., with 8 daus., all kng., rect. pl.

Fovant

c. 1500 Geo. Rede, rector, acad. dr., kng., rect. pl., Annun.

Ham

1590 John Hunt, c.d.
w. Christian, c.d., kng.

Lacock

1501 Robt. Baynard, arm., tab.
w. Eliz., her. mant., with 13 sons, 2nd a priest, 5 daus.

Lavington, West

1559 John Dauntesay, J.P., arm.

Mere

1398 John Bettesthorne, arm., lge.

c. 1425 Man, arm. (lower hf miss.).
w., c.d., bad. mut., was lge.

MINETY
1609 Nich. Poulett, arm., with 1 son, Ames.
w. Mary, c.d., with 3 daus., all kng., rect. pl.

NEWTON, LONG
1503 John Erton, rector, mass vests.

OGBOURNE, ST GEORGE
1517 Thos. Goddard, c.d.
w. Joan, c.d.

PRESHUTE
1518 John Barley, c.d. (ft miss.).
w. Maryon, c.d., with 7 sons, 3 daus.

SALISBURY CATHEDRAL
1375 Robt. Wyvil, bp., episcopal vests., mitre, crosier, hf-eff., stg. in a castle, marg. inscr., mut., lge.
1578 Edm. Geste, S.T.P., bp. of Rochester and Sarum, rochet, chimere, holding book.

SALISBURY, ST THOMAS
1570 John Webbe, mayor, c.d.
w. Anne, c.d., with 3 sons, 3 daus., marg. inscr.

SEEND
1498 John Stokeys, c.d.
w. Alys, c.d., sm.

STOCKTON
1590 Eliz. Poticary, 1st w. of below, with 1 son, 4 daus., all kng., rect. pl.
1596 Jerome Poticary, clothier, c.d.
2nd w. Eleanor, c.d., with 2 sons, 2 daus., all kng., rect. pl.

TISBURY
c.1520 Man, c.d.
w., c.d.
1590 Laur. Hyde, c.d., with 6 sons.
w. Anne, c.d., with 4 daus., marg. inscr., mut., rect. pl.

UPTON LOVELL
c.1460 Priest, mass vests., hf-eff.

WANBOROUGH
1418 Thos. Polton, c.d.
w. Edith, c.d., hf-effs.

WARMINSTER
1649 Eliz., Carter, c.d., with 3 sons, 1 dau., all kng., rect. pl.

WESTBURY
1605 Thos. Bennet, c.d.
w. Margt., c.d., mut.

WILTON
1585 John Coffer, c.d.
w. Phelipe, c.d., kng., ach.

WISHFORD, GREAT
1473 1 son, 3 daus. of Thos. Bonham, effaced, mut.

WOODFORD
1596 Gerald Erington, c.d.

WORCESTERSHIRE

ALVECHURCH
1524 Philip Chatwyn, usher to Hen. VIII, arm.

BIRLINGHAM
1600 Thos. Harewell, c.d.
w. Margt., c.d., with 1 dau., Mary, by 1st hus., Rich. Sheldon, all kng., rect. pl., ach.

BROADWAY
1572 Anth. Daston, arm. ach. [Pal., 16th cent. Flem.]

BUSHLEY
1500 Thos. Payne, c.d.
w. Ursula, c.d.

CHADDESLEY CORBETT
1511 Thos. Forest, park keeper of Dunclent Park, c.d.
w. Margt., c.d., with 5 sons, 6 daus., marg. inscr., mut., wn.

DAYLESFORD

1632 Wm. Gardiner, c.d., holding book, marg. inscr.

FLADBURY

1445 John Throckmorton, under-treasurer of England, arm.
w. Eleanor, wid. dr., marg. inscr.

1458 Thos. Mordon, LL.B., rector, in cope, hf-eff.

1488 Edw. Peytoo, arm., liv. coll.

1504 Wm. Plewme, M.A., rector, mass vests., sm.

KIDDERMINSTER

1415 Maud Harcourt, mant.
1st hus. Walter Cookesey, arm.
2nd hus. Sir John Phelip, arm., all with SS colls., trip. can., mut., lge., wn.

LONGDON

1523 Wm. Brugge, arm.
w. Alice, c.d., marg. inscr., mut.

MAMBLE

c. 1510 John Blount, arm.
w. Kath., c.d.

STOCKTON

1508 Wm. Parker, c.d.

STOKE PRIOR

1606 Hen. Smith, draper, c.d., kng.

1609 Robt. Smith, draper, c.d.
1st w. Thomasin, c.d., with 11 sons, 6 daus.
2nd w. Susan, c.d., all kng., rect. pl., ach.

STRENSHAM

c. 1390 Robt. Russell, arm., marg. inscr.

1405 Sir John Russell, arm., sin. can., marg. inscr., mut.

1502 Robt. Russell, arm.
w. Eliz., c.d.

1562 Sir John Russell, arm., tab., with only son, Sir Thos., arm.
w. Edith, her. mant., kng., ach.

TREDINGTON

1427 Rich. Cassey, rector, canon, in cope, marg. inscr.

1482 Hen. Sampson, rector, in almuce, kng.

1561 Alice Barnes, c.d.

WORCESTER, ST HELEN

1622 Stephen Maylard, proctor, c.d. v. wn. and corroded.

YARDLEY

1598 Isabel Wheler, c.d.
1st hus. Wm. Astell, c.d.
2nd hus. Simon Wheler, arm., all kng., rect. pl.

YORKSHIRE

(East, North and West Ridings are indicated by the letters E.R., N.R., and W.R.)

ALDBOROUGH (N. and W.R.)

c. 1360 Wm. de Aldeborough, arm., jupon and shield, holding heart, on br., lge.

ALLERTON MAULEVERER (W.R.)

1400 Sir John Mauleverere, arm., jupon.
w. Eleanor, c.d., rect. pl., sm.

AUGHTON (E.R.)

c. 1466 Rich. Ask, arm., salade.
w. Margt. wid. dr. (lower hf miss.).

BAINTON (E.R.)

1429 Roger Godeale, rector, mass vests., ch., marg. inscr., wn.

BEEFORD (E.R.)

1472 Thos. Tonge, LL.B., rector, in diapered cope, holding book, marg. inscr., mut.

BIRSTALL (W.R.)
1632 Eliz. Popeley, rect. pl. with shrouded eff. between 2 daus., kng.

BISHOP BURTON (E.R.)
1521 Joan Rokeby, c.d.
1579 Lady Isabel Smethelaye, c.d.
2nd hus. Christ. Estoft, c.d., mut., wn.

BOLTON-BY-BOWLAND (W.R.)
1520 Hen. Pudsey, arm., tab.
w. Margt., her. mant., kng., rest.

BOSSALL (N.R.)
1454 Robt. Constable, chancellor of Durham, arm. (head, middle miss.).

BRADFIELD W.R.)
1647 John Morewood, c.d., with 9 sons.
w. Grace, c.d., with 6 daus., all kng., rect. pl.

BRANDSBURTON (E.R.)
1364 Wm. Darell, rector, mass vests., hf-eff. (head miss.), marg. inscr., mut. wn.
1397 Sir John de St Quinton, arm., holding heart (head miss.).
1st w. Lora, c.d., lge.

BURGH WALLIS (W.R.)
1566 Thos. Gasgoign, arm.

CATTERICK (N.R.)
1465 Wm. Burgh, arm.
Wm. Burgh, son of above, arm.
1492 Wm. Burgh, arm.
w. Eliz., c.d.

COTTINGHAM (E.R.)
1383 Nich. de Luda, rector, prebendary, choir cope, sin. can. with super can., marg. inscr., lge., rest.
1504 John Smyth, c.d.
w. Joan, c.d.

COWTHORPE (W.R.)
1494 Brian Roucliff, baron of the exchequer, judicial robes, mut.

EVERINGHAM (E.R.)
1558 Dame Jane Constable, (L)?

FORCETT (N.R.)
1637 Anne Underhill, rect. pl. with recumbent eff. under arch with figs. of Labour and Rest, ach.

HAMPSTHWAITE (W.R.)
c. 1360 Man, c.d., mut., sm.
1570 *on the above brass has been scratched an inscr. to* Ad. Dyxon.

HARPHAM (E.R.)
1418 Sir Thos. de St Quinton, arm.
w. Agnes, c.d., dble. can., lge.
1445 Thos. de St Quinton, arm., liv. coll.

HAUXWELL (N.R.)
1611 Man, c.d. (Of the Thoresby fam.)
w., c.d., kng., rect. pl.

HELMSLEY (N.R.)
c. 1480 Wm. Overton, arm.
w. Eliz., c.d., both effaced.

HORNBY (N.R.)
1489 Thos. Mountford, arm. (legs miss.).
w. Agnes, wid. dr., with 8 sons, 3 arm., 1 a priest, acad. dr., 7 daus., 1 a nun.

HOWDEN (E.R.)
c. 1480 Man, arm.

HULL, HOLY TRINITY (E.R.)
1451 Rich. Byll, alderman, c.d.
w. Margt., c.d., hf-effs.

HULL, ST MARY (E.R.)
1525 John Haryson, alderman, c.d., with 3 sons.
1st w. Alys, c.d.
2nd w. Agnes, c.d., all kng., rect. pl., Trin., mut.

KIRKBY MALZEARD (W.R.)
1604 Wm. Mann, c.d.
w. Eliz., c.d., kng., sm.

KIRKBY MOORSIDE (N.R.)
1600 Lady Brooke, with 6 sons, 5 daus., all kng., rect. pl.

KIRKBY WHARFE (W.R.)
1492 Wm. Gisborne, canon, prebendary, in cope, sm., wn.

KIRKHEATON (W.R.)
1655 Adam Beaumont, arm., with 1 son.
w. Eliz., c.d., with 1 dau. and holding infant.

KIRKLEATHAM (N.R.)
1628 Dorothy, dau. of John and Eliz. Turnor, aged 4, sm.
1631 Robt. Coulthirst, mcht. tailor, c.d., holding book, marg. inscr.

LAUGHTON-EN-LE-MORTHEN, ST JOHN (W.R.)
c. 1620 John Mallevorer, arm.

LEAKE (N.R.)
c. 1530 John Watson, auditor, c.d.
w. Alice, c.d., sm., wn.

LEEDS, ST PETER (W.R.)
1459 Sir John Langton, arm., salade.
w. Eupheme, wid. dr.
1467 Agnes Langton, c.d., effaced.
1709 7 sm. effs of child., with inscr. to their f., Wm. Massie, rect. pl., ach.

LOWTHORPE (E.R.)
1417 Geo. Salveine, arm.

MARR (W.R.)
1589 John Lewis, c.d.
w. Mary, c.d., with 2 sons, 4 daus.

OTLEY (W.R.)
1593 Rect. pl. with recumbent eff., c.d., with genealogical tree of Lyndley and Palmes fams., ach.

OWSTON (W.R.)
1409 Robt. de Haitfeld, c.d.
w. Ade. c.d., both with SS colls., holding hands.

RAWMARSH (W.R.)
1616 John Darley, c.d., with 4 sons.
w. Alice, c.d. with 4 daus., all kng. except for 2 infants in cradles.

ROTHERHAM (W.R.)
1561 Robt. Swifte, c.d., with 2 sons.
1st w. Anne, c.d., with 2 daus., all kng., rect. pl.

ROUTH (E.R.)
c. 1420 Sir John Routh, arm.
w. Agnes, c.d., both with SS colls., dble. can., mut., lge.

ROXBY CHAPEL (N.R.)
1523 Thos. Boynton, arm.

SESSAY (N.R.)
1550 Thos. Magnus, archdeacon, in cope, scroll from hands.

SHERIFF HUTTON (N.R.)
1657 Mary Hall, c.d., holding chrysom, sm.

SKIPTON-IN-CRAVEN (W.R.)
c. 1570 Sir Hen. Clifford, arm., tab.
2nd w. Anne, her. mant., with 2 sons, 3 daus, all kng., rest. (Only 2nd son, Trin. are orig.)

SPROTBOROUGH (W.R.)
1474 Wm. Fitzwilliam, arm., salade.
w. Eliz., wid. dr.

TANFIELD, WEST (N.R.)
c. 1490 Thos. Sutton, M.A., rector, canon, in cope.

THIRSK (N.R.)
1419 Robt. Thresk, rector, mass vests., hf-eff. between two angels, wn.

TODWICK (W.R.)
1609 Thos. Garland, c.d., kng., rect. pl., sm.

TOPCLIFFE (N.R.)
1391 Thos. de Topclyff, c.d., anelace. w. Mabel, mant., rich can. with souls, angels etc., marg. inscr., mut., lge. rect. pl. Flem. [Pal., part of unfinished brass.]

WATH (N.R.)
1420 Rich. Norton, chief justice of the kings bench, judicial robes. w. Kath., mant., effaced.
c. 1490 Sir John Norton, arm.

WELLWICK (E.R.)
1621 Wm. Wryght, c.d. w. Anne, c.d., ach.

WENSLEY (N.R.)
c. 1375 Sir Simon of Wensley, rector, mass vests., head on cushion held by angels, Flem. ch. on breast.

WENTWORTH (W.R.)
1588 Mich. Darcy, arm., with 1 son, John. w. Margt., c.d., with 2 daus., all kng., rect. pl., wn.

WILBERFOSSE (E.R.)
1447 Robt. Hoton, arm. w. Joan, c.d., v. wn.

WINESTEAD (E.R.)
c. 1540 Man, arm. (lower hf miss.). w., c.d., mut., with 7 sons, eldest arm., 6 daus. (1 head miss.). (Poss. Sir Christ. Hildyard and 2nd w. Joan.) [Man pal., c. 1360, Flem.]

WYCLIFFE (N.R.)
1606 Ralph Wicklif, aged 14, c.d., kng., rect. pl.

YORK MINSTER
1315 Wm. de Grenefeld, archbp. of York, full vests. (lower hf miss.), lge.
1585 Eliz. Eynns, wid., lge. hf-eff., with open book with texts.
1595 Jas. Cotrel, c.d., cap, ¾-eff., rect. pl.

YORK, ALL SAINTS, NORTH ST
1642 Thos. Atkinson, tanner, sheriff, c.d., lge. hf-eff., rect. pl.

YORK, ST CRUX
1597 Robt. Askwith, mayor, c.d., cap, lge. ¾-eff., rect. pl.

YORK, ST MARTIN, CONEY ST
1614 Christ. Harington, goldsmith, c.d., hf-eff., wn.

Ireland

DUBLIN, CHRIST CHURCH CATHEDRAL
c. 1580 2nd and 3rd sons of Sir Arthur Grey, 1 a chrysom, rect. pl., sm., ach.

DUBLIN, ST PATRICK'S CATHEDRAL
1528 Robt. Sutton, dean, in almuce, kng., rect. pl., Trin., mut.
1537 Geoffrey Fyche, dean, in almuce, kng., rect. pl. with Our Lady in Pity above.
1579 Sir Edw. Fiton, c.d., with 9 sons. w. Anne, c.d., rect. pl., ach.

Scotland

ABERDEEN, ST NICHOLAS
1613 Duncan Liddel, M.D., eff. in c.d. seated in study with books around, marg. inscr., lge. rect. pl., Flem.

GLASGOW CATHEDRAL

1605 Man, arm., kng., rect. pl. (Poss. of the Mynto fam.)

In Dunfermline Abbey, Scotland, there is a modern brass to Robert the Bruce (1274–1329) in the style of the late 13th cent.

Wales

ANGLESEY

BEAUMARIS

c.1530 Rich. Bulkley, mcht., c.d., with 2 sons, 1 a priest, in almuce.
w. Eliz., c.d., with 1 dau., all kng.

LLANWENLLWYFO

1609 Rich. Williams, c.d., with 2 sons.
w. Marcelie, c.d., with 1 dau., all kng., rect. pl.

CAERNARVONSHIRE

CLYNNOG

1633 Wm. Glynne, aged 2, sm.

DOLWYDDELAN

1525 Maredith ap Ivan ap Robert Wynne, arm., kng.

LLANBEBLIG

1500 Rich. Foxwist, notary, rect. pl. with eff. in bed, holding shield with 5 wounds, penner and inkhorn at side, sm.

YSPYTTY-IFAN

1598 Maurice ap Robt. ap Robt. Gethin, c.d.
w. Anne, c.d., with 1 son, 3 daus. and infant, in shroud, rect. pl.

DENBIGHSHIRE

HOLT

1666 Thos. Crue, rect. pl. with skeleton on mattress, under arch, lightly engraved.

LLANRWST

1626 Sir John Wynn, c.d., bust, ach.

1632 Lady Sydney Wynn, w. of above, c.d., bust.

1658 Lady Mary Mostyn, dau. of above, c.d., bust, 2 achs.

1660 Sir Owen Wynne, bust, ach.

1669 Kath. Festyniogg, aged 16½, hf-eff., ach.

1671 Dame Sarah Wynne, c.d., ¾-eff. in frame, 2 achs, lightly engraved.

RUTHIN

1560 Edw. Goodman, c.d.

1583 Edw. Goodman, burgess, mercer, c.d., with 3 sons.
w. Ciselye, c.d., with 5 daus., all kng.

WHITCHURCH

1575 Rich. Middleton, c.d., with 9 sons.
w. Jane, c.d., with 7 daus., all kng., rect. pl.

WREXHAM

1673 Humph. Lloyd, rect. pl. with recumbent skeleton, under arch.

FLINT

MOLD

1602 Robt. Davies, c.d., kng., rect. pl.

GLAMORGAN

LLANDOUGH-NEXT-COWBRIDGE

1427 Wenllan Walsche, w. of Walter Moreton, c.d.

LLANGYFELACH
1631 Matthew Jones, c.d.
w. Mary, c.d., kng., rect. pl.

SWANSEA
c. 1500 Sir Hugh Johnys, arm.
w. Dame Mawde, c.d., with 4 daus., rest. Resurrection.

MONTGOMERYSHIRE

BETTWS CEDEWAIN
1531 John ap Meredyth de Powys vicar, mass vests., ch., wf.

LLANDYSILIO, NEW CHURCH
1674 Mary Eyton, in shroud.

PEMBROKESHIRE

HAVERFORDWEST
1654 John Davids, c.d., kng., rect. pl.

INFANTS IN SWADDLING CLOTHES

BEDFORDSHIRE

TINGRITH
1611 2 child. of Robt. Hogeson, with f.

TODDINGTON
c. 1480 Anon.

BERKSHIRE

BRAY
1610 Edw. Page, with parents.

BUCKINGHAMSHIRE

CHESHAM BOIS
c. 1520 Benedict Lee.

MARSWORTH
1606 Child of Mary West, with m.

WOTTON UNDERWOOD
1587 Son of Edw. Greneville, with parents.

DERBYSHIRE

CRICH
1637 Ephraim Shelmerdine.

DURHAM

HAUGHTON-LE-SKERNE
1592 Dorothy Parkinson, holding twin chrysoms.

ESSEX

AVELEY
1583 Eliz. Bacon, aged 13 weeks.

BARKING
1596 5 sons of John Tedcastell, with parents.

CHESTERFORD, GREAT
1600 John Howard.

CRESSING
1610 Child of Dorcas Musgrave, with m.

HALSTEAD
1604 Child of John Watson, with m.

ILFORD, LITTLE
1630 Wm. Hyde, died 1614, with s.

NETTESWELL
1607 Dau. of John Bannister, with parents.

STANFORD RIVERS
1492 Thos. Grevile.

TILTY
1590 3 infants, child. of Geo. Tuke, with m.

GLOUCESTERSHIRE

CLIFFORD CHAMBERS
1601 Eliz. Marrowe, holding chrysom dau.

WORMINGTON
1605 Infant in bed with m. Ann Savage.

HAMPSHIRE

DOGMERSFIELD
1590 Child of Anne Sutton, with m.

ODIHAM
1636 Margt. Pye.

WINCHESTER, ST MAURICE
1612 3 daus. and 1 son of John Bond, all born and died within three years.

HEREFORDSHIRE

MARDEN
1614 Francis Chute, with m.

KENT

BEARSTED
1634 Dau. of Wm. Cage, with parents.

BIRCHINGTON
1533 Child of Margt. Crypps (head miss.), with m.

CRANBROOK
c. 1520 Anon, with f.

DARTFORD
1590 Eliz. Death, holding chrysom.

DAVINGTON
1613 2 child. of John Edwards, with parents.

DEAL, ST LEONARD
1606 Anne Consant.

HARRIETSHAM
1603 Child of Susan Partheriche, with m.

TEYNHAM
1509 Child of Robt. Heyward, with f.

LANCASHIRE

MIDDLETON
1618 Rich. Assheton, with parents.

LEICESTERSHIRE

BARWELL
1614 Child of John Torksay, with parents.

LINCOLNSHIRE

COATES BY STOW
1590 Priscilla Butler, with parents.

SCOTTER
1599 Dau. of Marmaduke Tirwhit, with parents.

LONDON

HORNSEY, ST MARY
c. 1520 John Skevington.

MIDDLESEX

EDGWARE
1599 Anth. Childe.

HESTON
1581 Infant in childbed with m., Constance Bownell.

PINNER
c. 1580 Anne Bedingfel. [Pal. late Flem.]

MONMOUTHSHIRE

ABERGAVENNY
1637 Child of Margt. Robertes, with m.

NORFOLK

BLICKLING
1512 Anne Asteley, holding twin chrysoms in arms.

Ketteringham
c. 1530 John Colvyle.

Rougham
1510 John, died 1505, and Roger Yelverton, under can.

NORTHAMPTONSHIRE

Burton Latimer
1626 Child of Margt. Bacon, with m.

OXFORDSHIRE

Oxford, St Cross, Holywell
1622 Child in bed with m., Eliza Franklin, with 3 other child., in shrouds.

SOMERSET

Ilton
1508 Nich. Wadham.

SUFFOLK

Bradley, Little
1584 2 chrysoms, child. of John Daye, with parents.

Lavenham
1631 Clopton D'Ewes.

Melford, Long
1624 2 chrysoms, child. of Rich. Martin, with parents, v.sm.

SURREY

Stoke D'Abernon
1516 Elyn Bray.

Merstham
1587 Peter Best (renewed 1911).

YORKSHIRE

Sheriff Hutton (North Riding)
1491 Dorothy and John Dacre.
1657 Mary Hall, holding chrysom.

IRELAND

Dublin, Christ Church Cathedral
c. 1580 Son of Sir Arthur Grey, v. sm.

HANDS AND HEARTS

BUCKINGHAMSHIRE

LILLINGSTONE LOVELL

1446 John Merstun, 2 hands issuing from clouds holding bleeding heart, inscribed "Ihc".

CUMBERLAND

ARTHURET

c. 1500 2 hands holding heart.

ESSEX

ELMSTEAD

c. 1500 2 hands issuing from clouds holding heart, inscr. miss.

KENT

HALLING, LOWER

1401 John Colard, shield with five wounds.

MARGATE, ST JOHN THANET

1433 Thos. Smyth, vicar, heart, 3 scrolls and inscr.

SALTWOOD

1496 Dame Anne Muston, angel issuing from clouds, holding heart.

LEICESTERSHIRE

MELTON MOWBRAY

1543 Christ. and Eliz. Gonson, lge., inscribed heart., wn.

NORFOLK

FAKENHAM

c. 1470 4 inscribed dble. hearts.

HELHOUGHTON

c. 1450 Wm. and Margt. Stapilton, hands issuing from clouds supporting heart.

KIRBY BEDON

c. 1450 Heart, with scrolls, mut.

LODDON

1462 Denis Willys, 2 hands issuing from clouds, holding heart.

LUDHAM

1633 Grace White, inscribed heart.

MARTHAM

1487 Robt. Alen, vicar, inscribed heart, rest.

SOUTHACRE

1454 Sir Roger Harsyk, 2 hands holding heart. (In pieces in church safe.)

TRUNCH

c. 1530 Heart with scroll.

WIGGENHALL, ST MARY THE VIRGIN

c. 1450 Sir Robt. Kervile, heart and scrolls.

NORTHAMPTONSHIRE

HIGHAM FERRERS

c. 1500 Inscribed heart.

NOTTINGHAMSHIRE

WOODBOROUGH

1693 Mary Lacock, inscr. on heart-shaped pl.

OXFORDSHIRE

CAVERSFIELD

1533? Thos. Denton, 2 hands issuing from clouds, holding heart.

SOULDERN

c. 1460 Hands issuing from clouds, holding inscribed heart.

SOMERSET

BAGBOROUGH, WEST

1641 Robt. Kellett, inscribed heart.

WEDMORE

c. 1630 Capt. Thos. Hodges, heart, ensigns.

SUSSEX

CHICHESTER CATHEDRAL

c. 1500 2 hands issuing from clouds holding heart, inscribed "ihc".

CROSSES

Crosses with effs. are listed under appropriate church

BEDFORDSHIRE

SUTTON

1516 Thos. Burgoyn, floriated cross.

CORNWALL

SITHNEY

c. 1420 Roger Trewythynnyk, inscribed floriated cross, mut.

DURHAM

AUCKLAND, ST ANDREW

1581 Fridesmond Barnes, rect. pl. with cross, scrolls etc., sm.

HAMPSHIRE

EVERSLEY

1502 Rich. Pendilton, lge. plain cross.

HERTFORDSHIRE

ROYSTON

c. 1500 Anon, plain cross with 5 wounds.

KENT

PENSHURST

c. 1520 Thos. Bwllayen, plain cross, sm., part. rest.

LINCOLNSHIRE

GRAINTHORPE

c. 1380 Anon, lge. floriated cross (stem miss.).

LINCOLN, ST MARY-LE-WIGFORD

1469 Wm. Horn, plain cross, sm.

LONDON

WESTMINSTER ABBEY

c. 1270 Margt., dau. of Wm. de Valence (base and 20″ of stem only).

NORTHAMPTONSHIRE

FLOORE

1537 Alyce Wyrley, floriated cross, sm., mut.

HIGHAM FERRERS

1400 Thos. and Agnes Chichele, lge. plain cross with the Deity at intersection, Ev. syms. at extremities.

OXFORDSHIRE

CASSINGTON

1414 Roger Cheyne, floriated cross (one arm mut.).

CHINNOR

c. 1320 Anon, floriated cross, head of priest in centre (stem miss.).

STAFFORDSHIRE

STANDON

c. 1420 Anon, floriated cross, slightly mut., sm.

SURREY

BEDDINGTON

1425 Margt. Oliver, floriated cross, mut., sm.

PEPERHAROW

1487 Joan Brokes, plain cross.

SUSSEX

BROADWATER

1445 Rich. Tooner, vicar, cross with inscribed arms.

At Hever in Kent is a small cross which has been wholly rest. with the orig. inscr. to

c. 1520 Hen. Bwllayen.

CHALICE BRASSES

BEDFORDSHIRE

HOLWELL
1515 Robt. Wodehouse, rector, ch. and wf., 2 wild men.

KENT

SHORNE
1519 Thos. Elys, vicar.

NORFOLK

ATTLEBRIDGE
c. 1525 Geo. Cunynggam, vicar.

BAWBURGH
1531 Wm. Richers, vicar, ch. in hands issuing from clouds.

BELAUGH
1508 John Feelde, rector.

BINTRY
1510 Thos. Hoont, rector, chaplain, wn.

BUCKENHAM, OLD
c. 1520 Anon.

BURLINGHAM, SOUTH, ST EDMUND
1540 Wm. Curtes, priest.

BUXTON
1508 Robt. Northen, vicar.

COLNEY
1502 Hen. Alikok, rector.

GUESTWICK
1504 John Robertson, vicar.

K

HEDENHAM
1502 Rich. Grene, rector.

NORWICH, ST GILES
1499 John Smyth, chaplain.

SALTHOUSE
1519 Robt. Sevyr.

SCOTTOW
c. 1520 Nich. Wethyrley, chaplain, wn.

SURLINGHAM
1513 Rich. Louhawkys, rector, mut.

TAVERHAM
1515 John Thorp, priest.

WALSHAM, NORTH
1519 Edm. Ward, vicar.
c. 1520 Robt. Wythe, chaplain.

WALSINGHAM, NEW
c. 1520 Wm. Westow, chaplain, ch. in hand issuing from clouds.

WOOD DALLING
1510 Edw. Warcop, chaplain.

SUFFOLK

GAZELEY
c. 1530 Ch. only, anon.

RENDHAM
1523 Thos. Kyng, vicar.

YORKSHIRE

BISHOP BURTON (EAST RIDING)
1460 Peter Johnson, vicar.

LEEDS, ST PETER
1469 Thos. Clarell, vicar.

RIPLEY, (WEST RIDING)
1429 Rich. Kendale, M.A., vicar, wn.

YORK, ST MICHAEL SPURRIERGATE
1466 Wm. Langton, rector.

Norfolk clergy favoured the engraving of chalice brasses. The following have all lost their chalices but most indents remain. There are probably many more, hidden under wooden floors, pews, etc.

CATFIELD
c. 1500 Rich. Foo, rector. (Covered?)

CROSTWIGHT
1497 Hen. Lesyngham, rector, inscr. still intact.

FAKENHAM
c. 1510 Hen. Newman, rector.

HINDOLVESTONE
1531 Thos. Warde, vicar, inscr. still intact.

LODDON
Anon, indent.

MAUTBY
Anon, indent.

NORTHWOLD
1531 John Dawson, priest, inscr. still intact.

NORWICH, ST MICHAEL COSLANY
c. 1515 Thos. Coke, rector, inscr. still intact.

NORWICH, ST PETER PERMOUNTERGATE
Anon, indent.

SALL
1482 Simon Boleyn, chaplain, inscr. still intact.

SLOLEY
c. 1500 Wm. Ward, chaplain, inscr. still intact.
1503 Robt. Glaveyn, rector, inscr. still intact.

STRUMPSHAW
1500 John Hauys, clerk, inscr. still intact.

TRUNCH
c. 1500 Nich. Pylgrym, chaplain, inscr. still intact.

WALPOLE ST PETER
1537 John Whetom, parson, inscr. still intact.

WALSHAM, SOUTH
c. 1495 Miles Walker, rector.
c. 1500 Robt. Melton, chaplain, indents only.

WALSINGHAM, LITTLE
1532 Thos. Grandon, rector, inscr. still intact.
1532 John Thorp, chaplain, inscr. still intact.

WORSTEAD
Anon, indent.

MISCELLANEOUS BRASSES

not included in text

BUCKINGHAMSHIRE

EDLESBOROUGH

1412 John Killyngworth, sm., inscribed rose.

DEVONSHIRE

MONKLEIGH

1509 Jas. Seyntleger, 2 angels holding scroll.

ESSEX

WOODHAM WALTER

c. 1650 Death's Head, inscribed.

GLOUCESTERSHIRE

CIRENCESTER

15th cent. Angel Gabriel, and a lily pot from an Annun.

HAMPSHIRE

WEEKE

1498 Eff. of St Christopher, to Wm. and Annes Complyn, sm.

HEREFORDSHIRE

LLANDINABO

1629 Thos. Tompkins, sm. rect. pl. of boy stg. in pond.

ISLE OF WIGHT

CALBOURNE

1652 Dan. Evance, rector, rect. pl. with figs. of Time and Death.

KENT

BEXLEY

15th cent. Hunting horn with bawdrick enclosing shield with arms of Castelyn.

MARGATE OR ST JOHN THANET

1615 Roger Morris, ship of war in full sail, rect. pl.

OXFORDSHIRE

CHECKENDON

c. 1430 Walter Beauchamp, soul borne by 2 angels.

OXFORD, NEW COLLEGE

1623 Thos. Hopper, figs. of Aesculapius and fortune, circles, triangles etc.

SOMERSET

KINGSTON, ST MARY

1672 Thos. and Anne Dyke, lge. skull, with scrolls.

SUFFOLK

BOXFORD

1606 David, son of Joseph Bird, rector, aged 22 weeks, in cot, rect. pl., sm.

SURREY

COBHAM
c.1500 Adoration of the Shepherds, rect. pl., sm.

SUSSEX

FLETCHING
c.1440? Peter Denot, glover, pair of gloves.

WILTSHIRE

BROUGHTON GIFFORD
1620 Robt. Longe, rect. pl. with altar tomb, behind it a herald holding sheaf of shields from which Death draws one.

SCOTLAND

EDINBURGH, ST GILES
1569 rect. pl. with seated figs. of Religion and Justice, ach. [Pal., late 15th cent.]

THE HOLY TRINITY

not included in text

DERBYSHIRE

TIDESWELL
1462 Sir Sampson Meverell, inscr.

NORTHAMPTONSHIRE

CHACOMBE
c.1545 Myghell Fox, inscr.

SURREY

LEIGH
1499 Rich. Ardern, inscr.

THE RESURRECTION

not included in text

LONDON

BARKING, ALL HALLOWS
c.1500 Anon, corroded.

SURREY

CRANLEIGH
1503 Robt. Harding, inscr.

GENERAL BOOKS OF REFERENCE

ANDREWS, W. F. *Memorial Brasses in Hertfordshire Churches.* (2nd ed.) 1903

ASHDOWN, C. H. *British and Foreign Arms and Armour.* 1909

British Costume During XIX Centuries. 1910

BADGER, E. W. *The Monumental Brasses of Warwickshire.* 1895

BEAUMONT, E. T. *Ancient Memorial Brasses.* 1913

BELCHER, W. D. *Kentish Brasses* (2 vols). 1905

BOUTELL, C. *Monumental Brasses and Slabs.* 1847

Christian Monuments in England and Wales. 1854

BRISCOE, J. P. and FIELD, H. E. *Monumental Brasses of Nottinghamshire.* 1904

Cambridge Libraries List of Remaining Effigies in Cambridgeshire. 1970

CHANCELLOR, F. *The Ancient Sepulchral Monuments of Essex.* 1890

CLINCH, G. *Old English Churches.* 1900

English Costume. 1909

COTMAN, J. S. *Engravings of Sepulchral Brasses in Norfolk and Suffolk.* 1839

Engravings of Sepulchral Brasses in Suffolk. 1838

CROSSLEY, F. H. *English Church Monuments.* 1921

DAVIS, C.T. *Monumental Brasses of Gloucestershire.* 1899

The Monumental Brasses of Herefordshire and Worcestershire (Archaeological Section in the 'Transactions of the Birmingham and Midland Institute'). 1884–5

DRUITT, H. *A Manual of Costume as Illustrated by Monumental Brasses.* 1906

DUNKIN, E. H. W. *Monumental Brasses of Cornwall.* 1882

Encyclopaedia Britannica (Article "Brasses").

FARRER, E. *A List of Monumental Brasses Remaining in the County of Norfolk.* 1890

A List of Monumental Brasses Remaining in the County of Suffolk. 1903

The Church Heraldry of Norfolk. 1887–93

FIELD, H.E. *The Monumental Brasses of Derbyshire,* Vols. III, V, of the Transactions of the Monumental Brass Society.

GAWTHORP, W. E. *The Brasses of Our Homeland Churches.* 1923

GOUGH, R. *Sepulchral Monuments of Great Britain.* 1786–96

GRIFFIN, R. and STEPHENSON, MILL. *List of Monumental Brasses Remaining in the County of Kent in 1922.*

HAINES, H. *A Manual of Monumental Brasses,* 1861; reissued 1970

HARTSHORNE, C. H. *Funeral Monuments in Northamptonshire.* 1840

HOLLIS T. and G. *Monumental Effigies of Great Britain.* 1840–42

HUDSON, F. *The Brasses of Northampton.* 1852

ISHERWOOD, G. *The Monumental Brasses in Bedfordshire Churches.* 1906

JEAN, G. E. *A List of the Existing Brasses in Lincolnshire.* 1895

KITE, E. *The Monumental Brasses of Wiltshire.* 1860

MACKLIN, H. W. *Monumental Brasses.* (6th ed.) 1913

The Brasses of England. 1907

The Brasses of Huntingdonshire, Vol. III in the Transactions of the Monumental Brass Society.

McCALL, H. B. *Richmondshire Churches.* 1910

MORLEY, T. H. *Monumental Brasses of Berkshire.* 1924

OXFORD ARCHITECTURAL SOCIETY *A Manual for the Study of Monumental Brasses.* 1878

Oxford Journal of Monumental Brasses. 1897–1912

Oxford Portfolio of Monumental Brasses. 1898–1901.

PAGE, W. *The Brasses and Indents in St. Albans Abbey,* in Vol. I of the Home Counties Magazine. 1899

PLANCHÉ, J. R. *A Cyclopaedia of Costume* (2 vols). 1876–79

Portfolio of the Monumental Brass Society (4 vols). 1894–1914

ROGERS, W. H. H. *Ancient Sepulchral Effigies and Monumental and Memorial Sculpture of Devonshire.* 1877

Memorials of the West. 1888

SANDERSON, H. K. *The Brasses of Bedfordshire,* in Vol. II of the Transactions of the Monumental Brass Society.

SIMPSON, J. *A List of the Sepulchral Brasses of England.* 1857

STEPHENSON, MILL. *A List of Monumental Brasses in the British Isles.* 1926

STOTHARD, C.A. *Monumental Effigies.* (2nd ed.) 1876

SUFFLING, E.R. *English Church Brasses.* 1910

THORNELY, J. L. *The Monumental Brasses of Lancashire and Cheshire.* 1893

Transactions of the Monumental Brass Society.

VICTORIA and ALBERT MUSEUM *List of Rubbings.* 1915

WALLER, J. G., and L. A. B. *A Series of Monumental Brasses.* 1864

WARD, J. S. M. *Brasses.* 1912

WOODMAN, T. C. *The Sussex Brasses.* 1903

SPACE FOR NOTES

SPACE FOR NOTES

SPACE FOR NOTES

SPACE FOR NOTES

SPACE FOR NOTES

SPACE FOR NOTES

Dame Margaret Chute
Marden - Hertfordshire

SPACE FOR NOTES

SPACE FOR NOTES

SPACE FOR NOTES